BISON
BOOKS

D0962436

CUSTER'S LAST STAND

The Anatomy of an American Myth

BRIAN W. DIPPIE

University of Nebraska Press • Lincoln and London

The paper in this book meets the minimum requirements of American National
Standard for Information Sciences—Permanence of Paper for Printed Library
Materials, ANSI Z39.48–1984.

First Bison Book printing: 1994
Most recent printing indicated by the last digit below:
10   9   8   7   6   5   4   3   2

Library of Congress Cataloging-in-Publication Data
Dippie, Brian W.
Custer's last stand: the anatomy of an American myth / Brian W. Dippie.
p.   cm.
Includes bibliographical references and index.
ISBN 0-8032-6592-1
1. Little Big Horn, Battle of the, 1876.   2. Custer, George Armstrong, 1839–
1876.   I. Title.
E83.876.C983D56   1994
973.8′2—dc20
94-26029   CIP

Reprinted by arrangement with Brian W. Dippie.

FOR MY PARENTS
in admiration
with gratitude

TABLE OF CONTENTS

PREFACE TO THE BISON BOOK EDITION

By Brian W. Dippie

This book was originally published in 1976. Its roots went back further, to a paper I delivered as a fresh-faced undergraduate at one of the monthly Saturday-night meetings of the University of Alberta History Club in 1964. I titled it "Custer and His Last Stand: The Growth of an American Myth." Shortly after, a senior historian in the department went on record in the local paper that it was a good thing Canadians did not need Boones, Crocketts, and the other trappings of America's myth-encrusted culture. I must not have agreed, since I made the Custer myth the subject of my master's thesis at the University of Wyoming in 1966. Academic reality caught up to me soon after, and I had to shelve the subject until I had finished my doctorate and, in 1970, taken up the duties of an assistant professor at the University of Victoria in British Columbia, where I still make my home. When I returned to Custering, completed an extensive overhaul of the manuscript, and began shopping for a publisher, I discovered to my great surprise that not every university press was smitten with the Boy General's mythic last moments. Thus I was more than pleased when the University of Montana's publications program took on the project and in 1976 issued *Custer's Last Stand: The Anatomy of an American Myth*. Montana was where the Last Stand happened, after all, and 1976 was the battle's centennial year.

I can report that the book enjoyed a modest success. Reviewers were mostly kind, Custer buffs were intrigued, and fellow devotees of the myth became my friends. Paul A. Hutton, who fits all three categories, has recently listed this book among the ten essential Custer books, which I accept as a not strictly objective tribute to a pioneering effort. Because my book *is* flawed. It was conceived as a descriptive and interpretive treatment of the Custer myth, but I would agree it is more descriptive than interpretive. I felt the need to introduce readers to a substantial body of material—poetry, art, fiction, movies—that is not the usual stuff of cultural history, or even of Custeriana, as this historical subspecialty is known.

Thus my book is frankly descriptive in covering so much unfamiliar ground. Others have offered bolder intepretations of the Last Stand than I essayed—notably, Richard Slotkin in *The Fatal Environment: The Myth of the Frontier in the Age of Industrialization, 1800–1890* (New York: Atheneum, 1985). Broad studies of American culture have also incorporated the Custer myth in imaginative ways. Bruce A. Rosenberg's *Code of the West* (Bloomington: Indiana University Press, 1982), Edward Tabor Linenthal's *Changing Images of the Warrior Hero in America: A History of Popular Symbolism* (New York: Edwin Mellen Press, 1982) and *Sacred Ground: Americans and Their Battlefields* (Urbana: University of Illinois Press, 1991), and Michael Kammen's *Mystic Chords of Memory: The Transformation of Tradition in American Culture* (New York: Alfred A. Knopf, 1991) come to mind.

My interpretation of Custer's Last Stand, which derives from an older American Studies interest in myth and symbol, still strikes me as essentially correct. I agree with the premise underlying William H. and William N. Goetzmann's *West of the Imagination* (New York: W. W. Norton & Company, 1986) that "the West as people imagined it . . . was part of reality, too," and have had the opportunity to say why I agree in "The West That Was and the West That Is" (*Gilcrease,* July 1986), and "American Wests: Historiographical Perspectives" (*American Studies International,* October 1989), where I wrote: "Since cultural values shift over time, myths, in order to remain relevant, shift their meanings as well. If . . . the major challenge facing Western history is to relate past to present in a meaningful way, the mythic approach has much to offer. It accounts for continuity *and* change." *Custer's Last Stand* is faithful to this premise. So are related studies like Stephen Tatum's *Inventing Billy the Kid: Visions of the Outlaw in America, 1881–1981* (Albuquerque: University of New Mexico Press, 1982) and Susan Prendergast Schoelwer's *Alamo Images: Changing Perceptions of a Texas Experience* (Dallas: DeGolyer Library and Southern Methodist University Press, 1985). Paul Hutton, who wrote the introduction to the Alamo volume, has also written the best short treatment of the Custer myth, "From Little Bighorn to Little Big Man: The Changing Image of a Western Hero in Popular Culture" (*Western Historical Quarterly,* January 1976). He reworked his material for a general audience in "Custer's Last Stand" (*TV Guide,* November 26, 1977). The assumption that the Custer myth tells us about changing times also informs John P. Langellier's "Tracing the Legend of George Armstrong Custer" (*AB Bookman's Weekly,* October 5, 1992).

In its own time, Custer's Last Stand impressed itself so deeply on the American consciousness precisely because it was the exception that proved a rule. By 1876 white Americans were "winning the West" with astonishing rapidity, and the era of frontiering was coming to an end. It seemed important to affirm pioneering values and, at the same time, to make native defeat and displacement the unavoidable outcome of a fair contest between the forces of the past and those of the future, between savagery and civilization. Custer's Last Stand, that most atypical of frontier events, thus became the *typical* event of the Indian wars. It was a defeat that, paradoxically, stood for victory—and for conquest. George Armstrong Custer himself was critical to the process of mythicization. He was the buckskin-clad hero, steeped in frontiering tradition, who in death became a martyr to progress. By standing for endings, Custer stood for beginnings. That was the key to the Last Stand's appeal in the nineteenth century—it was a last stand for all of yesterday. The core image of doomed heroism remains central to the myth today, though subject to entirely different interpretation. Was it heroism that doomed Custer's men? Or foolishness? Or a murderous penchant that had wormed its way into the American soul?

Custer buffs (that is, amateur historical enthusiasts) still abound, and their primary concerns are unchanged: What happened at the Little Bighorn, and why? Who did what to whom? Who was responsible for defeat? (The question is not why the Indians achieved victory, since Custer's Last Stand is a white myth and explanations rest on white factors.) Custeriana is mostly an untrendy field. Though considerations of race and gender have dominated much recent social history, those who study Custer (usually men) are essentially military history buffs, not nearly as interested in right and wrong as they are in the fine points of orders and tactics and the character and performance of individual soldiers. Race and gender do enter Custeriana through rumor—Did Custer father a child by the Cheyenne prisoner Monahsetah?—an old chestnut that still carries weight in some Native American assessments and is the subject of Barbara Zimmerman's "Mo-nah-se-tah: Fact or Fiction" (*4th Annual Symposium, Custer Battlefield Historical & Museum Assn., Inc.*, held at Hardin, Montana on June 22, 1990). And gender also enters by the grace of Elizabeth, who went to war for the memory of her dead husband and, as Shirley A. Leckie has demonstrated in *Elizabeth Bacon Custer and the Making of a Myth* (Norman: University of Oklahoma Press, 1991), for herself. There was money to be made from myth, after all, and a living at a time when the independent, self-sufficient woman was not an accepted norm. Gay issues, too, have entered Custer literature through the story of Corporal John Nunan (or Noonan) of the Seventh Cavalry, who shot himself in 1878 after it was discovered his wife was a man. The best account is James V. Schneider's *An Enigma Named Noonan* (n.p., 1988).

The trendiest development in mainstream Custeriana in years has been the emergence of archeology. Long on the fringes, the subject took center stage at the battlefield when the National Park Service authorized an archeological survey in 1984–85. The digs led to a media bonanza. *Time, National Geographic, Natural History, Newsweek*, national television, and countless newspapers provided coverage. The digs also whipped up their own controversy (Robert M. Utley spoke for the dissenters in "On Digging Up Custer Battlefield," *Montana, The Magazine of Western History*, Spring 1986), promoted claims to archeological omniscience, and yielded new data that have reawakened interest in the basics of what happened at the Little Bighorn. Two recent works have drawn on this data to buttress novel interpretations of the fighting on June 25—John S. Gray's *Custer's Last Campaign: Mitch Boyer and the Little Bighorn Reconstructed* (Lincoln: University of Nebraska Press, 1991) and Richard Allan Fox Jr.'s *Archaeology, History, and Custer's Last Battle: The Little Bighorn Reexamined* (Norman: University of Oklahoma Press, 1993). Fox, rejecting the interpretation of the archeological evidence advanced in a book he coauthored just four years earlier, *Archaeological Perspectives on the Battle of the Little Bighorn* (Norman: University of Oklahoma Press, 1989), contends that there was no Last Stand as such, and that the final soldier casualties occurred after the guns were silenced on Custer Hill. Of course, this is mother's milk to Custer buffs—part of the old, honorable tradition of arguing over who did what at the Little Bighorn.

In the main, what the buffs resent—and resist—are not reinterpretations of the battle, but of the battle's meaning. They wage a rearguard action against Political Correctness (most will never accept the name change that in December 1991 transformed the Custer Battlefield National Monument into the Little Bighorn Battlefield National Monument), just as they never accepted the double-whammy of the appointment of a Native American woman as battlefield superintendent in 1989. Indeed, relations became so strained that the battlefield's forty-year "friends group" (or cooperating association) was divorced by the National Park Service in 1993 on the grounds of incompatibility, and has since taken up residence in Golden, Colorado, where it still proudly answers to the name Custer Battlefield Historical & Museum Association. The divorce raises the central question: What *should* Custer's Last Stand symbolize? Tragedy, certainly, but is it a white tragedy or a native one? Indian activists may have chosen Wounded Knee in 1973 as the most bitterly poignant symbol of white conquest, but Custer's Last Stand is the ultimate prize in the ongoing struggle over cultural meanings. Who won in 1876 is not at issue; the issue is, who wins today? The 1993 revised edition of Linenthal's *Sacred Ground* offers an up-to-date account of the battlefield monument's shifting significance, and the staff there have been studying its interpretive programs in the years from 1940 to 1986 (see Robert L. Hart, "Changing Exhibitry and Sensitivity: The Custer Battlefield Museum," *1st Annual Symposium, Custer Battlefield Historical & Museum Assn., Inc.*, held at Hardin, Montana on June 26, 1987.)

The five-hundredth anniversary of Columbus's "discovery" of America inspired a great deal of soul-searching about the subsequent destruction of what many posited as a New World paradise. An acclaimed public television documentary that aired in 1992, Paul Stekler's *Last Stand at Little Bighorn,* reduced the fabled battle to a fleeting, panic-stricken moment in the larger story of the defeat and dispossession of the Lakota, the Plains Indians, indeed all the Native peoples of North America. Stekler has provided an interesting account of its making in "Custer and Crazy Horse Ride Again . . . and Again, and Again: Filmmaking and History at Little Bighorn" (*Montana,* Autumn 1992). *Last Stand at Little Bighorn* was predictable in condemning Custer through the words of Native American informants, the descendant of one of his troopers, and historians. After all, "Custer-bashing" (as the buffs call it) has been all the rage for thirty years or more. But by adopting Richard Fox's premise and denying there even was a Last Stand, Stekler went a step toward creating something profoundly anti-mythic. Custer's Last Stand is a visual construct; the myth collapses when it cannot be seen. But Stekler pulled back from the brink by framing his story with several Last Stands out of the movies. Intended as ironic counterpoint to historical reality, they necessarily burden any retelling, including his own, with the weight of heroic tradition. That is the power of myth. A Native American activist like Russell Means can stand beside the monument on Custer Hill and pronounce it an abomination, about as welcome in Indian country as a Hitler monument would be in Israel. But he made his pronouncement in 1988 where he did because of the resonance the setting lent his words.

When *Custer's Last Stand: The Anatomy of an American Myth* made its debut in 1976, a few critics (friendly, I like to think) pointed out that my enthusiasm sometimes outran my discipline. Paul Hutton said that after reading my tenth description of the Last Stand, he was eager for the general to expire permanently. I can sympathize, since my theme is that Custer *never really gets to expire.* Over and over, he is doomed to repeat his grand finale. If there is truth to the slogan "Custer died for your sins," then Custer has more than atoned for us all. What harder fate than endlessly dying? Merrill G. Burlingame also commented on my stylistic excesses and noted, with wounding accuracy, that the topical arrangement, with its parallel treatment of the Custer myth in different forms of popular culture, ensures repetition, and that the parts of my book never quite add up to a unified whole. Guilty. But it was a young historian who wrote this book, and it was his central problem to analyze a myth that is overwhelmingly familiar through its component parts, which are not. If I sound defensive, I guess it is because I am still proud of *Custer's Last Stand* for all of its faults. It was my first book, and it is probably true that you love your first book like you love your first-born child. (No more than your second book, of course, my second-born son reminds me.)

I hope one day to revise *Custer's Last Stand* thoroughly—updating it, naturally, and correcting errors and omissions. The notes to the Epilogue, for example, are misnumbered. Note 12 was inadvertently deleted, creating confusion with the next three, which are actually 13, 14 and 15. (Note 12, by the way, should read: "It Was Only 75 Years Ago: Custer Anniversary Is Observed," *Life* [July 9, 1951]: 41.) The need for updating is obvious. The Custer bibliography has swollen since 1976—for the best recent guide, see Paul Hutton's bibligraphical essay in his *Custer Reader* (Lincoln: University of Nebraska Press, 1992). There are four additions to my "Chronological Bibliography of Custer Biography" (Appendix A), not one a conventional biography: Stephen E. Ambrose's *Crazy Horse and Custer: The Parallel Lives of Two American Warriors* (Garden City, N.Y.: Doubleday & Company, 1975), Evan S. Connell's phenomenally popular *Son of the Morning Star: Custer and the Little Bighorn* (San Francisco: North Point Press, 1984), Eddie Dieber's *General George Armstrong Custer's Biography in Pictures* (Grand Forks, N.D.: Washburn Printing Center, n.d.), and Robert M. Utley's masterly *Cavalier in Buckskin: George Armstrong Custer and the Western Military Frontier* (Norman: University of Oklahoma Press, 1988). I have also had my biographical say in an interpretive essay on Custer in Paul Hutton's anthology *Soldiers West: Biographies from the Military Frontiers* (Lincoln: University of Nebraska Press, 1987).

Though Custer has not been my principal scholarly concern since 1976, the myth has never released its hold on me. Custer poetry is an uncommon obsession, as I know from having edited and published a 344-page compendium in collaboration with the late John M. Carroll, *Bards of the Little Big Horn* (Bryan, Tex.: Guidon Press, 1978). It reprints 155 poems and songs on the Custer theme—more verses, I might add, than there were readers for the book, though I am still proud of such quirky entries as Richard Brautigan's "General Custer Versus the Titanic," and I will always remember the kindness of distinguished contemporary poets like the late William E. Stafford in permitting their work to be anthologized without fee. *Bards of the Little Big Horn*'s "Bibliography of Custer Poems" included titles for which reprint permissions were unavailable; it is expanded and corrected in the poetry section of a bibliography I co-authored with Paul Hutton, "Custer and Pop Culture," in Gregory J. W. Urwin and Roberta E. Fagan, eds., *Custer and His Times, Book Three: A Publication of the Little Big Horn Associates, Inc.* (Conway: University of Central Arkansas Press, 1987). Paul and I earlier collaborated on another esoteric offering, *The Comic Book Custer: A Bibliography of Custeriana in Comic Books and Comic Strips* (1983, Publication No. 4, Brazos Corral of the Westerners, Bryan, Tex.), and this, as well, is updated and corrected in "Custer and Pop Culture," along with the entire "Bibliography of Custer Fiction" offered here. Apart from Vincent A. Heier's "Fiction Stranger Than Truth: A 'Novel' Approach to Custer in Literature" (*3rd Annual Symposium, Custer Battlefield Historical & Museum Assn., Inc.*, held at Hardin, Montana on June 23, 1989), there has been little recent comment on Custer fiction, though individual authors like Thomas Berger and Will Henry continue to receive attention, and a few of the many Custer novels published since my book appeared have enjoyed popular success—notably Douglas C. Jones's *The Court-Martial of George Armstrong Custer* (New York: Charles Scribner's Sons, 1976) and George MacDonald Fraser's *Flashman and the Redskins* (London: Collins, 1982), "edited and arranged" from the papers of what wonderful Victorian scoundrel, Sir Harry Flashman, V.C.

The Last Stand remains an enormously popular theme for western artists. Don Russell supplemented his 1968 book *Custer's Last* with an article, "What Really Happened at Custer's Last Stand?" (*ARTnews*, December 1978), and updated his 1970 *Custer's List* with "Custer's List—Continued," in Paul A. Hutton, ed., *Garry Owen 1976: Annual of the Little Big Horn Associates* (Seattle: Little Big Horn Associates, 1977). It needs updating again, since the artists are still hard at it. A 1976 exhibition in Billings "commemorating the 100th Anniversary of the Battle of the Little Big Horn" showcased the work of thirty-four painters and sculptors (see Judy Henry's "A Centennial Commemoration of the Custer Battle," *Southwest Art*, May 1976). The same year, *Smithsonian* (June 1976) reproduced Eric von Schmidt's new oil *Here Fell Custer,* a huge (five-by-thirteen foot) frieze-like painting that downplays heroism to create a brutally realistic vision of chaotic defeat. Von Schmidt has told the story behind its creation in an entertaining essay, "Sunday at the Little Big Horn with George" (*Montana*, Spring 1992). Von Schmidt's iconoclastic breakthrough has not won the day in Custer art, however. It is the ghost of his father, Harold von Schmidt (see page 48), that hovers over the Last Stands painted by Joe Grandee (1982), Mort Kunstler (1986), and Frank McCarthy (1987). Ralph Heinz, whose crisp imagery and precise detail recall the style of military artist H. Charles McBarron, has succeeded the late James K. Ralston as Montana's premier painter of Custer subjects, though other artists, including Michael Schreck, have specialized in the battle. Thom Ross of Seattle has brought a welcome touch of humor to the subject reminiscent of the work of Warrington Colescott. His stylized paintings, in which the combatants often resemble toy soldiers in formation, are also reminiscent of the Custer parodies by native artists like Fritz Scholder, T. C. Cannon and Randy Lee White, though Ross's variations on the heroic conventions of Last Stand art actually salute the myth.

The sculptors have been almost as busy as the painters, producing single figure studies of Custer (mounted and unmounted) and complex Last Stand groups. The artistic interest in Custer is not confined to his last battle. Branching out, painters have depicted episodes from his Civil War career, his stint in Kansas, the Black Hills Expedition, and all phases of the Sioux Expedition of 1876. But the Last Stand remains the ultimate challenge, and it continues to lure artists outside the western art tradition like John Hull, who finished a five-by-eight foot *Custer's Last Stand* in 1992.

Interest in the older Custer paintings and artists is undiminished. Biographies of William M. Cary, Edgar S. Paxson, W. Herbert Dunton, William R. Leigh, Olaf C. Seltzer and E. W. Deming, all published since 1976, treat their Last Stands. Specialized studies include John M. Carroll's "Anheuser-Busch and Custer's Last Stand," (*Greasy Grass*, May 1987), Anne Weber-Scobie's "Paintings, Politics, and Pickles: The Life and Work of Irish-American Artist John Mulvany (1839–1906)," an unpublished research paper (Binghamton, N.Y., July 1989), and Bruce R. Liddic's "The Letzte Schlacht of Custer," *Research Review: The Journal of the Little Big Horn Associates*, N.S. (January 1992), on Elk Eber. I am guilty of constantly sneaking Custer into my own writing on western art—for example, "Remington, Russell and the Western Tradition" (*Art Today*, Spring 1986), "Frederic Remington's West: Where History Meets Myth" (in Chris Bruce, et al., *Myth of the West*, New York: Rizzoli, for the Henry Art Gallery, University of Washington, Seattle, 1990), and "The Visual West" (in Clyde A. Milner, Carol A. O'Connor, and Martha A. Sandweiss, eds., *The Oxford History of the American West*, New York: Oxford University Press, 1994). Others have offered well-illustrated overviews of Custer art since 1976, notably James S. Hutchins in "Still Dodging Arrows," *Gateway Heritage* 1 (Winter 1980), Christopher M. Summitt in "Apologia Pro 'Custer's Last Stand'" (*Greasy Grass*, May 1989), and Gregory Lalire in "Custer's Art Stand" (*Wild West*, April 1994).

The legends that cluster around the Custer battle have inspired a literature of their own. Elizabeth A. Lawrence has written the ultimate book on Comanche, *His Very Silence Speaks: Comanche—The Horse Who Survived Custer's Last Stand* (Detroit: Wayne State University Press, 1989), a complete review of the known evidence that is equally attentive to the legend. Comanche's master, Captain Myles Keogh, is the subject of two recent books of his own: Charles L. Convis, *The Honor of Arms: A Biography of Myles W. Keogh* (Tucson: Westernlore Press, 1990), and John P. Langellier, Kurt Hamilton Cox, and Brian C. Pohanka, eds., *Myles Keogh: The Life and Legend of an "Irish Dragoon" in the Seventh Cavalry* (El Segundo, Calif.: Upton and Sons, 1991), a virtual compendium on the Keogh-Comanche legend. Other old standards like Rain-in-the-Face, notorious for dining on Custer's heart, and Curley, the Crow scout once celebrated as the sole *human* survivor of Custer's Last Stand, have been relatively neglected, though the late John S. Gray offered "A Vindication of Curly" (*4th Annual Symposium, Custer Battlefield Historical & Museum Assn., Inc.*), and featured him as a much-abused but reliable witnes in *Custer's Last Campaign*. I addressed the perennial issue of sole survivors in "Why Would They Lie?; or, Thoughts on Frank Finkel and Friends," in Paul A. Hutton, ed., *Custer and His Times: A Publication of the Little Big Horn Associates* (El Paso: Little Big Horn Associates, Inc., 1981), and the equally hoary issue of how Custer died in "The Custer Mystery; or, The Strange Deaths of George A. Custer" (in Ferenc

Morton Szasz, ed., *Great Mysteries of the West*, Golden, Colo.: Fulcrum Publishing, 1993).

Video has revolutionized film study. The hit-and-miss days of catching a particular film on late-night television are over. Classics like *Custer's Last Fight* (1925 re-release), *They Died with Their Boots On*, *Fort Apache*, and *Little Big Man* are now readily available for home viewing; so are *Santa Fe Trail*, *Little Big Horn*, the Custer episodes from television series like *Time Tunnel* and *Twilight Zone*, one-shot documentaries like *Last Stand at Little Bighorn*, television mini-series like *Son of a Morning Star*, and documentary series like *West of the Imagination*, *Wild West* and episodes from the long-running A&E series *Real West*. As Hollywood continues to rummage through its backlist for salable items, more of the "B" Westerns of the 1940s and '50s will become available.

Most books on the western mention the Custer movies. Jon Tuska, who believes films have a responsibility to be accurate and rejects the argument that they are more useful as cultural indicators than historical sources, devoted a few pages of *The American West in Film: Critical Approaches to the Western* (1985; reprint, Lincoln: University of Nebraska Press, 1988) to the Custer movies, while Wayne Michael Sarf gave them a full chapter in his *God Bless You, Buffalo Bill: A Layman's Guide to History and the Western Film* (Rutherford, N.J.: Fairleigh Dickinson University Press, 1983). Studies of the image of the American Indian in film have also paid attention to the Custer movies, if only to deplore them. See, for example, Ralph E. and Natasha A. Friar's *The Only Good Indian . . . The Hollywood Gospel* (New York: Drama Book Specialists, 1972) and John E. O'Connor's *The Hollywood Indian: Stereotypes of Native Americans in Films* (Trenton: New Jersey State Museum, 1980). Gretchen M. Bataille and Charles L. P. Silet edited a compilation, *The Pretend Indians: Images of Native Americans in the Movies* (Ames: Iowa State University Press, 1980), and published an annotated bibliography, *Images of American Indians on Film* (New York: Garland Publishing, Inc., 1985).

Writing about the western as genre and as source of Indian stereotypes faded in the late 1980s when the western itself faded from the screen. But the genre's recent resurgence in guises as variant as *Lonesome Dove*, *Dances with Wolves*, and *The Unforgiven* suggests the likelihood of a critical resurgence as well. Cultural historians of the American West have never lost sight of the influence of the movies on the popular imagination. Paul Hutton, who has written on the cinematic treatment of various events (the Alamo) and characters (Billy the Kid, Wyatt Earp), first examined the Custer films in "The Celluloid Custer," *Red River Valley Historical Review* (Fall 1979), and most recently in "'Correct in Every Detail': General Custer in Hollywood" in *Montana* (Winter 1991). I updated my discussion here in "Custer Stories on the Screen—II," *Newsletter* (Little Big Horn Associates, December 1976), but others besides Hutton have done much more. John

Phillip Langellier, at work on a book on the Custer myth in fiction and film, has published "Custer's Last Fight and the Silver Screen" (*Gateway Heritage*, Winter 1981–82), and "Movie Massacre: The Custer Myth in Motion Pictures and Television," *Research Review: The Journal of the Little Big Horn Associates*, N.S. (June 1989). Besides reporting on the television miniseries *Son of the Morning Star* for *Western Horseman* (March 1991) and for *Montana* (Winter 1991), Dan Gagliasso has offered an overview in "Custer's Last Stand on Celluloid" (*Persimmon Hill*, Spring 1991). Ronald Reagan, who played Custer in the 1940 Errol Flynn vehicle *Santa Fe Trail*, contributed to a feature on the film in *Greasy Grass* (May 1990), while Flynn's own 1941 Custer epic is the subject of Tom O'Neil's "The Making of *They Died With Their Boots On*" (*Research Review: The Journal of the Little Big Horn Associates*, N.S. (June 1990).

The showmen who anticipated the movies and had much to do with establishing Wild West heroics in the public's mind have never lost their appeal for scholars. William F. (Buffalo Bill) Cody leads the pack, as well he should. He has been much maligned of late, but "In Defense of Buffalo Bill: A Look at Cody in and of His Time" by Paul Fees provides perspective (in Bruce, et al., *Myth of the West*). Works on Cody almost always mention Custer, the man and the symbol portrayed in the Wild West's reenactment of the Last Stand. See, for example, the exhibition catalog *Buffalo Bill and the Wild West* (New York: Brooklyn Museum, 1981) and Joseph G. Rosa and Robin May's *Buffalo Bill and His Wild West: A Pictorial Biography* (Lawrence: University Press of Kansas, 1989). Sarah J. Blackstone focuses on the reenactment in "Custer Joins the Wild West Show" (in Urwin and Fagan, eds., *Custer and His Times, Book Three*). John Wallace (Captain Jack) Crawford, Cody's stage partner on occasion and author of perhaps the worst verse ever written on the Last Stand—a notable distinction!—now has a biography of his own, Darlis A. Miller's *Captain Jack Crawford: Buckskin Poet, Scout, and Showman* (Albuquerque: University of New Mexico Press, 1993).

In earlier days, reenactments of the Last Stand were sometimes staged as community promotions. Several interesting photographs of a 1902 reenactment illustrate my essay "'The Thrillin'est Fight Ever!': Sheridan Re-enacts Custer's Last Stand" (*Annals of Wyoming*, Fall 1982). It would be useful to have more case studies since there were direct tie-ins between reenactments and the early Custer films. Perhaps the revival in June 1990 of the annual Crow Indian reenactment of Custer's Last Stand outside Hardin, Montana, will inspire more scholarly interest in the subject; certainly the revival has attracted media attention.

In the past, reenactments occasionally played a part in official anniversary observances at the battlefield. Given current racial sensitivities, that will not happen again. But the anniversaries still provide symbolic occasions that vividly demonstrate the power of the Custer myth. The controversy surrounding the 1976 centennial commemoration is a story in itself, more about what did not happen than what did. The impassioned introduction to Michael J. Koury's compilation *Custer Centennial Observance 1976* (Fort Collins: The Old Army Press, 1978) indicates how high emotions were running at the time. They were running high again in 1988 when a large group of Indians congregated on the battlefield on the anniversary day to lay a plaque honoring the Native American dead. I was there, watching, as several men began to dig up the grass at the base of the Custer Monument. The tension was palpable. If some in the crowd had had their way, the National Park Service rangers would have intervened forcibly. Fortunately, the rangers could count—the Indians must have outnumbered them twenty to one—and we were spared a repeat of history on Last Stand Hill. That day was an unforgettable reminder that myth speaks, *urgently,* in the present tense.

Thanks as always to my family—Donna, Blake, and Scott—and the friends who not only tolerate my obsession but have attended our Custer's Last Stand party (more or less faithfully) each June since 1974—Alison, Anna, Angus, Arlene, Barb D, Barb K, Barb L, Barry, Brian L, Brian Sh, Brian Sy, Carol, Charlie, Chuck, Connie, David, Den, Dorothy, Erin, Fran, Gary, Ged, Greg, Jack, Jane, Jaron, Jeanne, Jesse, Jim, Joe, Joy, Judy, Kay, Ken B, Ken D, Leslie, Lorraine, Maia, Margo, Nathaniel, Paddy, Patrick, Phyllis, Rick, Ron Pe, Ron Po, Rory, Roy, Sean, Ted, Terry, Tomiko, Werner, Winston.

Victoria, B.C.
April 1994

PREFACE

Custer's Last Stand was fought on June 25, 1876, now almost a century ago. One of the earliest press dispatches from the field reported "The Terrible Details" in sparse yet vivid prose:

> At the highest point of the ridge lay Gen. Custer, surrounded by a chosen band. Here were his two brothers and his nephew, Mr. Reed, Col. Yates and Col. Cooke, and Capt. Smith, all lying in a circle of a few yards, their horses beside them. Here, behind Col. Yates' company, the last stand had been made, and here, one after another, these last survivors of Gen. Custer's five companies had met their death. . . . Not a man had escaped to tell the tale, but the story was inscribed on the surface of the barren hills in a language more eloquent than words.[1]

Here, simply put, were all the ingredients of epic tragedy — the dead Custer, the Seventh Cavalry's "last stand," the compelling fact that "not a man had escaped to tell the tale." These raw data made a deep impression on the minds of contemporary Americans. Shaped and refined by the artistic imagination they became the basis of a heroic national myth.

The historian can trace the growth of this myth by demonstrating how misinformation combined with misjudgment on the part of supposedly informed persons — participants, journalists and, later, students of the battle — led to the propagation of many fallacies that have since filtered down to the public and won acceptance. This approach is ably explored in Robert M. Utley's *Custer and the Great Controversy: The Origin and Development of a Legend.* I have attempted instead to show how the familiar concept of Custer's Last Stand is largely a creation of nonhistorical materials, of popular culture which, omniverous, feeds upon fact and fancy, history and legend, and, turning cannibal, upon itself. The popular culture of the Last Stand is both a source and an embodiment of the Custer myth. The extent of its direct influence can be suggested by reference to a few historians.

John A. Carroll once noted that "many have become competent in historical analysis by studying the Custer controversy."[2] As for what first attracted them to the subject, often enough the answer is the popular culture inspired by the battle. Robert Utley admits that he became addicted to Custeriana as a boy of twelve when he saw the movie *They Died With Their Boots On.*"This so aroused my interest in the great man," he writes, "that I could talk of little else for some time."[3] So began a search for the truth behind the Custer legend, and a distinguished career as a National Park Service historian. In turn, Harry H. Anderson, author of several important articles on the Sioux War of 1876, was drawn into the field after reading Will Henry's novel *No Survivors.*[4]

It was a color reproduction of William Reuswig's painting *Custer's Last Stand* in a 1951 *Collier's* that first won me over. Reuswig's dramatic tangle of soldiers and Indians made an indelible impression on my mind; at an early age, I was bitten by the Custer bug. Custeriana *is*, to be certain, a virus of sorts, and a contagious one at that, since few who are stricken seek a cure.

As I worked on the present analysis of the Custer myth, I came to see how Custeriana spreads and takes hold. Custer himself might be resistible — after all, his personal reputation is currently at best mixed. Too, the Last Stand, while providing a fascinating "problem in historical reconstruction," is of slight enough significance that it need not become a chronic affliction. [5] But, as William A. Graham once observed, because Custer "went out in a blaze of glory that became the setting for propaganda which caught and held, and still holds, the imagination of the American people, what began in controversy and dispute has ended in Myth; a myth, built like other myths, upon actual deeds and events, magnified, distorted and disproportioned by fiction, invention, imagination and speculation."[6] The myth, then, is the main carrier of the Custer bug, and it comes in a number of irresistible forms — touched with something of the absurd, no doubt, but nevertheless irresistible. Its major forms are my concern.

It is my pleasure to acknowledge a number of debts that I have incurred while working on this book. Professor Wallace D. Farnham, now of the University of Illinois, helped give form and substance to my enthusiasm for Custeriana while I was still an undergraduate at the University of Alberta, Edmonton. Professor Herbert R. Dieterich supervised the original draft of this manuscript as a master's thesis at the University of Wyoming back in 1966, and accepted exposure to Custeriana with patience and without complaint. Professor Gene M. Gressley allowed me a free hand to ferret out Custer materials in the Western History Research Center at the University of Wyoming, and Professor William H. Goetzmann of the University of Texas, Austin, read an earlier version of the manuscript and, while doubting the wisdom of such a longstanding obsession on my part, offered several valuable suggestions.

For ideas, advice, materials and many other courtesies I wish to thank the following: Mr. Thomas J. Carroll, Anheuser-Busch, Inc., St. Louis, Missouri; Professor Austin C. Fife, Utah State University, Logan; Mr. James T. Forrest, formerly of The Bradford Brinton Memorial, Big Horn,

Wyoming; Mrs. Thomas K. Garry, formerly of the Custer Battlefield National Monument, Crow Agency, Montana; Mr. James S. Hutchins, Smithsonian Institution, Washington, D.C.; Mr. Edward T. LeBlanc, Fall River, Massachusetts; Professor James D. McLaird, Dakota Wesleyan University, Mitchell, South Dakota; Mr. Edward B. Mayo, The Museum of Fine Arts, Houston, Texas; Mr. William Edgar Paxson, Whittier, California; Mr. Jerome Peltier, Spokane, Washington; Mr. James K. Ralston and his late wife, Willo, of Billings, Montana; Professor Morton L. Ross, University of Alberta, Edmonton; Mr. and Mrs. Myron F. Steves, Houston, Texas; friends and fellow members of the Little Big Horn Associates; and Mrs. Joan Whitfield, History Department secretary at the University of Victoria, British Columbia, who did an expert job of typing the final draft, and put up with my "shorthand" quirks and certain stylistic afterthoughts with perfect equanimity.

I am very much indebted to a small coterie of writers who have treated aspects of my subject in detail, and have done my best to acknowledge their work in my bibliographical essay. Don Russell, in particular, has been of great assistance. His monographs on Custer art and the Wild West Shows contain a fund of useful material, and our correspondence over the years has been most enlightening for me. Mr. Hugh W. Shick, North Hollywood, California, exhibited a deep, personal interest in my book at a critical point in its evolution, and Mrs. John L. Lockwood, San Rafael, California, went to enormous trouble to answer my inquiries and to share her own research, particularly in Custer poetry, with me.

All of my friends have contributed generously to this book, if simply by lending a "willing" ear while I expounded. Mr. Charles Odell, of Victoria, combines an abiding interest in Custer and the cinema with a retentive memory, and has filled in many details about the Custer films and television shows that I long ago forgot. Mr. William C. Hine, Orangeburg, South Carolina, with a perverse delight in seeing justice done to one of Ohio's great native sons (whom he regards as at least on par with Warren G. Harding), has contributed clippings, moral support and a guided tour of the little town of New Rumley, the General's birthplace. Professor Brian D. Sykes of the University of Alberta, Edmonton, abandoned his test tubes to spend a week with me in September, 1964, visiting Western art galleries, museums and battlefields in Montana and Wyoming, including one broiling hot day traipsing over the Custer Battlefield, gingerly sidestepping the cactus, loading my camera, watching out for snakes and listening patiently as I talked on and on and on . . .

A preliminary version of Chapter Two and a portion of Chapter Four have appeared in *Western American Literature*. Passages from Chapters Three and Five were used, respectively, in articles published in *Montana: the Magazine of Western History* and *Cultures*. Travel and research grants from the University of Victoria for other projects have given me the opportunity to work with Custer materials in the Bancroft Library, University of California, Berkeley; the Cadiz, Ohio, Public Library; and the Leonard Jennewein Collection, Dakota Wesleyan University,

Mitchell, South Dakota. The State Historical Society of South Dakota provided me with photocopies about early Last Stand re-enactments, and I greatly profited from a few days' work at the Billings Public Library, with its excellent holdings in Montana history.

My wife Donna, in keeping with the fate that usually befalls wives in acknowledgements, gets put "last but not least." She more than all the others has suffered from exposure to Custeriana through me. Without her continuous encouragement over a decade — and, occasionally, her strategically-timed insistence — I, for one, am certain that this book would never have been completed.

October, 1975
Victoria, B.C., Canada

CUSTER'S LAST STAND:

The Anatomy
Of An American Myth

Chapter 1

MYTH AND HISTORY:
Custer and His Last Stand

Long after this generation has passed away, long after every vestige of the merciless Sioux has passed from the continent, long after this Yellowstone country has become the seat of towns and cities and a prosperous civilization, the name of Custer and the story of his deeds will be fresh in men's memories. The story that comes to us to-day with so much horror, with so much pathos, will become a part of our national life.

New York Herald, July 12, 1876

Now, stark and cold,
Among thy fallen braves thou liest,
And even with thy blood defiest
The wolfish foe:
But ah, thou liest low,
And all our birthday song is hushed indeed!

Edmund C. Stedman, "Custer" (1876)

Almost any mention made of Custer's Last Stand today is a reference not to history but to myth. The words themselves have become visual ones, summoning up the image of a man standing tall on a western hill, oblivious to personal danger, facing a swarm of Indians who will in a matter of seconds annihilate his whole command. The setting, the Indians and the other soldiers in this mental picture are indistinct; only that solitary figure, surrounded and doomed, is sharply defined. He may be clothed in buckskins or dress blues, armed with sabre, rifle or pistols, with long golden hair or even with his hair clipped short. The details are inconsequential. All that matters is that defiant stance with which he confronts his destiny.

How this picture came to be planted in the American mind is the subject of my study. Obviously, the picture can bear only coincidental relationship to reality, since we have no exact knowledge of what happened on that ridge above the Little Big Horn River. It can tell us nothing of cause or responsibility, though that lone figure arouses just enough curiosity for most Americans to have formed an opinion about both. This picture can, however, and does serve as a striking example of the fearless individual at bay, of courage in the face of insuperable odds, of, simply, good form in dying. And it is also an ironic summation of one part of the American experience — the winning of the West. As such, Custer's Last Stand has become a national myth.

I

In using the term "myth" here, I mean to elicit its richest connotations. For Americans, the word implies everything from the hero tales of preliterate cultures through to the ideological fallacies held by advanced societies, and, in its plainest sense, refers to "a notion based more on tradition or convenience than on fact; a received idea."[1]

Henry Nash Smith, in his provocative study of the West in the American mind, Virgin Land, employed "myth" and "symbol" to designate "larger or smaller units of the same kind of thing, namely an intellectual construction that fuses concept and emotion into an image."[2] Myths exist only in our minds. They are, in effect, the fusion of what we see with what we want to see, the end product being that reality upon which we act, what we believe we see. In cultural terms, they are ingrained beliefs shared by the whole society. As Smith defines it, myth is essentially static, although capable of inspiring action. Myth also, and more familiarly, involves movement. As another scholar has written, "a myth is a story, a narrative, a plot, an explanatory account; it may be historically true, legendary, or invented; but, for the believer, it is 'truer than truth' and therefore highly impervious to refutation by a show of facts to the contrary."[3] In short, it "conveys a poetic truth more majestic and significant than mere fact."[4] Such are the meanings commonly associated with "myth." For my purposes, the word embraces the whole concept of Custer's Last Stand, a static image within a frame of story. The frame can be altered to meet changing conditions, but the image is immutable.

The Last Stand myth is larger than Custer's personal legend. Indeed, the myth subsumes the legend, its imagery unimpaired despite the fact that Custer's reputation has undergone a complete transformation over the past forty years.[5] In the nineteenth century Custer was a genuine national hero. But heroism is a fickle thing, and heroes, as one student of the American variety pointed out, "have cycles of popularity."[6] Custer, yesterday's hero, today is most frequently considered a villain or, worse yet, perhaps, a monumental fool. Either way, he is not forgotten. "For a nation that is supposedly obsessed with competing and winning," the Saturday Evening Post editorialized in 1966, "we show a strange affection for losers. Gen. George Custer . . . was something less than a hero, but we have always cherished a certain admiration for the foolishness with which he went down to utter defeat."[7] A newspaperman expressed the same thought epigrammatically: "Any fool can be right occasionally. Only Heaven's favored fools can be finally, gloriously wrong."[8]

2

Americans had traveled far from the previous century's reverence for the heroic individual. With Thomas Carlyle's musings *On Heroes and Hero-Worship* freshly in mind, Ralph Waldo Emerson in 1841 summarized his and his age's conclusions on the subject: "Heroism feels and never reasons, and therefore is always right; . . . for the hero that thing he does is the highest deed, and is not open to the censure of philosophers or divines."[9] Longevity, however, has proven to be more the property of myths than heroes. Custer's personal reputation has fluctuated enormously over the years, but Custer's Last Stand lives apart, uncompromised and "cherished" even by the General's critics. Like other American myths, it possesses a permanent appeal.

Because the span of United States history is relatively so short, one would expect American mythology, with its pervasive pietism and its jingoistic overtones, to be both shallow and dull. Yet its variety is surprising, and its importance should not be underestimated. Sociologist Orrin E. Klapp has argued that American "social typing," "if properly interpreted, . . . is a key to our national character." But, as Klapp added, much of what we remember of social types "consists of parts they have played in certain [historical] dramas that struck the popular imagination."[10] That is to say, sometimes the great event and the rare personality blend into myth.

Not only do Americans respond directly to myth (in Henry Nash Smith's sense), but they are subtly influenced by it. Ideally, Parson Weems' tale about George Washington and the cherry tree would inclucate in Americans an aversion to dishonesty on principle. This failing, Charlie Brown of *Peanuts* fame, catching his sister in a fib, need only shout "GEORGE WASHINGTON!!!" to reduce her to tears — and to extract the promise "You're right! I'll never lie again!" National myths — even more than heroes, who serve as examples — are instructional devices that, indirectly and painlessly, instill in the citizens those values and beliefs that constitute their country's tradition. In just over four and a half centuries, an amazing number of heroes and villains, real personalities encrusted in legend and obscured by emotionalism, have become mythical characters in the American story.

No other area in the United States rivals the trans-Mississippi West as a breeding ground of national myths. Tennessee's Davy Crockett, the epitome of Jacksonian frontier democracy, found his immortality in Texas, "Where freedom was fighting another foe / And they needed him at the Alamo." The memory that Americans hold dear is not of Crockett the bear-hunter, Indian-fighter and comic hero, but of Davy swinging Old Betsy over his head and knocking Santa Anna's soldiers down like so many bowling pins before sheer weight of numbers tramples him under.

Moreover, in the supposedly individualistic West, types became myths. First there were the Lewis and Clarks, government explorers who blazed the trails westward, and the Jim Bridgers and Kit Carsons, mountain men who cherished the wilderness and yet were instrumental in taming it. Then there were the pioneers, sun-bronzed husbands and their sun-bonneted wives, hardy souls made even tougher by a demanding environment. There were plains Indians and cavalrymen, sheriffs and outlaws, gold miners and cattle kings. And there were cowboys. It would be difficult to imagine a more monotonous vocation than riding behind a herd of steers all day getting a face full of dust. But add cards, whiskey, six-guns and honky-tonk girls at the end of the trail, and the cowboy assumes mythic proportions.

What was it, then, that transformed the mundane into high romance and adventure? Simply, the Far West was the best of all possible settings for the final act in the American drama of continental expansion. As Charles M. Russell, Montana's cowboy artist, wrote: "The mountains and plains seemed to stimulate man's imagination. A man in the States might have been a liar in a small way, but when he comes west he soon takes lessons from the prairies, where ranges a hundred miles away seem within touchin' distance, streams run uphill and Nature appears to lie some herself."[11] To an Easterner who only dreamed of such country and the men who strode across its surface, the gulf between possibility and impossibility grew even narrower, and suddenly Westerners were eight feet tall and made of steel, and the West — America's *last* West — was a myth.

II

Like the moon, General Custer's reputation has two sides, one bathed in light and the other cast in deep shadow. To those who saw only the brightness, Custer was a modern Lancelot, and the epithets applied to him make stirring reading: Murat of the American Army; the Napoleon of the Plains; *Beau Sabreur*; the Boy General; Bravest of the Brave; the Last of the Cavaliers; the Darling of the Gods. One writer described his visit to the Custer Battlefield in the following terms: "I remained alone at the 'monument,' memories flooded my mind — I thought of many things. I thought of another bleak and barren hill — in a land far away — and of a MAN who stood there long, long ago — His garments stripped from his body. I thought of an old parable: 'Take the shoes from off thy feet — you stand on sacred ground,' "[12] To those who saw only the darkness, however, Custer was a very different man. He was a modern Machiavelli, an egotist, foolhardy, unprincipled and vain, and they called him Glory-Hunter. Yet this duality, far from impairing the Custer legend, has only served to propagate it. Custer becomes either hero or villain, as you wish him.[13]

George Armstrong Custer was born in the small farm community of New Rumley, Ohio, on December 5, 1839, and graduated from West Point in 1861 at the bottom of a thirty-four man class. The Civil War was his proving ground, and his personal courage — an attribute that even his bitterest critics grant him — soon made him a conspicuous figure. At twenty-three Custer was a brigadier general of volunteers, and at twenty-five earned the rank of brevet major general, the youngest man ever to achieve this distinction in the United States Army. His flamboyant manner and striking appearance — flowing blond locks set off by a red cravat, a sailor's blouse and a blue jacket agleam with gold braid — were bound to attract attention. They combined with courtly, magnanimous gestures towards vanquished foes and thundering cavalry charges to capture the imagination of an American public hungry for cavalier-heroes comparable to those who rode for the Confederacy. Custer was the North's "Jeb" Stuart in style at least, and from the welter of Union Civil War generals the Boy General ascended to the rarified rank of a national hero.

A year after the war ended, Custer received a permanent commission as lieutenant colonel of the newly-formed Seventh Cavalry regiment. From 1867 to 1871 the Seventh served with distinction on the Southern plains against the Comanches, Kiowas, Arapahoes, and Southern Cheyennes. But Custer's own record was a motley one. In 1867 he was court-martialled on a variety of charges ranging from absence without leave from his command to conduct prejudicial to good order and military discipline (the most damaging specification being that he had ordered deserters tracked down and shot on the spot). Found guilty on all counts, though with "no criminality attached" to the most serious charges, Custer was suspended from rank and pay for one year.[14] However, he was reinstated in time to lead the Seventh at Washita, November 27, 1868, a victory, but also a turning point in the Custer story. After successfully routing a large Cheyenne village, Custer had found himself confronted by a swelling body of Indian reinforcements and had ordered a hasty retreat. In the attendant confusion, nineteen men who had ridden off with Major Joel H. Elliott — and, as it turned out, perished — were left behind with no effort made to ascertain their fate. This incident proved to be the wedge that split the Seventh Cavalry's officers into two factions, the Custerphiles and the Custerphobes — groupings maintained to this day by Custer's more impassioned advocates and detractors. Regimental harmony was shattered, and Custer never did succeed in repairing the rift. In 1873 the Seventh headed north to Dakota Territory, where it took part in major expeditions in 1873, 1874 and 1876. From the last of these, only half of its men returned.

On January 31, 1876, a Bureau of Indian Affairs directive ordering Sitting Bull's Sioux followers to come into their agencies or be deemed hostile and punished accordingly expired. The next day, Secretary of the Interior Zachariah Chandler notified the Secretary of War that "the said Indians are hereby turned over to the War Department for such action on the part of the Army as you may deem proper under the circumstances."[15] The Army, long restive under civilian management of Indian affairs, had been waiting for this very opportunity, and it was quick to act. Three military columns took the field: one, under General George Crook, set out from Fort Fetterman in Wyoming; the second, under Colonel John Gibbon, from Fort Ellis in Montana; and a third, under General Alfred H. Terry, from Fort Abraham Lincoln, Dakota Territory. It was hoped that by working in concert the three columns would trap the Indians and force their surrender.

Custer was not commanding the Dakota Column because, once again, he had fallen from official favor. Impetuous, outspoken and sometimes tactless, he had testified in March and April before a Congressional committee investigating charges of corruption in the War Department. Custer had no firsthand knowledge to offer, but his testimony implicated both W. W. Belknap, the Secretary of War, and Orvil Grant, the President's brother. The President immediately suspended Custer's command, and it was only through the intervention of General Terry that Custer was allowed to accompany the Dakota Column in a secondary capacity as commander of the Seventh Cavalry.

Crook's column, after an abortive campaign in March, set out for the second time on May 29. Gibbon was underway by the end of March. The Dakota Column, plagued as it was with difficulties, did not leave Fort Lincoln until May 17. On June 17 Crook met the Indians on Rosebud Creek, was fought to a standstill, and then withdrew to his base camp on Goose Creek, near the present site of Sheridan, Wyoming. The next day, a young lieutenant with Gibbon's Montana Column jotted in his field diary, "No move, anniversary of Waterloo, both as to day of the week and day of the month."[16] Americans were exactly one week away from having a Waterloo of their own.

Crook's setback remained unknown to Gibbon and Terry when they rendezvoused at the mouth of Rosebud Creek on June 21. They did, however, know the approximate location of the Indians, and a rough battle plan was drawn up. The Dakota Column was to position itself south of the valley of the Little Big Horn, where it was rightly suspected that the hostiles would be found, while the Montana Column was to approach from the north, thereby precluding escape in that direction. Caught between the two forces, the Indians would either have to fight or capitulate; they could not simply run away.

Terry elected to accompany Gibbon's slower-moving infantry, and on June 22 Custer, now in sole command of his regiment and independent of authority, started up the Rosebud. During the early hours of the 25th, hot on the trail of a large body of Indians, the Seventh marched cross-country towards the Little Big Horn. At daybreak the scouts sighted the Indian encampment. That noon, Custer led his 675 men against a force of perhaps 3,000 warriors, termed by one of his officers "good shots, good riders, and the best fighters the sun ever shone on."[17] Furthermore, he divided the Seventh into three battalions: Major Marcus A. Reno and Captain Frederick W. Benteen were assigned three companies each, while Custer himself commanded a battalion of five companies. Captain Thomas M. McDougall, with one company, was left to guard the pack-train. Benteen's battalion headed south to scout the area to the left of the main column, with instructions to pitch into anything it encountered. Reno, meanwhile, was ordered to attack the village directly, with the promise that he would be "supported by the whole outfit."[18]

6

During the subsequent action, Custer's support failed to materialize and Reno's charge was stopped cold. Reno managed eventually to retreat to the bluffs across the Little Big Horn, but suffered almost one-third casualties in the process. Benteen, then McDougall, joined him shortly after, and the combined units dug in for a siege which was lifted only with the arrival of the Terry-Gibbon column on June 27.

What of Custer? He, and the 225 men in his battalion, five whole companies of the Seventh Cavalry, had been annihilated five miles down the Little Big Horn from Reno's position. This was the famous Custer's Last Stand, shrouded in mystery and speculation — for there were no survivors.

It is often said that no other battle in American history except Gettysburg has had more written about it, and one Custer bibliography, never exhaustive and now outdated, lists some six hundred items.[19] From any objective standpoint the battle of the Little Big Horn was a minor episode in the history of the United States. At the same time, to quote a student of the subject, "in another kind of history . . . it was a mammoth event and Custer is a mammoth figure. Most Europeans know about Custer when they know very little else about American history."[20] This "other kind of history" is the study of popular traditions that have become part of the American heritage and have moulded the American identity at home and abroad.

Custer's Last Stand had from the outset all of the qualities of which myths are made. If it was not removed in time, it was in distance, and to the average American the Little Big Horn was as unreal as Thermopylae, and such names as Sitting Bull and Rain-in-the-Face as exotic as Leonidas and Xerxes. Savagery and civilization had clashed on the frontier, and 225 soldiers had been swallowed up in mystery. What was more, the psychological timing of the battle was acute, the East receiving its first intimations of disaster on July 6, 1876, just two days after celebrating the nation's hundredth anniversary. Henry Wadsworth Longfellow voiced the general shock:

> Whose was the right and the wrong?
> Sing it, O funeral song,
>   With a voice that is full of tears,
> And say that our broken faith,
> Wrought all this ruin and scathe,
>   In the Year of a Hundred Years![21]

The times themselves launched Custer and his Last Stand into mythic immortality.

III

1876, marking the centennial of American independence, was a conspicuous date in the nation's history. It was a time both for reflection on the past and contemplation of the future. Many developments seemed to be converging to lend substance to the automatic symbolism of the "Year of a Hundred Years." The United States was moving into a new phase of its career. No longer young and innocent, tempered by civil war and transformed from an overwhelmingly rural, agrarian society into an increasingly urban, industrial one, the nation still paid allegiance to progress as to a god. Musing over what the second century of American independence might bring, one journalist smugly wondered: "Will it equal the century which has just closed, in material development and intellectual progress? It would seem that, in invention, in the arts and sciences, little has been left to be done by this century."[22]

With the completion of the transcontinental railroad in 1869, the West and the country as a whole had moved into a period of accelerated change, and technological innovations followed one another in quick succession. In 1875, Alexander Graham Bell discovered the principle of the telephone. The instrument itself was patented in March, 1876, and displayed at the United States International Exhibition, a gala hundredth birthday party held in Philadelphia and popularly known as the Centennial Exposition.

Self-congratulation was the order of the day. The fair's theme was a "Century of Progress," and crowds thronged through Machinery Hall to marvel at the latest advances in American technology. Dwarfed in the shadow of the thirty-nine foot high Corliss steam engine, by size alone the center of attention, were seven smaller internal combustion engines, including one designed by a Bostonian that ran on crude petroleum. The gasoline-powered automobile was less than a decade away. The next year, as the telephone was going into general service, Thomas A. Edison, who would shortly develop the incandescent lamp, invented the phonograph. America had a new hero: the technological wizard, whose fertile brain was the source of an almost magical material progress.

Yet even as they were celebrated, change and progress inspired uneasiness. Nostalgia — lingering, regretful backward glances — vied with confidence in the future. Much that was familiar and comforting was being lost in the rush to grow bigger and better and richer. Old values had been abandoned. The small, independent farmer, repository of republican virtue and a social model since the nation was founded, was losing ground to that business-oriented hero, the self-made man. More profoundly, creation was being transformed. Dogmatic old-school theologians like Charles Hodge of Princeton might still reject Darwinism out of hand ("What is Darwinism? . . . It is atheism"), but the theory of evolution was winning almost unanimous acceptance in scientific circles. Its ramifications, of course, went far beyond science. While avowed Darwinians like Asa Gray and American Spencerians like the popularizer John Fiske would continue to insist that evolution and Christianity were entirely compatible and that God, in one form or another, still ruled the universe, others like mathematicians Chauncey Wright and Charles Sanders Peirce had arrived at the conclusion that man inhabited a universe devoid of moral purpose. The only law of life was change, with chance its primary agent. In terms of social thought, evolutionary

8

naturalism would lead to the pessimism of a William Graham Sumner, who saw man descending inevitably to an elemental level of competition for survival where the law "Root, hog or die" would operate without restraint or amelioration. It would at the same time inspire the optimism of a Lester Frank Ward, who saw man progressing ever upwards to a Utopian "sociocracy" governed according to the precepts of a dynamic sociology that would ensure the greatest possible happiness for everyone.[23]

Confirmation of human progress was certainly one conclusion that could be derived from evolution. In 1876, Lewis Henry Morgan, a lawyer by profession and an ethnologist by choice, was busily putting the finishing touches on his monumental study *Ancient Society; or, Researches in the Lines of Human Progress from Savagery through Barbarism to Civilization*, which described in precise, categorical terms man's social evolution upwards to the heights of nineteenth-century industrial civilization. Morgan set his labors aside long enough in July that year to respond to the "hue-and-cry" occasioned by Custer's Last Stand. He patiently pointed out that America's Indian problem, of which that sanguinary encounter was but the latest manifestation, could be directly attributed to the government's failure to make policy conform to the laws of evolutionary progression that he was even then elucidating in his book. In the past, policy had struggled to achieve an overnight transformation of the Indian from free-roaming hunter to sedentary farmer. President Grant's policy, for example, had been conditioned by the philosophy of "conquest by kindness." Sometimes referred to as the Quaker Policy because of its attempt to combat corruption in the Indian service by allowing the participating Christian sects to nominate agents for the reservations, the Peace Policy, as it was more broadly known, involved the use of coercion to get the Indians onto their reservations, and training to raise them to civilization and citizenship once they were there. While the motive was laudatory, Morgan insisted that policy must accept ethnological reality and, with patience and foresight, raise the Indians gradually through the successive ethnic periods that stood between them and the reformer's goal of civilization. Progress was inevitable — but at an evolutionary pace.[24]

One could find comfort, albeit cold, in all of this. Progress was still the rule of life in a post-Darwinian world. But evolution correctly understood meant that all life was eternal flux, and perhaps even meaningless flux. The loss of faith in an ordered universe with its attendant stability became the common intellectual malaise of the time, and many Americans besides the restless, questing, superficially-cynical Henry Adams felt trapped in an industrial epoch that worshiped the dynamo while they still yearned for the simple security of the Virgin. Nostalgia, in short, was the other side of progress. Indeed, so sharply was America's machine-made future limned at the Centennial Exposition that an arts and crafts movement sprang up in reaction to revive the homey skills that were disappearing before the mechanical efficiency of factory production.

In the past, the West had always provided Americans with an option.

Metaphorically, it represented a future of untried possibilities, of hope and dreams without limitation. As long as there was a frontier and virgin land out West, the opportunity existed for perpetual renewal, and thus perpetual youth. In 1874, Custer had led a reconnaissance into the forbidden and still-mysterious Black Hills of Dakota, exposing to the public eye one of the last wilderness strongholds in the area of the United States, and leaving behind a legacy of place names and a diminished realm for discovery in the future. At one point, the expedition passed through a valley carpeted with flowers and watered by a crystal-clear stream "so cold as to render ice undesirable even at noonday." "Its equal I have never seen," Custer wrote in an enthusiastic official dispatch:

> Every step of our march that day was amid flowers of the most exquisite colors and perfume. So luxuriant in growth were they that men plucked them without dismounting from the saddle. . . . It was a strange sight to glance back at the advancing columns of cavalry, and behold the men with beautiful bouquets in their hands, while the head-gear of the horses was decorated with wreaths of flowers fit to crown a queen of May. Deeming it a most fitting appellation, I named this Floral Valley.[25]

Few such enchanting valleys remained to delight an unsuspecting world. By the Centennial Year, the exploration of *terra incognita*, so long synonymous with the American West, had shifted from the United States, where F. V. Hayden's Colorado Survey was engaged in a mopping-up operation, to "Darkest Africa," where Stanley's exploits were winning a name for himself and thrilling an American public no longer so infatuated with its own wilderness.

America had been tamed, domesticated, by its century of progress. Indian wars, like discovery, were a thing of the past. Then "like a clap of thunder from a cloudless sky" had come the news of the Little Big Horn disaster.[26] While Americans had been marvelling over the mechanical wonders on display at the Exposition in Philadelphia, Custer and his men had fallen at the hands of Indians out on the Western plains. In 1876, Custer's Last Stand was an anachronism. As such, almost from the moment of its occurrence, it was treasured as a heroic memory. Apparently some of the old values — a sense of duty, love of country, courage, self-sacrificing heroism — had survived intact through a century of change. Custer's Last Stand was a sign; God had not forgotten His Republic.

IV

Because 1876 was a presidential election year, political conditions, too, were ripe for national significance to be attached to the Little Big Horn. The Democrats had been out of power since 1861. Following the Civil War, they had had to fight the imputation of disloyalty and treason directed at the South and the Democratic Party in particular as the

Republican Party claimed the victorious Union cause for its own. In 1874, with the country mired in a severe depression, the Democrats had enjoyed a resurgence, capturing a majority in the House of Representatives that boded well for the presidential contest. By 1876 they were effectively challenging for the presidency. The Republican Reconstruction policy in the South had about run its course, and as the ex-Confederate states regained their full political rights it became apparent that the Democrats would dominate the South for the foreseeable future. As Republican incumbents struggled to regain the credibility lost during Grant's scandal-plagued second administration, their Democratic rivals found the conjunction of the Belknap impeachment trial and Custer's death under a cloud of official displeasure entirely too fortuitous to be missed. There was the rank odor of corruption in the air, of old Union generals bumbling in high office, and Custer's defeat was immediately converted into political ammunition as the Democratic press blasted holes in the administration and its Indian Peace Policy. An editorial in the Atlanta *Constitution* blamed "the Quaker idiocy and post-trader and contractor corruptions of the administration" for arousing the Indians' ire, while another Atlanta paper carried front-page stories with the self-explanatory headlines "The Custer Massacre — The Administration Responsible" and "Grant, the Murderer of Custer."[27]

The Republican press responded in kind. "Politics Run Mad," the *New York Times* editorialized. Noting that grief over the disaster was "mixed with indignation at the use made of this tragic affair by a besotted partisan press," the *Times* charged that "the Sioux, bloody and vindictive though they are, have never yet touched the depth sounded by the [New York] *World*, which parades the streets beating a tattoo on the coffins of the dead, and calling on all men to vote the Democratic ticket."[28] So virulent were the accusations which flew back and forth that it seemed for a while as though the election of 1876 might be fought over Custer's corpse. (Even yet the strand of politics is woven into the fabric of the Custer legend. Some contend that he died in a reckless attempt to erase the humiliation he had suffered at Grant's hands; others interpret his behavior differently, and speak of a dream that died with him — the Democratic Party's nomination, his for the asking if he but scored a smashing victory over the Sioux.)

V

Such a barrage of publicity could only distort the Little Big Horn out of all just proportions. Controversy's fires were soon raging, and every additional word intensified the heat. While Custer's Last Stand was being engulfed in partisan dispute, the poets, painters, novelists and showmen stepped in and, embracing fact and fantasy alike, salvaged from the flames the Last Stand's essence: its element of desperate heroism. And so the myth was born.

11

Chapter 2

"CHIVALRY'S AFTERGLOW:" The Poets and Custer's Last Stand

> Poets best understand the name and nature
> of heroes.
>
> Marshall W. Fishwick, *American Heroes.*

> His name with age
> On history's page
> Shall shine with greater glory,
> And bards shall tell
> How Custer fell,
> And sing his thrilling story.
>
> William Ludlow, "Custer's Last Charge."

"Of Custer's fight we at present know nothing, and can only surmise," wrote Lieutenant Edward Maguire on July 10, 1876, from "Camp on the Yellowstone River, Near the mouth of the Big Horn River." He continued: "We must be content with the knowledge gleaned from the appearance of the field, that they died as only brave men can die, and that this battle, slaughter as it was, was fought with a gallantry and desperation of which the 'Charge of the Light Brigade' cannot boast."[1] Maguire's analogy was appropriate, if not particularly imaginative. Alfred, Lord Tennyson, had transformed the blunder at Balaclava into a thrilling display of British courage in "The Charge of the Light Brigade." Similarly, the battle of the Little Big Horn, fought twenty-two years later, was immortalized by American poets seeking to translate disaster into a kind of moral victory.

The *Saturday Review,* an English weekly devoted to "Politics, Literature, Science and Art," observed with fascinated disapproval the American attempt to apotheosize Custer's Last Stand. Its merciless analysis of a poem which had appeared in the New York Herald on July 15 ("Amid 'heroes' gore,' 'corpses,' 'spouting wounds,' and 'savage foes,' ... [Custer] made a perfect melodramatic end") was followed by the relatively gentle admonition that "Americans, like ourselves, are better at doing things than commemorating them:"

> The unfortunate General Custer has received the dubious honour of comparison with Lord Cardigan, and an American rival of Tennyson has composed a poem on "Custer's Last Charge," while a sculptor has named a price for which he will undertake to represent in bronze "Custer with his long hair, and in his cavalry costume brandishing his sabre." These poets and artists will go near to add a new terror to death by making its victims ridiculous.[2]

But the British plea for moderation was to no avail.

General Bosquet, watching the Light Brigade charge to immortality, reputedly remarked, "C'est magnifique, mais ce n'est pas la guerre." Certainly, if Custer's Last Stand was not war, it was *magnifique*, and the sour remonstrances of the British press were not about to inhibit America's soaring muses. Newspapers which reported the story of the Little Big Horn under such Tennysonian headlines as "INTO THE JAWS OF DEATH!" "Custar's [sic] Ride Into the Jaws of Destruction" and "Custer's Balaklava" were duty bound to give the battle full poetic treatment. Occasional verse eventually yielded place to retrospective verse, and Custer's Last Stand was enshrined in the pantheon of conventional patriotic subjects.

This chapter deals with the poetic celebrations of Custer, his Last Stand and the legends that surround both. A few twentieth-century verses are included, for the battle remains a source of inspiration. Recently a number of unusually gifted poets have discovered Custer and, utilizing the fact that he is today a symbolic figure, have cast him in the role of villain to comment on militarism, racism and the red man's continuing struggle for political and cultural survival. There is also a long-standing tradition of amateur verse about the Custer battle, some of it as ingratiating as it is ingenuous, that tends to follow the heroic formula in its sympathies. But the focus for purposes of the present discussion is on the nineteenth-century poets who were commemorating a current event at a time when the public read verse and the newspapers were wont to publish reader contributions. I have come across approximately 150 poems on the Custer theme. About half of these were written in the nineteenth century, and more than thirty appeared in 1876 alone. These spontaneous reactions to the tragic news set the tone for later writers. Though their efforts often seem designed to corroborate Edmund Wilson's contention that "the celebration of current battles by poets who have not taken part in them has produced some of the emptiest verse that exists," the ranks of the Custer bards did include several of America's favorite poets.[3] They, along with their less distinguished fellows, were widely read in an age that had more time for poetry than our own, and all played a part in converting the Last Stand into a popular myth.

13

Narrating the story of the battle in verse seems the most agreeable method of acquainting the modern reader with the texture and tenor of the poets' efforts. What follows is a chorus of voices offering a one-sided commentary on the action at the Little Big Horn, as well as a distillation of all that was heroic in it.

I

With Nebraska's poet laureate, John G. Neihardt, we join the Seventh Cavalry as it sets out from the camp on the Yellowstone River, June 22, 1876, to complete the last leg of the campaign against the hostile Sioux and Cheyenne. Custer, brimming with confidence, waited impatiently with General Terry as the Seventh passed in review. Then, "waking from a dream at last / With still some glory of it in his eyes," he

> Shook hands around and said his last goodbyes
> And swung a leg across his dancing bay
> That champed the snaffle, keen to be away,
> Where all the others were.[4]

M. F. Bigney, in a verse submitted to the *New Orleans Republican*, observes the Seventh heading to its rendezvous with the wily Sioux:

> With [Custer] proudly three hundred ride,
> Each a hero, in martial pride,
> Thinking how deeds that must soon be done
> May add to honors already won.[5]

A quick change of lens and we are with Henry Wadsworth Longfellow surveying the Indian village:

> In the meadow, spreading wide
> By woodland and river-side
>   The Indian village stood;
> All was silent as a dream,
> Save the rushing of the stream
>   And the blue-jay in the wood.

But, Longfellow warns us, it is all a trap:

> In his war paint and his beads,
> Like a bison among the reeds,
>   In ambush the Sitting Bull
> Lay with three thousand braves
> Crouched in the clefts and caves,
>   Savage, unmerciful![6]

With Frederick Whittaker we return to Custer, now on the ridge above the Little Big Horn River, studying the camp spread out before him and gloating over his anticipated victory:

Down in the valleys the ages had hollowed,
There lay the SITTING BULL's camp for a prey!
Numbers! What recked he! What recked those who
    followed!
Men who had fought ten to one ere that day?

It was the moment of decision, and Frances Chamberlain Holley put words into Custer's mouth certain to rouse the romance in any soul:

"Come on, my boys! We will strike for yon hills,
    There Victory's waiting with garlands fair,
We will pluck from her hands the bay wreath
    green,
Which she twines for the bold that dangers
    dare."[8]

So, "with the blast of bugles," to quote John Greenleaf Whittier,

Straight into a slaughter pen,
With his doomed three hundred men,
    Rode the chief with the yellow hair.[9]

Immediately the Indian village burst into activity:

. . . the camp outspewed
    Its savage brood
And the locust swarm expanding,
    Was a blast from hell
    That withering fell,
The lives of all demanding.[10]

The showdown was at hand:

See the reeling, stricken squadrons!
    Dying man and dying steed!
They fly, they halt, they rally!
    But in vain they fight and bleed.
Still the ravines send their legions,
    Pouring onward like a flood!
And the air is black with terror,
    And the sands are red with blood![11]

Francis Brooks brings us into the very midst of the advancing braves:

Closing and closing
Nearer the redskins creep;
With cunning disposing,
With yell and with whoop,
(There are women shall weep)
They gather and swoop,
They come like a flood,

15

> Maddened with blood,
> They shriek, plying the knife,
> (Was there one begged for his life?)[12]

In turn, Ernest McGaffey offers us a trooper's eye view of the battle:

> Grim cavalry troopers
> Unshorn and unshaven,
> And never a craven
> In ambuscade caught,
> How like demons they fought
> Round the knoll on the prairie that marked their last haven.[13]

Slowly the Last Stand fades into myth as

> In front, in rear, on flank and flank,
> Death's darkening circles sweep,
> And horrid whirlwinds on each rank,
> Red as the lightnings, leap![14]

Though "Never a cap that had worn the bright SEVEN / Bowed till its wearer was dead on the strand," bow they all soon did.[15] For "of that gallant band / Not one returned again."[16] John Oliver Bellville rings the curtain down on the scene:

> When the sun had climbed the mountains,
> Death-like shades obscured the light,
> For the sullen war-cloud bound it
> In its blood-stained folds of night,
> And this sad and solemn message
> Floated over hill and plain;
> "In the valley of the Big Horn,
> Custer and his men lie slain."[17]

It was all over.

However, Longfellow relying on newspaper gossip current at the time, added a macabre touch that has become one of the most enduring of the Custer legends:

> . . . the foeman fled in the night,
> And Rain-in-the-Face, in his flight,
> Uplifted high in air
> As a ghastly trophy, bore
> The brave heart that beat no more,
> Of the White Chief with yellow hair.[18]

The best comment on these lines appeared in an anecdote, no doubt apocryphal, relating Sitting Bull's reaction to "The Revenge of Rain-in-the-Face:" "His attitude toward the paleface had always been tinged by dour conservatism, and after Major Kossuth Elder translated to him Longfellow's awful poem on the death of Custer . . . he was heard to state a preference for Negroes."[19]

16

The other half of the battle of the Little Big Horn, the Reno-Benteen engagement, has always had limited appeal for poets. Perhaps sensitive to the criticisms that abounded after the disaster, one rhymester in 1885 fashioned a ringing vindication of Captain Benteen, "the 'Chief with the Silvery Crown:' "

> one bright star in the Cimmerian sky,
> Too careless of life, too defiant to die.
>   Ah! a braver hero never was seen
> Than the white-haired Chieftain, brave Benteen![20]

Reno, who always needed one more, never found a poetic champion. Instead, Irving Bacheller sketched a picture of his men cowering on "the Hill of Fear," confused, demoralized, incapacitated by doubt: "The scattered troops of Reno look and listen with bated breath, / While bugle strains on lonely plains are searching the valley of death."[21]

John Neihardt, less partisan, recounted Reno's fight in memorable terms. He vividly described the troopers on the hill, surrounded by death and suffering from thirst under a June sun that was "like a wound / Wherewith the day bled dizzy." That night, "petulant with dread," they dug into the hilltop, and

> . . . talked of Custer, grumbling at a name
> Already shaping on the lips of Fame
> To be a deathless bugle-singing soon.[22]

Indeed, the person of Custer inspired the poetic muse to an almost frenzied rapture.

II

Custer! "The soul of chivalry was he — / He was [the Seventh's] boast and pride."[23] Custer! "He, whose brave heart went down to death/ Knew not what 'twas to fear."[24] Custer! "Young lion of the plain,/Thou of the tawny mane!"[25] Custer! "Thou wert a peerless one, a fearless one / With soul of poet, heart of cavalier."[26]

The very name Custer was to the poets quite truly a "deathless bugle-singing"— though it was they who shaped the notes of praise:

> Brave Custer! Fame's trumpet resounding
> Throughout every nation and clime,
>   Shall not oft sound a name
>   More worthy of fame,
> Through the echoing ages of time.[27]

Moreover, the poets have proven faithful, and if Neihardt speaks of Custer as "the Wolf of Washita,"[28] and others characterize his role at the Washita Battle of 1868 in an unfavorable light,[29] the Custer of the Last

Stand remains by and large transcendent and glorious. This is true despite the fact that Custer's most unabashed poetic partisans have unwittingly been among his most damning critics. They characterize his last charge as not only heroic, but also daring and impetuous — claims which the General's detractors would turn into a devastating condemnation.

"Ah, grand as rash was that last fatal raid /The little group of daring heroes made," Ella Wheeler Wilcox sighed,[30] and Edmund Clarence Stedman simply exclaimed, "O gallant charge, too bold!"[31] C. B. Davis was capable of extolling Custer in the following words:

> Outnumbered, still he would not yield
> And knowing well the cost,
> For glory's sake on that lone field
> He staked his all — and lost.[32]

A contemporary poet expressed the same thought:

> That wondrous "Charge" of CUSTER
> So dauntless and so brave,
> Is the noblest act of daring
> That History ever gave;
> For CUSTER knew full well the fate
> That awaited his command,
> Was, to conquer the revengeful Sioux,
> Or, sacrifice his band![33]

The point, of course, is that while it may have been fine for Custer to "stake his all" for "glory's sake," it was hardly right that he "sacrifice his band" in the process. Joseph Clarke's poem in the *New York Herald* had blithely concluded:

> . . . Fame will never forget that ride,
> That wild mad dash to the riverside,
> Where the glorious Custer, fearless, died.[34]

These lines moved the *Saturday Review* to observe that "the leader of a 'wild, mad dash' at an ambushed enemy ought never to have been allowed to lead at all. But perhaps General Custer was not such a fool as he looks in poetry."[35]

Nevertheless, the self-contradictions of Custer's poetic admirers could not compromise their earnest devotion to the dead General's memory, and they would brook no unfriendly criticism of his actions. Joaquin Miller challenged Custer's detractors:

> Yea, who shall call him rash, or chide
> From some safe place this man who died,
> With all his kindred at his side?

The "strong, sweet singer of the West," whose reputation straddled two mountain ranges ("Byron of the Rockies," "Poet of the Sierras"), answered himself by echoing Tennyson: "Not his to question wrong or right,/They bade him seek the foe to fight!"[36] "Old age will say 'Twas rashly done,' " a Massachusetts poet conceded,

> But Youth, "Behold the flags he won!
> There are enough for every son,
>   For him and all his dead; he won them all by
>   charges like this final one."[37]

Although their appraisals of Custer might suffer from internal inconsistency, the poets rose above such a mundane consideration, convinced that future ages "shall swear that the cup of his glory / Needed but that death to render it full."[38]

There was, finally, something exhilarating — indeed, beautiful — in Custer's Last Stand:

> Not when a hero falls
> The sound a world appalls:
> For while we plant his cross
> There is a glory, even in the loss.[39]

With this theme in mind, poets like Joaquin Miller consciously elevated the disaster into a moral victory:

> O Custer and thine comrades, where
> Have ye pitched tent in fields of air?
> Above the Rocky Mountains' brow —
> In everlasting glory now,
> Ye shine like some high shaft of light,
> Ye march above the bounds of night,
> And some strong singer yet shall rise
> And lift your glory to the skies
> In some grand song of wild delight.[40]

Truly, all of the other voices chanting the heroic saga of Custer and his Last Stand were drowned out by the dominant tones of one "strong singer," Walt Whitman.

In Custer's defeat American poets had found something precious, a new myth, a genuine tragedy with the qualities of a classical epic. Appropriately, it was Whitman, that most American of bards, who first detected in the carnage at the Little Big Horn "a trumpet-note for heroes:"

> Continues yet the old, old legend of our race!
> The loftiest of life upheld by death!
> The ancient banner perfectly maintain'd!
> (O lesson opportune — O how I welcome thee!)

Whitman's excitement was palpable on July 7 when he submitted "A Death-Sonnet for Custer" to Whitelaw Reid at the New York Tribune. "If it comes in time, get it in tonight," he urged, "as earliness is everything."[41] The country must be apprised of the real meaning of

Custer's Last Stand as Whitman perceived it, and as he had compressed it into a few memorable lines:

> Thou of the sunny, flowing hair, in battle,
> I erewhile saw, with erect head, pressing ever in
>   front, bearing a bright sword in thy hand,
> Now ending well [in death] the splendid fever of thy deeds,
> (I bring no dirge for it or thee — I bring a glad,
>   triumphal sonnet;)
>   There in the far northwest, in struggle, charge, and
>   sabre-smite,
> Desperate and glorious — aye, in defeat most desperate,
>   most glorious,
> After thy many battles, in which, never yielding up a
>   gun or a color,
> Leaving behind thee a memory sweet to soldiers,
> Thou yieldest up thyself.[42]

John Hay, a fellow poet, wrote Whitman on July 22 to say that his "Death-Sonnet" was "splendidly strong and sustained and full of a noble motive."[43] Here was a tale of American heroism. Indeed, here was the outline of a national myth.

III

In what have been called the "Sentimental Seventies," the fact that Custer's Last Stand involved pathos and tears was as important to its mythicizing as the core element of tragedy. Confirmation of the disaster in all its details stunned a nation that by 1876 had grown complacent about the dangers of Indian warfare. Just days before news of the Little Big Horn reached the East, one New York paper had smugly noted that "while all the world . . . is in a seething, angry condition; while Europe resounds with the tramp of armed men; . . . we close our century in profound peace."[44] As if in repentance for such premature self-congratulation, Americans were caught up in a wave of recrimination, sorrow and sympathy for the fallen General, his gallant men, his beautiful young widow and all the others personally bereaved by the tragedy.

Custer, cavalier sans peur et sans reproche, was dead, and William Lawrence, a Congressman from his native state of Ohio, voiced the prevalent feeling when he stood up in the House of Representatives to mourn

> this unfortunate war by which the lives of some of our best, truest, bravest, most valuable, faithful officers and men have been sacrificed. . . . we know beyond doubt that the brave and good and daring Custer and his brave and good and daring men acted in the line of duty in obedience to orders. History will do them justice, and I shall venerate their names and cherish their memories.[45]

20

Lawrence's eulogy was merely prelude to the Congressional reaction to the Little Big Horn disaster, much of which was lachrymose in nature, ranging from proposals for the erection of "suitable monuments" to fervent pleas that pensions for the widows be rushed through committee.[46]

But no official expressions of sympathy could rival those of the poets. "Weep, fathers and mothers throughout the land — / Weep, sisters and brothers where'er you stand," one Colorado poetaster lamented:

> But oh! to think of those who stand
> And wait for what can come
> No more to fill the household band
> Or hear the welcome home!
> God of the sorrowful, pity such lives;
> Lighten the burden of each who survives,
> Waiting these absent faces.[47]

Harper's Weekly aimed directly at the prevalent sentimentality with an anonymous verse titled "Romance and Reality." The contrasting scenes — a fair young cadet at West Point wooing his lady love under a full moon, and the same soldier lying on the plains, an arrow in his breast and a picture of his sweetheart fluttering from his lifeless fingers — were calculated to sunder every heart:

> Look! how silent a brave form lies!
> The sun glares down from the tearless skies.
>
> No soft hand touches the matted hair,
> No lips of woman are resting there.
>
> Only a veteran stern and grim,
> Pauses a while with eyes grown dim.
>
> There's a pictured face on the blood-stained grass;
> O'er the smiling eyes, no shadows pass.
>
> There are other eyes that are dim with tears,
> That will smile no more in the coming years,
>
> That turn in pain from the cheerless moon
> As the weeks bring round the month of June,
>
> And lips that whisper a simple name
> That has never rung on the blast of fame.

A pair of equally sentimental illustrations by C. S. Reinhart completed *Harper's* assault on its readers' sympathies.[48]

Because Custer was a Yankee war hero, Southern newspaper readers were spared the more lugubrious of the occasional verse which graced papers elsewhere in the nation. The poetic eulogies by Walt Whitman, Joaquin Miller and Edmund C. Stedman were reprinted, and a few restrained original contributions appeared. But not until Laura S. Webb's thin volume *Custer's Immortality* was published later that summer did the nation get a dose of Southern sentimentality.

Mrs. Webb, whose "lonely, widowed heart" lay "buried with the 'Gray,'" was no Emmeline Grangerford, perhaps, but she did manage to draft a tribute almost before her subject was cold. The news of the Little Big Horn had awakened in her "the string of slumbering lute," and she felt compelled

> To sound this feeling lay,
> For the gallant, graceful CUSTER,
> Who wore the foeman's "Blue,"
> And fought the Southern soldiers
> As a hero grand and true.

One can almost imagine Mrs. Webb fighting back the tears as she described Custer making his decision to attack:

> . . . not the faintest pulse was stirred
> Of fainting in his heart;
> Though, doubtless, thoughts of home and wife
> Caused the quick tear to start;
> For "the bravest *are* the tenderest,
> The loving are the daring,"
> While Love and Duty, Fame, Renown,
> The soldier's thoughts are sharing.

"A thousand tears for that princely man," she intoned, and concluded in the same vein:

> then hang around his glorious name,
> A wreath of *immortelles,*
> And let the diamond tear-drop light
> The tale which Glory tells.

Asked by the author to comment on her poem, William Cullent Bryant diplomatically replied: "You have given voice to a sadness which was in all men's hearts and have fervently expressed the general sorrow."[49]

Twenty years later another poetess composed a moving picture of Custer at his Last Stand spurning the offer of an Indian scout to lead him to safety:

> A second's silence. Custer dropped his head,
> His lips slow moving as when prayers are said —
> Two words he breathed — "God and Elizabeth,"
> Then shook his long locks in the face of death,
> And with a final gesture turned away
> To join the fated few who stood at bay.
> Ah! deeds like that the Christ in man reveal
> Let Fame descend her throne at Custer's shrine to kneel.[50]

Thus did poets steeped in classical imagery and ever-mindful of their republican heritage encase the fallen hero in clusters of ivy and immortelles, cypress branches and evergreen bows, wreaths of laurel, myrtle, bay leaves — everything short of a crown of thorns.

The nation's emotional reaction to the Little Big Horn disaster was given concrete expression at West Point on August 30, 1879, with the unveiling of Wilson Macdonald's statue of Custer — a preposterously overblown affair depicting the General mid-stride, pistol and sabre in hand, that managed to earn Mrs. Custer's undying hatred and a few cynical sneers from officers at the Academy who considered Custer a creature of the press.[51] Certainly the monument to him was the result of a vigorous campaign undertaken by the *New York Herald* whose publisher, James Gordon Bennett, an old acquaintance of Custer, recognized in the news of his death an opportunity not only to castigate the Republican administration and honor the General's memory, but also to sell papers. The *Herald* kept the story alive by proposing the erection of a monument to Custer and his men, and appealing to its readers for contributions. Money did not exactly pour in, but there was a steady trickle of small donations, carefully recorded with the sum totaled up each day. In promoting its own scheme, the *Herald* editorially pounded home the constant theme that in the Centennial year Custer's sacrifice offered the nation a fit model of valor, courage and devotion to duty. Perhaps the *Herald's* ultimate monument to Custer was the heroic aura with which it so consciously surrounded his name.

Whatever one thought about the West Point statue and the nature of Custer's fame, the dedication ceremonies in 1879 were properly reverent. A "Distinguished Tragedian" recited most of the *Herald* poem "Custer's Last Charge," and five "eminent artists" performed "Hail! and Farewell to Custer," which was written for the occasion by Henry Morford and sung to the tune of "Annie Laurie:"

> His name makes classic the Rosebud;
> His death at the Little Big Horn
> Gives a theme of song and story
> To the ages yet unborn —
> To the ages yet unborn.

Morford also provided one of the featured speakers with "words of apostrophe to our dead hero," a little poem that "press[ed] for utterance:" "Ah, if the Days of Chivalry are gone,/We have an afterglow that shames the dawn."[52]

Today we are far removed from the spirit that informed these lines, and the contemporary reply to such nineteenth-century sentimentality was succinctly phrased in the refrain of a popular novelty record of 1960: "Please, Mr. Custer, I don't wanta go!"[53] But the battle occurred in an age which could appreciate the grand gesture, no matter how futile. It was also an age which deemed a delicate refinement of sensibility to be the mark of the gentleman as well as the lady. Blushes might be reserved for the latter, but both were disposed to shed a tear when the occasion demanded it. Novels, melodrama and the genteel verse that graced the monthly journals all catered to this taste for the romantic and sentimental. So did the newspapers. The *Atlanta Times* on July 21 carried one story under a heading that requires no elaboration: "The Grief for the Gold-Haired Cavalryman in His Adopted State [Michigan] — At the Home — A Gray-Haired Father's Cureless Grief — 'They Were Brave, Good Boys.' " In the same issue the *Times* printed the only statement that could be obtained from the General's prostrate widow: "All the world is gone!"

Custer's Last Stand prompted admiration and tears in equal measure, and the two responses, intertwined, found perfect expression in the sonnets, songs and dirges that flowed from busy pens. Here clearly was a moment in the nation's history destined for reverent remembrance.

IV

The poets not only forged Custer's Last Stand into a glowing affirmation of American ideals, but they also perpetuated certain minor legends deriving from the battle by incorporating them in the larger mythic structure. It was Longfellow's verse that made Rain-in-the-Face's name a blood-curdling synonym for savagery long after the original newspaper accounts of his nefarious deed were forgotten. Similarly, the paeans sung over the battlefield monument and Comanche, "the horse that survived the Custer massacre," have contributed to a myth most fully realized in the traditions of the Seventh Cavalry, symbolized by its regimental march "GarryOwen." Here the poetic apotheosis is fully realized, and the transformation complete: defeat has become victory.

The *Saturday Review* had fretted that Americans in attempting to honor Custer with poems and monuments would only add "a new terror to death" by making him look ridiculous. The English weekly did not go far enough. American poets were soon celebrating not just the dead General, but also the field upon which he died — and eventually the monument that crowned the fatal hill. On the tenth anniversary of the Seventh Cavalry's doomed charge, an Indianapolis poet called on the nation to "carve high their names on glory's scroll,"

> And let the spot where Custer fell
> Be marked by shaft enduring, high,
> That to all ages e're shall tell
> The story that can never die.[54]

A few years later, a journalist recorded his impressions of "Decoration Day on the Little Big Horn" in verse:

> Over the trail that Custer trod
>   March the troopers with reverent tread;
> Every step is on blood-bought sod —
>   Bought with the lives of the valiant dead.

Sprinkle the soil with manly tears,
    Weep for the heroes who died that day;
Here on this spot a country rears
    Tributes of love to the lifeless clay.

Over each headstone hang a wreath,
    Weeds and the tangled briars efface;
Mutter a prayer for the soul beneath —
    Death such as theirs is a saving grace.[55]

The Custer Battlefield had become a spot sacred in American affections. Designated a National Cemetery in 1879, it was declared a National Monument in 1946. Six years later a modest museum opened its doors. The site of a slaughter shrouded in controversy is now a patriotic shrine and an obligatory side-trip on any Northwestern tour. Three-quarters of a century ago, Freeman E. Miller rhapsodized:

Where Custer fell! The nation strows
The brightest garlands Honor knows
    Upon the marbles that alway
    Mark holy mounds of yellow clay,
And wreaths of glory there bestows.[56]

Now more than a quarter of a million tourists annually make the pilgrimage, treading

. . . with rev'rent foot this mound
    Where heroes grandly died;
This soil is consecrated ground;
    By their blood sanctified.[57]

A number of visitors have been inspired to verse. "In the valley of the Little Big Horn," one distinguished poet has written, "history explodes into quiet."[58] The active imagination hears taps in the wind and sees soldiers and Indians instead of white markers. Arthur Chapman, the author of "Out Where the West Begins," stood early one morning on the hogback above the Little Big Horn River, his mind drifting in reverie:

The fluttering bonnets breast the hill;
    Now silenced is the bugle's blare;
And all the forms in blue are still —
    All save the group with Yellow Hare;
But now the morning breaks the spell —
    The phantom hosts fade swift away;
Behold the cross where Custer fell,
    White in the smiling Western day![59]

The typographical error in the fourth line that turns the dauntless Yellow Hair into a frightened rabbit "breaks the spell" of Chapman's reverie before morning has a chance. But there was an animal — a horse — that won lasting renown as the sole survivor of the Little Big Horn.

No Last Stand legend is more generally cherished than that of Comanche, the charger ridden into battle by Captain Myles W. Keogh.

25

Indeed, Keogh himself has become a legendary figure. A soldier of fortune, handsome, hard-drinking and fearless, a bachelor and a rake with the necessary touch of Irish melancholy in his soul, Keogh had always regarded June with superstitious fatalism. It was his unlucky month, one that never passed, he wrote his brother, "without something very unpleasant occurring to me." June, 1876, was to be no exception: Keogh perished along with the company he commanded at the Little Big Horn.[60] His mount, wounded in the fighting, recovered to become the Seventh Cavalry's official mascot.

General Orders No. 7, issued at Fort Abraham Lincoln on April 10, 1878, charged every member of the regiment with the "kind treatment and comfort" of the horse known as Comanche: "Wounded and scarred as he is, his very existence speaks in terms more eloquent than words ... of the heroic manner in which all went down that fatal day." Pampered for the duration of his life, Comanche died in November, 1891. His remains were mounted and are still on display in the Dyche Museum at the University of Kansas. The object of curiosity ever since 1876, Comanche's exploits have inspired historical monographs, novels, comic books, paintings, movies, songs and verse.[61]

The most popular poem about Comanche is John Hay's "Miles Keogh's Horse." Since it was first published in 1880 it has been reprinted with such frequency that one Custer historian deemed it "almost as familiar as the famous Anheuser-Busch painting."[62] This is an exaggeration. Probably the best known Custer poem is Longfellow's "The Revenge of Rain-in-the-Face," and it does not begin to rival the Anheuser-Busch lithograph in popularity. But the dramatic impact of Hay's lines cannot be discounted:

> ... of all that stood at noonday
> In that fiery scorpion ring,
> Miles Keogh's horse at evening
> Was the only living thing.
>
> Alone from that field of slaughter,
> Where lay the three hundred slain,
> The horse Comanche wandered,
> With Keogh's blood on his mane.[63]

"Miles Keogh's Horse" is merely the most famous among several poetic tributes to Comanche. An anonymous and obviously amateur writer who may have been a trooper in the Seventh Cavalry anticipated Hay's theme in 1878:

> Honor to Keogh's charger!
> Only his flashing eye
> Saw the Three Hundred Fighting —
> Saw the Three Hundred die!
> . . .

26

And let a trooper lead him,
　　The horse that saw Custer die,
Forth to the place of honor
　　In the front of Company I!

　　　　　. . .

Honor to old Comanche,
　　While strength and life remain!
But, O, to see the Captain
　　Upon his back again![64]

A few years after Comanche's death Francis Brooks, a more polished craftsman, compressed the horse's tale into a few words:

Down the Little Big Horn,
(Tramp of the hoof, champ of the bit)
A single steed in the morn,
Comanche, seven times hit,
Comes to the river to drink;
Lists for the sabre's clink,
Lists for the voice of his master,
(O glorious disaster!)
Comes, sniffing the air,
Gazing, lifts his head,
But his master lies dead.[65]

At the heart of Comanche's appeal, of course, is the notion that he held the key to the Custer mystery. William V. Wade saw the "great Commanche" at Fort Lincoln in 1877 and was so inspired that he hastened from the stable to the banks of the Missouri River and, perched above the muddy waters, dashed off a poem:

Old Commanche, Old Commanche,
Tell us of that dreadful day
Tell us of that bloody fray,
　　Tell us true,
Of days past and gone
Of the battle of the Little Horn,
When Custer led his troopers on
　　To doom, all of you.[66]

The dream of the story straight from the horse's mouth expired with Comanche's death. But the fame that surrounded him in life continues to defy time.

Various schemes to bring Comanche's remains back to Montana have periodically flourished and failed in the face of the University of Kansas' stout resistance, and when it was proposed in the late 1940's that Comanche be transferred to Fort Riley, Kansas, another controversy ensued.[67] In September, 1949, the New York Herald Tribune carried a poem by Robert E. Haggard arguing that the gallant old warhorse would have nothing in common with today's "cavalry-on-wheels:"

What would Comanche, given to the keeping
Of modern cavalry, have felt to see
Platoons of armored motorcycles sweeping
The praise [prairies?] of his time, unfenced
   and free?[68]

Defenders of the status quo eventually won out, and the time-worn symbol of a legendary episode in American history reposes undisturbed in Lawrence, Kansas, where he continues to receive the attention that has been his ever since that June Sunday in 1876. "The battle was over / At Custer's Last Stand," the plaintive wail of singer Johnny Horton informed the generation of the 1960's:

And taps were sounding
For all the brave men,
While one lone survivor,
Wounded and weak,
Comanche, the brave horse,
Lay at the General's feet.[69]

To this day, "the brave horse" remains the most poignant and popular hero of Custer's Last Stand.

Over the years, Comanche has served conspicuously as part of the tradition of the Seventh Cavalry and its modern descendants. So too has "GarryOwen," a quick-march or drinking song of Irish origin that was supposedly adopted as the Seventh's regimental tune in 1867 at the behest of Comanche's master, Captain Keogh. Whatever the truth might be, "GarryOwen" is still closely identified with the Custer myth. It was played during a musical interlude at the unveiling of the West Point statue of the fallen hero in 1879, and, since 1941, has often accompanied the Seventh Cavalry on its march to glory in successive Custer movies. This baffled at least one film critic who, attuned to cinematic history exclusively, could only account for the Irish air by invoking John Ford's pervasive influence on the cavalry Western.[70]

Since "GarryOwen's" charm is to the ear, balladeers have been most successful in conveying its jaunty, devil-may-care appeal. The lilting strains reputedly can even raise a ghost from its grave. To the tune of "GarryOwen," Cliff Carl tells how the wraiths haunting the banks of the Little Big Horn still await the return of their commander, whose remains had been removed to West Point for burial in 1877:

Troopers talk of the battle on that bloody day
And keep waiting for Custer to lead them away
With his "Yo!" and "Away!" they'd be mounted and gone
To heaven in two's singing their "GarryOwen."[71]

"Sergeant Flynn'" as performed by the U.S. Army Band and Chorus, relates the destruction of the Seventh amid blasts of "Boots and Saddles," "Charge!" and "GarryOwen." Then comes a further word from the ghosts of Custer's men:

28

Though your bones to dust will crumble, Sergeant Flynn,
Down the years our drums will rumble, Sergeant Flynn,
In the annals of the brave
Comes our whisper from the grave,
On the breeze we're singing dear old "GarryOwen."[72]

"GarryOwen" arouses so many ghosts because it is one memento of disaster. Newspapers in 1876 had Custer shouting as he charged at the Washita, "Play Garry Owen — a good tune to die by!"[73] Yet, unconscious of any irony, members of today's "Fighting Seventh" bellow out the words with which the gay drinking song was saddled in 1905:

We are the pride of the army,
    And a regiment of great renown,
Our name's on the pages of history
    From sixty-six on down.
If you think we stop or falter
    While into the fray we're goin',
Just watch the steps with our heads erect,
    While our band plays "GarryOwen."

It is necessary to remind oneself that all of this enthusiasm stems from the Custer years and a dark day of slaughter on the Little Big Horn. Not a man armed with the wisdom and technology of nineteenth-century civilization survived that encounter with the representatives of an "inferior" culture. Five companies of the Seventh Cavalry were entirely annihilated. Nevertheless, "No other regiment ever can claim / Its pride, honor, glory and undying fame."[74] Utter defeat has become a source of pride; the vanquished are the real victors.

V

Ultimately, no one is more responsible for this seeming paradox than the poets themselves. Seizing upon the bleak news of a military debacle on the frontier, they proceeded to transform unadorned fact into a glorious myth. They narrated the story of the battle in such a way as to provide the public with its terms of reference, emphasizing the heroic to the virtual exclusion of all other considerations. They apotheosized Custer, making a monument of the man, and rendered such favorite legends as those of Rain-in-the-Face and Comanche in quotable verse. Moreover, there was nothing accidental about this mythicizing process. In the nation's hundredth year, poets were on the lookout for a sign, some evidence of national grandeur. They found it in Custer's Last Stand: " 'Oh, the wild charge they made.' Here is a theme for our poets to stir the heart, as with the purple blasts of a war trumpet."[75] The United States had come of age. It had been endowed with that most precious of traditions, an epic tragedy, a great "legend of total annihilation."[76]

The Alamo would not do. It was basically a Texas tradition before Walt Disney and John Wayne made it a national one. Previous defeats at the hands of the Indians had possibilities, but they had rarely been total. One exception, the Fort Phil Kearny Massacre, had shocked the country ten years before Custer's Last Stand. But Captain William Judd Fetterman, who led his eighty men to their graves in apparent defiance of orders, lacked heroic stature despite the magnificent stupidity of the boast attributed to him: "With eighty men I can ride through the whole Sioux nation." Perhaps in 1866 the public was still inured to casualty figures from the battlefront. At any rate, no Walt Whitman or Henry Wadsworth Longfellow, no John Greenleaf Whittier or Edmund Clarence Stedman, no Joaquin Miller or John Hay was inspired by Fetterman to step forward and tell the nation that there was "no better man." Rather it was Custer whose death ten years later sent poet and poetaster alike in hopeless search for suitable rhymes: "Custer, bold Custer, / The brighter your lustre"[77] . . . "Through the battle's storm and bluster"[78] . . . "The boys are beginning to muster"[79] . . . ". . . on his name shed luster."[80]

Custer's Last Stand was America's Thermopylae, her Waterloo, her Charge of the Light Brigade. A profusion of historical precedents tumbled from poets' pens:

> But never again shall the roll of fame
> Be called without mention of Custer's name;
> And the brave three hundred shall ever be
> Kin to those who fell at Thermopylae.[81]

"Oh, Custer — gallant custer!," another tribute began:

> . . . Man foredoomed
> To ride, like Rupert, spurred and waving plumed,
> Into the very jaws of death and hell,
> That Balaklava scarce could show so well.[82]

Though one newspaper headlined a story "Custer's Waterloo," and many likened the impetuous Yellow Hair to Napoleon's hotspur, General Joachim Murat, it was Balaclava, finally, with its innuendo of recklessness and blundering completely overshadowed by Lord Cardigan's superb charge, that afforded the closest parallel to Custer's Last Stand. There was in both "something higher than war . . . the utter consecration of one's life to his duty, the sublimest thing man can do."[83]

No poet captured these sentiments more effectively than Leavitt Hunt, an officer on General Samuel P. Heintzelman's staff during the Civil War. In "The Last Charge," he wrote:

> At eve all lay, by Death enrolled,
>   In ghastly bivouac,
> Alone Death stalked, the story told
> Of men of more than Spartan mould,
>   That column of attack.
>
> The sun sunk down, deep-dyed in blood,
>   When lo! a phantom shade

Of kindred spirits capped with hood
In battle line, to greet them, stood
    The deathless Light Brigade.

In low salute their colors dip,
    As Custer moves before;
Their sabres sink, in veteran grip,
One gleam illumines every tip,
    To comrades, as of yore.

They wheel in rear, with pennon lance,
    An escort, man for man
Their champing chargers proudly prance,
Through arch of glory they advance,
    And Custer leads the van.[84]

To the accompaniment of such poetic tributes, Custer and his men
passed into glory and into myth.

Chapter 3

"TO THE LAST MAN:" The Artists and Custer's Last Stand

Long before the cowboy and the sheriff commenced to haunt the movies, the West was having its influence. Lithographs, Currier & Ives pictures, steel engravings in the magazines and in the publicity pamphlets of the railroads as these pushed westward, copies of favorite pictures — a late example is almost any one of the paintings of Custer's defeat at the Little Big Horn — these became the Great West in the popular mind.

Howard Mumford Jones, *O Strange New World*

The many soldiers, their faces and attitudes, the carbines, the broad-brimm'd western hats, the powder-smoke in puffs, the dying horses with their rolling eyes almost human in their agony, the clouds of war-bonneted Sioux in the background, the figures of Custer and Cook[e] . . . indeed the whole scene, dreadful, yet with an attraction and beauty that will remain in my memory.

Walt Whitman, on viewing John Mulvany's
Custer's Last Rally (1881).

In a paper on "Fact and Fiction in the Documentary Art of the American West," ethnologist John C. Ewers argued that "a fictitious picture can do more harm than a false statement, for it may be retained in the viewer's memory long after the written words are forgotten."[1] Parsed of its value judgment, Ewers' contention seems unarguable. Certainly a scholar's prose account of a historical event, no matter how painstakingly researched and scrupulously accurate in detail, usually proves something less than deathless, while a picture of the same event may linger in the viewer's mind and leave a lasting impression. This proposition is demonstrably true in the case of Custer's Last Stand.

It was left to the artists to create a visual equivalent of that self-sacrificing heroism that had so enraptured the poets in 1876. They did not fail in their duty. By one recent count, some three hundred Custer's Last

Stands have appeared.[2] They crop up everywhere, though children's books are the most fertile single source. Nearly every turn-of-the-century school history of the United States, for example, contained an illustration that outdid the text's glowing description of doomed bravery on the Little Big Horn. "To impress great scenes upon the mind of the young is as important as to paint them on canvas," the author of one history that included a modest sketch of the Last Stand contended.[3] Generations of American youth were educated with scenes of Custer's Last Stand firmly in mind; the event lent itself to pictorial treatment, and was instantly recognizable. It probably goes without saying that most of the three hundred representations of the battle exhibit more fantasy and imitativeness than aesthetic merit. Unskilled hacks have given the subject the benefits of their talents with a distressing persistency. But many artists of substantial ability have also been fascinated by the Last Stand, and it is almost as obligatory for the Western painter as the Madonna and child was for his Renaissance predecessor.

The combined efforts of all those attracted to the subject have resulted in the familiar image of Custer's Last Stand as a high point in the annals of American heroism: "There was a man: Custer's Last Stand — The Massacre that Will Never Be Forgotten."[4] Different Last Stand styles have evolved, but each in its own way contributes to the central image of a doomed squadron fighting to the end, without a chance for victory, without a hope of succor or escape, yet unyielding in the determination to go down with honor. The picture that leaps to mind at the mention of Custer's Last Stand is the artists' contribution to myth.

Besides endowing the public with a mental picture of the Last Stand, the painters have inspired one another to attempt fresh interpretations of the theme. Successive artists have modified innumerable details and rearranged the composition of the picture, seeking through research or sheer imagination to get at the deeper meaning of the battle as they construe it. In the end, they have revitalized rather than revised the image of Custer's Last Stand, and have simply reaffirmed the myth.

The quantity of Custer art makes it impractical to attempt more than a brief consideration of the basic Last Stand styles and some significant examples of each. Since the various pictures tend to repeat one another ritualistically, similarity rather than novelty is their keynote. The heroic conception embodied by the many is thus fairly represented by the few. Moreover, that conception can be traced back to its immediate origins.

I

Although garbled account of the Little Big Horn disaster reached the East by July 6, 1876, it was not until the next day that confirmation was received and the story fully elaborated on the front pages of the nation's newspapers. As the details accumulated, a sharp impression of the action began to emerge. "The more we learn about the circumstances of the

33

late terrible fight in which Gen. Custer and his men lost their lives, the more we become impressed with the magnificent heroism they displayed," a Texas paper averred:

> Overwhelmed by blood-thirsty and yelling thousands, enclosed with "the jaws of hell," with certain death staring every man in the face, there was no panic, no rout, but each company took its place in turn to fight and die, Custer and his staff taking their turn last.
>
> There is nothing superior to it in all history.[5]

Such prose begged for pictorial representation.

On July 19, the New York *Daily Graphic* featured a full-page drawing, *The Battle on the Little Big Horn River — The Death Struggle of General Custer,* by William M. Cary. In less than two weeks an artist had crystallized his conception of what would ever after be known as Custer's Last Stand. Cary showed a heroic figure clad in army blues, standing with one foot on the haunch of a dead horse, his left arm stiffly extended, fingers gripping a pistol, and the right poised overhead, sabre in hand, about to deliver a devastating blow to a nearby Indian. The pure drama of the pose, augmented by the long curly locks floating from beneath a hat set at a rakish angle, made a memorable picture, and set the style for a legion of Last Stand artists to follow.

Writing five years later, Judson Elliott Walker observed that "almost numberless paintings, chromos, engravings and various other life-like illustrations [of Custer's Last Stand] adorn the walls to-day of almost untold numbers of art galleries, drawing rooms, studios, and public places."[6] This was more than a slight exaggeration in 1881, but the fact remains that Cary's New York *Graphic* sketch was only the first of many contemporary attempts to portray "the death struggle of General Custer" and, more importantly, its lessons for Americans.

Several nineteenth-century artists, captive to the convention of equestrian heroism, favored a "Last Charge" over a "Last Stand." They found some corroborating evidence in the press, particularly in a letter from one James Mannion, "a private in Gen. Reno's command," to his father in Detroit. If nothing else, the letter qualifies Mannion as an early entrant in the field of liars who rallied at the first news of total disaster on the Little Big Horn. Having burst through the circle of Indians and successfully run "the gauntlet of at least 2,000 rifles for the whole distance," Mannion wrote, Custer realized that his men were not behind him, but were still trapped back on the hill. Though his trusty Indian scout implored him not to throw his life away, "Custer only laughed, and, putting the reins of his horse between his teeth, with a revolver in each hand, he gave a wild cheer [no mean feat in itself!], and dashed back through the hell of smoke and flying bullets." "As if by a miracle," Custer returned safely, but on the third try, as he endeavored to lead the forty remaining troopers "from their place of peril over the path of his solitary charge," his luck finally ran out.[7]

34

Two lithographs published in 1876 bore the identical legend *Custer's Last Charge*. The one issued by America's master printmakers, Currier & Ives, was a perfunctory job, showing the single figure of Custer, sword raised above his head, staring out as if to have his portrait taken by some Matthew Brady of the Indian wars while his walleyed steed transported him to glory. Much more intriguing was a version signed by the lithographer, Feodor Fuchs, which isolated the figure of an unruffled Custer, omnipresent sabre about to split the skull of a feathered chieftain, in full gallop across the foreground while behind him his troopers charge and fall in precise military formation. The best work in this vein, John A. Elder's 1885 oil *Battle of the Little Big Horn*, has Custer in his buckskins, red cravat flying, still brandishing a sabre as he hacks his way through the redskins. The picture suffers from the fact that the cavalry, not the Indians, appears to be winning. Only one warrior, with bow drawn taut, arrow pointed at the General's breast, conveys the impression that this is Custer's *last* charge.[8]

Although other artists did equestrian Custers, these ultimately have a limited appeal. The hero on horseback is too commonplace. In *Battle of the Little Big Horn* Elder was responding as much to his training at Dusseldorf, Germany, as he was to a specifically American event. European painters delighted in depicting gallant soldiers astride their chargers. Thus Custer, as a consummate leader of the cavalry, must also dash to his end on horseback. Dismounted, however, Custer takes on a new dimension. The cavalryman afoot becomes a lion at bay, advance and retreat alike cut off. He is brought down to earth literally and now must confront a destiny made palpable. Consequently it is Custer's Last Stand and not Custer's Last Charge that has gripped the artistic and the popular imagination.

If William Cary instinctively embraced the notion of a Last Stand, his dramatic conception of it was further refined in an Alfred R. Waud sketch illustrating a popular life of Custer published in the autumn of 1876.[9] Like Cary, Waud drew upon a personal acquaintance with the West, a long experience as an illustrator and his imagination to recreate the final moments of Custer's Seventh Cavalry. Though Waud had earned a solid reputation as an accomplished field artist for *Harper's Weekly* during the Civil War, his *Custer's Last Fight* is nevertheless pristine melodrama, stripped of every nonessential that might detract from the person of Custer. The onrushing Indians part on either side of a solid triangle of troopers. His head forming its apex, a slightly quizzical expression on his face, Custer stands, a pistol stuck in one boot top, his light buckskin outfit a splendid contrast to the dark uniforms of his men, holding a rifle in his left hand and taking careful aim along a revolver in the other. He is the model of unflappable, icy calm.

Tribute to the vivid impression created jointly by Cary and Waud was soon forthcoming in the form of a popular print, *General Custer's Death Struggle: The Battle of the Little Big Horn*, lithographed by Henry Steinegger and published by the Pacific Art Company of San Francisco in 1878. Cary provided Steinegger with his basic composition and the majority of his figures, including a Custer with one foot planted on a dead horse's rump. Waud, in turn, contributed the idea of a captured American flag in the hands of a whooping warrior — as well as three figures from the right side of his triangle of troopers. One of these is his buckskin-clad Custer. The result is a quandary: two Custers strike heroic poses, and the viewer is left to choose for himself between them! The repercussions of the 1876 Cary and Waud sketches thus registered far beyond their original audiences, leaving an indelible impression on many Last Stands subsequently painted in the nineteenth century.[10]

One reasonably safe generalization can be ventured about these later works. With few exceptions, Custer is instantly visible. Erect, assuming the spread-leg posture that was a heroic convention in Victorian times, he quite literally commands the situation and the viewer's eye.

Three distinctive Last Stand styles can be distinguished. First, and most familiar, is the classic tangle of red and white locked together in mortal combat. The key to this form, naturally, is Custer, who will almost always be squared off against a particular Indian — and usually in the process of dispatching him with pistol or sabre.

The other two styles take their departure from the idea of a surround. They feature an island of troopers with a sea of Indians swirling about them. The major variations within this form constitute the second and third Last Stand styles. Most frequently in nineteenth-century versions, the attention is on the beleagured soldiers, sometimes to the virtual exclusion of the Indians assailing them. Custer, of course, completely dominates such pictures, occasionally exhibiting a composure that borders on disinterest, even boredom in the proceedings at hand.

Alternately, the focus may be on the Indians as they dash around a distant knot of troopers. It is worthy of note that even in this third style, Custer, indistinct though he might be, is often still visible, and sometimes even prominent along the sky line. Since this style entails a certain artistic detachment and necessarily plays down the heroism of Custer's Seventh, it did not really come into its own until this century. One of the earliest works in this mode is also one of the best. It was painted by Ernest L. Blumenschein in 1897, a year before he settled in Taos, New Mexico, with Bert G. Phillips and made that little pueblo the center of a bustling art colony committed to preserving the culture of the American Indian on canvas. Blumenschein's painting was done to illustrate the Cheyenne Two Moon's account of the Little Big Horn in *McClure's Magazine*, and bore the self-descriptive caption "We Circled All Around Him."[11] As Americans began to consider certain episodes in their history from the Indian viewpoint, this perspective would become increasingly common.

There is a whole other vision of the battle, representing a first-hand knowledge often enough, that is only now coming into its own. This is the Indians' pictographic history of Custer's Last Stand. Many participants recorded just their personal exploits, but others treated the fight in general terms, as an exciting contest in which gorgeously-costumed warriors rode down their blue-coated adversaries. The Indians are the individuals in such scenes, identifiable by dress, medicine charms and pony markings, while the soldiers are the depersonalized foe. These two-dimensional compositions serve to remind us that the American myth of Custer's Last Stand is a white man's myth. For the Indians the battle was neither a massacre nor a mystery. There were thousands of survivors, and a few of them have seen fit to depict the victors' view of victory, of what was after all a memorable day for the winners as well as the losers.[12]

But if recent scholars are responsive to such highly stylized eyewitness pictures of Custer's Last Stand, the average American still conceives of that event as it has been immortalized by the Carys, the Wauds and their hundreds of successors. The list of Custer artists reads like a *Who's Who* of Western painting. A glance at the contributions of some of the more illustrious permits us to see how the nineteenth-century conception of Custer's Last Stand has been carried forward, its mythic qualities unimpaired, into our factual, skeptical twentieth century.

II

Frederic Remington and Charles M. Russell, heralded as the "Titans of Western Art," both dealt with Custer's Last Stand. Remington, a friend of Theodore Roosevelt and Owen Wister and, like them, an Eastern aficionado of the West who did much to popularize the strenuous life in the wide-open spaces, painted and sketched the Custer battle without ever producing a particularly memorable version. It was not for want of trying.

One of Remington's biographers has suggested that Custer's death made a profound impact on the fourteen-year-old future artist. He had grown up steeped in the lore of his father's service as a cavalry officer in the Civil War, and apparently Custer became one of his "greatest youthful idols." Remington's first trip West, in the summer of 1881, was to Montana, and it seems likely that he visited the Custer battlefield at that time since he subsequently presented a rusty Colt .45 to a friend as a memento of the fight picked up on the spot.[13]

In 1887 and again in 1890, Remington provided illustrations for two volumes of Mrs. Custer's recollections of life out West with the General. He had formed his own strong opinions about who was responsible for the debacle on the Little Big Horn, siding with Custer against his subordinates, Reno and Benteen, on the simple-minded premise that "a soldier cannot afford to be anything else than a 'dead lion.' "[14] In 1899, he wrote Wister: "I am doing a big picture for Paris [the Paris Exposition] now — derived from Reno's repulse — where they all crossed the ford in a huddle — its kind of unpatriotic but art is impersonal I am told." In fact, Remington's cavalry pictures were always warmly partisan, even adulatory; perhaps for this reason the painting was never completed.[15] But Remington, who fancied himself *the* artist-historian of the Indian-fighting army, did not abandon his intention of "doing" Custer, and his assumption that he should have a monopoly on the subject led to one of the better documented feuds in the history of Western art.

Charles Schreyvogel, a mild-mannered, gentlemanly Hoboken painter had come into prominence in 1900 when his oil *My Bunkie* won the coveted Thomas B. Clarke Prize of the National Academy of Design — an honor that had eluded Remington. The painting showed a daring rescue during an Indian-cavalry skirmish, and the interest it aroused inspired Schreyvogel to turn out a series of spirited, if somewhat melodramatic, cavalry action pictures. Remington was annoyed by Schreyvogel's popularity, particularly since he regarded his rival's work as phony and ignorant. He continued to nurse his resentment until an auspicious moment in 1903 — the exhibition of Schreyvogel's latest work, a meticulous reconstruction of a peace parley between Custer and his staff and several Kiowa headmen on the Southern plains in 1869 titled *Custer's Demand*. Remington waded in, contemptuously dismissing Schreyvogel's work as "half-baked stuff," "very good" for a man who knew as little as he did "about such matters," but full of errors and hardly worthy of the favorable notice it had received. The counterattack was swift and decisive: Mrs. Custer expressed her admiration for the oil; John S. Crosby, who was actually present at the conference depicted, defended Schreyvogel's accuracy; and even Remington's old friend Theodore Roosevelt praised the painting and criticized Remington for his pettiness. Muttering his regrets at having engendered a controversy that now involved the widow of the lamented Custer, Remington "pulled in his horse" and let the issue die. The significance of this tempest in a teapot, and the immediate explanation for Remington's unbecoming outburst, seems to have been his belief that Schreyvogel had trespassed on his territory. "I have been getting ready for years to make a try at General Custer," Remington confessed to an unsympathetic Colonel Crosby. Now he had been scooped by an Eastern upstart.[16]

In retrospect, it is obvious that Remington need not have worried. As exuberant and exciting as some of Schreyvogel's cavalry paintings are, the simple truth is that they are not in the same class as Remington's best work. But it is also the simple truth that Remington never did a painting on the Custer theme as good as Schreyvogel's *Custer's Demand*. A black and white oil reproduced as *Custer's Last Fight* in 1903 was Remington's most direct contribution to the body of Last Stand art and it is, by any standards, a surprisingly bland work. Its foreground is crowded with warriors whose interest in the soldiers clustered on the ridge behind them is so slight that they could be riding by on a carousel, mildly bored by the whole business of having to circle the hill. It is hard to imagine how the man recognized as the premier Western action painter of his time could have conceived a less bellicose Last Stand.[17]

Remington also did a pen and ink sketch that was called *Custer's Last Fight* when it appeared in 1891 "by courtesy of Mrs. Custer." Despite its apparently impeccable credentials, however, the drawing does not really seem intended to illustrate the Custer battle. The men are wearing chaps and resemble cowboys more than soldiers, while the inevitable figure of Custer — prominent in the distance in Remington's oil — is nowhere to be seen. Instead, a wounded trooper is the focal point, his legs awkwardly outstretched and a pistol at ready to greet the foe.[18]

Remington has been subject to careless titling, and one wonders if this pen and ink *Last Fight* is a case in point. Doubt is raised despite the seemingly conclusive evidence to the contrary because Remington was often purposely vague. A thoroughly professional illustrator, he frequently generalized from personal experience and often produced "typical" rather than specific scenes. Thus while he painted many "last stand" groupings (soldiers, cowboys, scouts or trappers making a defense against Indians or one another), few illustrated a single historical event. His oil *Custer's Last Fight* is clearly an exception. The pen and ink of the same title is another matter, and even if it is accepted as a depiction of the Custer battle certain other Remington works do not pass the test.

A Remington painting that has usually been called *Custer's Last Charge* in its infrequent reproductions is also known as *A Sabre Charge*, and though the lead cavalryman could very well be Custer, there is nothing in the scene to actually link it to the Little Big Horn. The Museum of Fine Arts in Houston includes in its excellent Remington collection a strange watercolor with the title *Custer's Last Stand*. A group of scouts and soldiers crouch behind their dead horses and, screened by a few clumps of bush, fire into the faces of war-bonneted Indians dashing at them across a shallow stream. A close examination of the original painting convinces me that, to the extent it was intended to represent a historical event, its inspiration was the battle of Beecher's Island, where a company of fifty scouts under Major George A. Forsyth held off a large Cheyenne war party in eastern Colorado in 1868, and not the battle of the Little Big Horn.[19]

The problems Remington creates for the art historian are best suggested by his most familiar "last stand." *Harper's Weekly* for January 10, 1891, featured a two-page reproduction of a Remington oil with the noncommittal title *The Last Stand*. An accompanying note queried: "How many scenes of which this is typical have been enacted on this continent, who can say?"[20] Obviously the painting was meant to be generic rather than specific. Yet today the same canvas hangs in the Woolaroc Museum at Bartlesville, Oklahoma, as *Custer's Last Stand*, and it has gained wide acceptance as a representation of that event. When *American Heritage* used the painting on its cover in 1957, readers were informed that while it does "nothing to dim the romantic Custer legend," it does take note of "a few known facts." Just what these facts are is unclear. The troopers are perched on a rocky hilltop, their sabres planted in the ground before them, ignoring "known facts" of both terrain and equipment. Moreover, the central figure in the composition is an old, scraggy-bearded scout clad in a long buckskin coat and beaded mocassins. This, *American Heritage* confidently asserted, is Custer because he is "garbed about right." And so *The Last Stand* becomes *Custer's Last Stand*.[21]

Remington did in fact do two Little Big Horn subjects besides the black and white oil and Mrs. Custer's pen sketch. Of peripheral interest is his 1891 wash drawing of the Custer monument dedication which illustrated "On the Big Horn" in certain editions of John Greenleaf Whittier's collected poems. Of immediate interest, though usually overlooked, is a Remington painting bearing the descriptive title *The Rushing Red Lodges Passed Through the Line of the Blue Soldiers*. Within the context of the novel that it illustrated, Remington's own *The Way of an Indian*, it was definitely intended to depict the action at Custer's Last Stand. Several warriors are shown galloping over the bodies of their fallen foes, trampling them under their ponies' hooves. The conception is striking, and the painting constitutes Remington's most original, if least known, variation on the Custer theme.[22]

Charles M. Russell, though he was Montana's own celebrated cowboy artist, never felt the personal interest in Custer's Last Stand that Remington expressed. Indeed, while Russell loved to paint the plains Indian, fur trapper and cowboy, he virtually ignored the frontier army. In this respect he was Remington's antithesis. His viewpoint, too, was very different. Remington judged everything by a martial standard, and found in the white-red conflict a compelling symbol of civilization's inevitable victory over savagery, the essence of the "winning of the West." Russell, in contrast, mourned the old West's passing and, in looking back nostalgically on the good times he had enjoyed before barbed wire tamed the cattle country, identified with the Indian in his sense of loss. Nevertheless, he did do four Custer-related subjects, including two watercolors painted in 1903.

One, a small monochrome titled *Custer's Last Battle* in its first reproduction, shows the General and his men blasting away at some distant Indians. It was done on commission and is an uninspired effort at best, bearing a resemblance to the earlier, saloon-style oils *A Desperate Stand* (1898) and *Trappers' Last Stand* or *Attack on the Plains* (1899) in terms of composition, while its figure of Custer is evidently based on a popular 1897 illustration by J. Steeple David.[23] Clearly Russell was out of his element in his negligible, trooper's eye view of the battle. Critics have often commented on his propensity for recording events in American history from the red man's perspective, and his second version of the Last Stand, a full-color painting of the circling Indians called *The Custer Fight*, conforms to this preference. It is also a notably superior performance. As several warriors begin their charge up Custer Hill, a superb foreground figure, wearing a buffalo hide cap and with rifle in hand, wheels his pony preparatory to riding into the fray. Russell favored this composition in his red-white battle scenes, and did similar studies of parties of warriors attacking stagecoaches and wagon trains, as well as a pen and ink often titled *The Last of the Fetterman Command* that was meant by the artist to illustrate the Indians celebrating their victory over Custer.[24] He was at his best in *The Custer Fight*, however, and his skill at portraying the power and grace of the mounted plains Indian was never more evident. Consequently his watercolor, far more appealing than Remington's stiff, decorative oil, sets the standard for this particular Last Stand style.

A full-color reproduction of *The Custer Fight* appeared in *Scribner's Magazine* in 1905, and a lithograph was published by Charles Scribner's Sons the same year.[25] These and subsequent reproductions familiarized the public with Russell's composition.[26] Certainly it had a pronounced impact on other artists who wanted to try a Last Stand. A painting by the German Carl Lindeberg that has been reproduced as *Gall's Warriors Gathering for the Final Rush* is simply Russell's watercolor with three foreground figures from a Remington drawing superimposed over it.[27] Similarly, the Last Stand by a fellow Great Falls, Montana painter, Olaf C. Seltzer, bears an unmistakable resemblance to Russell's version. Seltzer included seven Custer subjects in a series of 102 miniature oils portraying major incidents in Montana's past, and his paintings of Custer dividing the Seventh prior to battle, a trumpeter delivering the last message to Captain Benteen, Reno's fight in the valley, and the discovery of the corpses of Custer's men two days later all represent original contributions to the pictorial record of the Little Big Horn. But Seltzer's own creativity was occasionally overwhelmed by his close association with Russell, and several of his conceptions are entirely derivative. His Last Stand is a case in point, while his oil *Curley Bringing News of the Custer Massacre to the Steamer "Far West"* is a virtual copy of a Russell pen-and-ink drawing of the same title.[28]

Russell's influence is also apparent in the *Custer's Last Stand* by the Taos painter W. Herbert Dunton, and, distilled through Dunton, traces of it remain in the version by a fine Arizona artist, R. Farrington Elwell.[29] In these and similar works, it can be detected in the grouping of the foreground figures (the central one will be carrying a rifle) and in the ubiquitous buffalo cap, which, sometimes inconspicuously, continues to turn up.[30]

Much of the popularity of this Last Stand style in the twentieth century, it would seem, can be attributed to Russell. Even Edgar S. Paxson, who is chiefly known for his enormous 1899 oil "showing the heat of the fray, with soldier, Indian and horse in the tangle of a sanguine melee," stepped back in 1906 to view things from a more detached perspective.[31] In the modest watercolor that resulted the hand-to-hand combatants whom he had once labored so arduously to portray became insignificant specks atop a distant rise, while mounted warriors thundered by in the foreground.

Of course, the other Last Stand styles continued to have their adherents. Henry F. Farny, later an adept interpreter of Indian camp life, in 1881 drew a *Custer's Last Fight* that included no Indians at all, though sprawling troopers and several fallen horses attest to their deadly proximity.[32] Rufus F. Zogbaum, a military illustrator of considerable reputation in the 1890's, produced a Last Stand scene that might charitably be termed mediocre. It is not altogether certain that the drawing, which appeared in *Harper's Monthly* in 1890, was actually meant to represent the Custer fight, though the central figure, down to the A. R. Waud buckskin suit, was certainly inspired by Custer. At any rate, this routine grouping of soldiers at bay is too poorly done to warrant extended comment. Suffice to say that Zogbaum redeemed himself in two later illustrations depicting the discovery of the corpses on the battlefield and an episode of Reno's fight in the valley.[33]

Almost as bad as Zogbaum's Last Stand was the oil finished about 1926 by a noted Western illustrator, Edwin Willard Deming. Deming's failure was magnified because he had lavished so much time upon it, the original idea of painting "an historical picture of the engagement" having occurred to him during a visit to the Sioux Agency at Standing Rock, North Dakota, in 1889. Deming was captive to the belief that Custer's men had been swept away by a massive Indian charge — a "red wave of destruction" that broke over the soldiers' line of battle. His first version of the Last Stand, done in 1904, was designed to illustrate those very words in a popular historian's article on the Custer disaster.[34] The same writer a decade later gave fuller expression to what was once a generally-accepted interpretation of the fighting on Custer Hill:

> In a little group stood Custer, his brother Tom, and [Captain George] Yates. The Indians were fearfully nearer now . . .

> The next moment out of the smoke surged a red wave. Revolvers cracked, pistols were thrown into the faces of the advance, carbines were clubbed. . . .

> How did the white man die? Standing like a stone wall and striking back like mad. Without a prayer for pity, without a murmur of repining, fighting to the last, high and low, officers and men, they were shot, overridden, and trampled down.[35]

Deming could not get these images out of his mind, and when he worked on the preliminary sketch for his large oil Custer's Last Stand, the idea of the "grand charge that ended the fight" still guided his hand. But in the process of refining and polishing this concept, Deming had lost the animation and vigor of his original 1904 version. The finished oil was flat and lifeless, without a hint of the frenzy that such a scene would necessarily entail.[36]

Three important artists commonly associated with Southwestern scenes — Blumenschein, Dunton and Elwell — adopted the Indian viewpoint in depicting Custer's Last Stand. So did a fourth, W. R. Leigh, a major transitional figure in Western art whose career stretched from the turn of the century to his death in 1955. His large 1939 oil Custer's Last Fight is a particularly effective example of the surround style. A highly trained, technically proficient draftsman, Leigh created a tableau of meticulously sculpted Indian figures set off against a thick dust that transforms the soldiers on Custer Hill into dim grey silhouettes. The haze separating the viewer from the lost troopers of the Seventh provides an evocative touch that is exactly right. Across the gap, we are aware only of a doomed but splendid resistance. All the terror of violent death has vanished. Leigh's canvas consequently is almost a summation of the artists' contribution to myth — a visual image of the Last Stand pared down to its essential heroism and, as such, a cherished cultural memory.

These considerations led Robert Taft to conclude his examination of Last Stand art with the remark that Leigh's painting was perhaps the "most satisfactory picture of all the Custer battle scenes."[37] But like those other scenes, Leigh's Custer's Last Fight is open to charges of inaccuracy in concept and in detail, and it has been scored on these grounds. Behind such criticisms lies a twentieth-century literalism, an obsession with historical authenticity that has left its stamp on a number of artists' work and, at the same time, has contributed to the continuing popularity of Custer's Last Stand as a subject for the Western painter.

III

William Cary's seminal *The Battle on the Little Big Horn River — Death Struggle of General Custer* not only set the heroic tone for those that followed, but also fostered several common fallacies. Custer actually carried no sabre at the Last Stand, and his long, golden locks had been trimmed close shortly before he set out on his final campaign. But the sword and flowing hair, details that lent themselves so well to artistic treatment, were too precious to be entirely abandoned in the interest of historical fidelity, and they still appear in pictures of Custer's Last Stand. Similar misrepresentations abound, particularly in relation to the apparel of soldiers and Indians, the guidons and battle flags and the terrain.

It has been the mission of a few serious-minded artists, especially since the Second World War, to set the record straight. Interestingly, they have generally tried to accomplish their ends with a minimum of damage to the splendid nineteenth-century Custer whose long locks and flashing sword were, after all, frills that could be dispensed with without emasculating the heroic concept. When Deming, for example, stripped Custer of the sword he had shown him wielding in 1904 and made him settle for a single pistol in his later versions of the Last Stand, he necessarily tamed the General down. But the basic stance with which Custer confronted the Indian charge was carried over intact. Only the details had changed. Hair short and receding at the temples, bereft of sabre, aged by the rigors of field duty and the responsibility of command, the Boy General has lost some of his glamour over the years. But much derring-do remains to be performed with two pistols and a heart still brimful of reckless courage. Even as modern realists purge their Last Stands of historical error, they continue to conceive of the subject in a nineteenth-century spirit. The results often are anachronisms admirably correct in detail but permeated with old-fashioned values. Consequently, Custer's Last Stand remains in art a heroic ideal, a myth inviolate despite the demands of the documentary approach.

In order to achieve historical accuracy in art, John Ewers has proposed that painter and historian work as a team. Continuing research into Western history has brought us to the point where the artist, properly advised, can re-create many events more accurately today than could a contemporary who was not himself an eyewitness. Finally, the work completed, "it would be a contribution if articles were written . . . listing the basic references used for developing the pictures and bringing out the relationship between written history, collections of historic specimens, and the paintings of historical reconstructions."[38] Several modern Custer artists have in fact anticipated certain of Ewers' recommendations.

Theodore B. Pitman first essayed the Last Stand in 1923, following a visit to the battlefield. The result was a surround scene that was something of a cliche in its own time. Its composition resembled that of a painting by Charles H. Stephens which had been illustrating a popular school history since 1898, and among its features were a buffalo hat and a gun-bearing warrior in the foreground.[39] Almost thirty years later Pitman painted what John S. du Mont, an armaments expert and a student of the Little Big Horn campaign, described as "a significantly improved version." Du Mont commissioned the oil to serve as the wrapper illustration for a monograph on the firearms in the Custer battle, and under his supervision Pitman produced a study that is accurate as to uniform and equipment. Yet the overall conception is uninspired, even dull. Like a poorly composed photograph, the top half of the picture is all sky, while the action depicted in the bottom half differs from the earlier oil's only in that the Indians' charge has carried them into the very ranks of the troopers. The setting is indistinctive, no sense of desperate struggle is conveyed, and, though Du Mont writes of Pitman's work that "an immense amount of research and attention to detail are what make a painting historically accurate," this *Custer's Last Stand* is not completely free from error.[40]

Nicholas Eggenhofer, a skilled Western artist now resident in Cody, Wyoming, rendered Custer's Last Stand twice in oil and several times in pen and ink during the early 1950's. While these efforts exhibited Eggenhofer's unmistakable talent, they were conceptually routine, showing the classic tangle of Indians and soldiers on the hill and a long-haired Custer, sabre and all.[41] But Eggenhofer, too, came under the guidance of a knowledgeable patron, James S. Hutchins. A recognized authority on the accoutrement of the plains cavalry, from uniforms through horse accessories, Hutchins has made an in-depth study of the Little Big Horn, reaching the conclusion that Custer's men "did not go down in hand-to-hand combat but were shot down from a distance and practically all *hors de combat* by the time any of their Indian opponents actually ventured into the so-termed 'Last Stand' area." Research had discredited the theory of a massive Indian charge overwhelming Custer's forces. Feeling that the battle should be represented in conformity to the newer interpretation of the fighting that day, Hutchins commissioned Eggenhofer to paint another, different Last Stand. In Hutchins' words:

> Nick was to handle all the artistic end of it. I would supply him with all data necessary to insure that all details of the terrain, arms, equipment, etc., were properly portrayed. And it was a stipulation that the "Last Stand" would be depicted in the way I had become convinced that it really happened. In a few months the completed canvas was in my hands.[42]

Eggenhofer's artistry shone through the restrictions of technical accuracy and his oil, appropriately titled *To the Last Man*, stands as a landmark in Custer art.

The concept is not new — several nineteenth-century Last Stands had focused entirely on Custer's men. But Eggenhofer's painting is far the best done in this style. Much of the theatrical heroism of his earlier versions has vanished. Weariness and a foreknowledge of the futility of the defense are engraved on the soldiers' faces. Custer himself is a man at bay, still calm and poised, a pistol in each hand, but the pervasive mood of the painting is one of despair. Dust begrimed, sweaty troopers gaze out hopelessly at their unseen assailants. The ground about them is studded with arrows. Some have found their mark, and the wounded troopers project anguish and pain, not a conventionalized, stoic forbearance. Though the painting is all portent, it realizes perfectly the implications of its title. No viewer could mistake the fact that this is Custer's Last Stand, and that every man shown will die there on that bleak hillside.[43]

While Pitman and Eggenhofer aspired to historical accuracy under the direction of others, some artists who have attempted to reconstruct the Last Stand on canvas have themselves been students of the battle. Gayle P. Hoskins' first version was completed in 1928 and reproduced as a calendar illustration by Brown & Bigelow the next year. In this early work, the ring of Indians converge on Custer's men, who lie barricaded behind their horses, peering out through the smoke at the advancing mass of warriors. A strong sense of impending disaster hangs in the air, and in its own right this painting is an impressive effort.[44]

But in 1953 Hoskins completed his masterpiece, a bird's eye view of the destruction of all five companies under Custer as it might have appeared were the time factor ignored. The canvas is panoramic, embracing not just the Last Stand (indeed, that culminating event is occurring on the furthest distant rise), but the separate actions which successively eliminated the various elements of Custer's immediate command. In order to accomplish this artistic feat and master the difficult perspective involved, Hoskins familiarized himself with the battlefield terrain, studied the United States Geological Survey's contour map of the area and produced a clay model of the ground. Then, in conjunction with the Custer authority whose book the finished oil was to grace, Colonel William A. Graham, Hoskins determined the positions of the Indians and troopers and set to work. The resulting *tour de force* should establish conclusively that a seemingly hackneyed subject still offers fresh possibilities for the unhackneyed mind.[45]

Ernest L. Reedstrom's initial entry into the field of Custer art was a traditional Last Stand done in 1955. Gorier than most, with blood spewing abundantly from a profusion of wounds, the oil featured a dauntless, two-gun Custer, a guidon that the Seventh Cavalry would not have recognized and a massive Indian charge rolling up the slope from the direction of the Little Big Horn River. Though *Custer's Last Campaign* was the product of five years of research and three of actual painting, Reedstrom has since surpassed it in a continuing series of pen drawings.

Each of the battalion commanders, Custer, Reno and Benteen, has received his due. Other sketches show the burial of the bodies on Custer Hill, the horse Comanche after the battle, and various phases of the action at the Little Big Horn. Particularly successful is Reedstrom's drawing of *Custer's Last Shot*. The mortally wounded General struggles to rise up on his elbow and squeeze off a parting round in a scene that eliminates the Wild West heroics without denying Custer a kind of final heroism.[46]

Joe Grandee, a Texas painter who prides himself on being a stickler for historical accuracy in his work, accepted a commission to do four studies of the Custer battle. Three years of research followed before he finished the first painting in 1967, *A Gathering of the Chiefs*. The idea of several prominent Indians huddling over strategy while the battle rages before them makes for a striking composition. Taken with the Custer theme, Grandee has subsequently worked back from the Little Big Horn to the attack on the Washita and the General's sojourn in Texas following the Civil War. In all of his work, Grandee has been fastidious about detail, and the Custer battle naturally presents a formidable challenge since the answers to even basic questions about armament and field uniforms have been lost in the confusion of defeat. Should the General be shown in full buckskins, or just in buckskin trousers with a blue shirt? Unable to decide, Grandee has portrayed him both ways. Niggling in themselves, such uncertainties plague the artist-historian in pursuit of strict accuracy. In another sense, they are microcosms of the large imponderables embraced by the ultimate question "What *really* happened on the Little Big Horn?" It is this question, and the search for answers, that lies at the bottom of the artistic quest for detailed authenticity.[47]

Other contemporary painters have repeatedly delved into facets of the Little Big Horn, including William Reusswig, Byron Wolfe and Lorence Bjorklund. But James K. Ralston of Billings, Montana, in his own distinctive manner has undoubtedly devoted most attention to it. *After the Battle*, the most ambitious of the dozen major oils he has done on Custer subjects, was unveiled in 1955 on the occasion of the seventy-ninth anniversary of the fight. Impressively researched, encompassing thirty-nine documented incidents, this 4½' x 18' study of the carnage that followed Custer's Last Stand represents the culmination of another, somewhat macabre artistic tradition.[48]

An early report describing the battlefield noted that "the mysterious silence which reigned over those mutilated dead must have been more eloquent than any words, because amid such surroundings conjecture, aided by imagination, must have drawn a more dreadful picture of the battle than the tongues of the dead could have given had they been able to speak."[49] The corpses, then, told the story as fully as it would ever be known with any certainty. A surprising number of artists have seen fit to depict the battle's aftermath, from the Indians looting and mutilating their victims to the discovery of the corpses by the Montana Column and the burials a few days later. A first-hand account carried in the papers of the time provided the inspiration. "I was standing by General Custer," a lieutenant wrote, "when General Terry came up, and as he looked down upon the noble General the tears coursed down his face as he said: — 'The flower of the army is gone at last.'" In lieu of Custer's dying words it made for a good epitaph, and the New York Herald expressed its belief that "this picture would make an appropriate bas-relief upon the proposed Custer monument."[50] Several artists agreed, and the dead hero's unrumpled corpse, as natural in death as in life, served as another pictorial reminder of his self-sacrificing dedication to duty. Recently Leonard Baskin, an artist of national reputation who was commissioned to illustrate a new edition of the government's handbook on the Custer Battlefield National Monument, made a stark drawing of the General's naked corpse that introduced a measure of realism but was considered too graphic for inclusion in the booklet.[51] To date, however, no other work in this vein has even approached the magnitude of Ralston's After the Battle.

For all of his interest in Custeriana, Ralston has painted only two Last Stands as such. Both present unique historical interpretations. Custer's Last Hope features the usual band of soldiers fighting on Custer Hill; unusually, however, they are watching one of their numbers, a courier, gallop off into the distance. While there is no direct corroborating evidence, a Sergeant James Butler apparently did attempt to break through to Reno's position, and a lonely marker stands today on the field as testimony to his thwarted effort. Similarly, Ralston's Call of the Bugle is a variation on the familiar Last Stand. Commissioned by the Custer Battlefield Historical and Museum Association and finished in 1965, the large painting shows the troopers gathering on the slope of the hill for their final defense, and effectively captures the feverish activity compressed into the fleeting minutes of life left to them. Custer, hat in hand, gesturing and yelling, does his best to rally his men and stave off the panic that has already seized a few. Around him, all is confusion, and even the attempt to make a Last Stand seems pointless in the face of such absolute calamity.

As the most prolific of all the Custer painters, Ralston has always exhibited wide-ranging interests. His work on the Little Big Horn blends accuracy with imagination. Five separate oils treat the prelude to battle and two others besides the 1955 oil are concerned with its aftermath. Tired of painting clusters of dead Indians, soldiers and horses, Ralston expressed a longing in 1963 to desert Custer's doomed command and join the troopers with Reno and Benteen. "I have often made the remark . . . that I could paint pictures for the rest of my life without ever getting a mile away from Reno Hill," he observed. "The subject matter there is unlimited."[52]

Yet Reno's part in the fray remains as neglected by the painter as by the poet. A few pictures showing the fight in the valley and the retreat across the Little Big Horn River and up the bluffs, the occasional sketch of some episode that occurred during the two-day siege, a diorama in the Battlefield Museum, and that about covers the artistic record of the Reno-Benteen engagement. Dixon Wecter has observed that while "the crowd loves victory, . . . it also likes the salty sacrificial taste of disappointment and tragedy."[53] Soldiers walked away from Reno Hill, but not one left Custer Hill alive. It is the totality of the disaster that fires the artistic imagination. Inspired by utter defeat, and unrestrained by precise fact, painters have naturally found Custer's finale the most congenial of subjects. As a 1968 exhibition of Last Stand art held at the Amon Carter Museum in Fort Worth, Texas, clearly demonstrated, it is a subject whose appeal is far from exhausted.

For example, as the seventy-fifth anniversary of the battle drew near, two national magazines commissioned Last Stand paintings. *Esquire* featured a superbly-executed version by the veteran illustrator Harold Von Schmidt as a color gatefold in its September, 1950 issue. The Indians are depicted rushing up the slope towards a pinnacle occupied by a magnificent Custer, unconcernedly blasting away at his enemies with two pistols.[54] *Collier's* marked the anniversary with a full page color reproduction of a Last Stand by William Reusswig showing Custer receiving his death wound. One historian has described it as "in many respects probably the best picture of the fight."[55] Actually, while Von Schmidt's and Reusswig's paintings have exceptional artistic merit, they continue many questionable Last Stand traditions, most notably the notion of a fierce hand-to-hand encounter that was decided by an overwhelming charge. Both works also contain a number of factual errors. And, perhaps most interesting of all, neither does a thing to diminish the heroic Custer image.

Historical fact and changing historical interpretation, in truth, cannot easily alter the heroic image of Custer's Last Stand. A painting by an experienced military artist, H. Charles McBarron, suggests why. Commissioned by the American Oil Company and completed in 1962, McBarron's *Custer's Last Stand* exhibits the crisp, linear style which enables the artist to achieve an almost photographic clarity in rendering details of arms, equipment and uniform. But, combined with McBarron's fondness for vibrant colors, this very style makes his Last Stand visually unreal, no matter how technically accurate. No clouds of dust and powder smoke are permitted to obscure the mechanisms of Springfield carbines or the colors of battle flags. There is no sense of frenzy or movement, though each individual figure is frozen in a pantomime of violent exertion. Realism has been sacrificed to surface authenticity, and the result is a Hollywoodish Last Stand acted out on a pleasant, sunny afternoon against a sky of robin's egg blue. Moreover, Custer still goes about his business with a deadly revolver, the legendary hero immaculately groomed for his appointment with destiny.[56]

Authenticity, then, is no ultimate guarantor of historical truth in art. If the conception itself remains inviolate, details can be altered and rearranged almost at will without changing anything basic. Indeed, there is nothing new in the modern desire to achieve historical fidelity. Some of the most preposterous nineteenth-century Last Stands came from the brushes of artists who claimed to have inspected the battlefield, interviewed the more prominent warriors and a few of the surviving officers of the Seventh and gathered together genuine battle relics in order to ensure verisimilitude in their paintings. The result of all this

48

activity is a visual realism of sorts that merely lends credence and authority to conceptions that are in fact wholly imaginary. Myth is thereby "documented" or "proven."

To this day, despite the demand for historical accuracy, artists still portray the Last Stand in the heroic terms of Cary's and Waud's sketches — or, more precisely, in those of the huge compositions by three relatively obscure Western painters, John Mulvany, Edgar S. Paxson and Cassilly Adams. Influenced by the European and native traditions of battle art then current, all three Last Stands convey a visual impact to which no book-sized reproduction can do justice. They are creations on the grand scale, as inflated as their subject, an epic American myth.

<h1 style="text-align:center">IV</h1>

John Mulvany's 20' x 11' oil *Custer's Last Rally*, completed in 1881 after two years of research and painting, focuses on the General and the troopers huddled about him who, taking their cue from their leader, face without flinching what appears to be a solid wall of charging Indians.[57] In its own time the painting created a considerable stir as a uniquely American achievement; however, it strikes the modern viewer as a typical gargantuan nineteenth-century battle piece, stiff, pompous, a little ridiculous — in short, a perfect mirror of the artist's Dusseldorf, Munich and Antwerp schooling.

Today there is less interest in Mulvany's masterpiece than in Walt Whitman's reaction to it. The poet studied the painting while it was on tour in New York in August, 1881, and, after examining it for over an hour, pronounced his ringing verdict: "Altogether a western, autochthonic phase of America, the frontiers, culminating, typical, deadly, heroic to the uttermost — nothing in the books like it, nothing in Homer, nothing in Shakespeare; more grim and sublime than either, all native, all our own, and all a fact." It was, he concluded, an "artistic expression for our land and people."[58]

That "trumpet-note for heroes" which Whitman had heard while many around him were responding with shocked horror to the news from the Little Big Horn was still echoing in the poet's ear four years later. Custer's Last Stand was a symbolic moment in American history, and a painter had successfully captured its essence. By 1881, Whitman's contemporaries were also prepared to view things in the same light. "Upon Mulvany's canvas one can see the poetical magnificence of that slaughter in the lonely valley of the Little Big Horn as it appeared to the mind of genius," one journalist wrote, while a Kansas City reporter, in an enthusiastic commentary on *Custer's Last Rally*, actually anticipated Whitman's whoop of patriotic joy. Describing the figure of Custer, he noted: "His face is flushed with the heat of battle, his broad-brimmed hat lies carelessly on one side, and the long yellow locks, which added so greatly to his manly beauty, are tossed impetuously back [a detail that

Mulvany subsequently modified]. He stands erect, undaunted, and sublime."[59]

Exhibited across the country over the next decade, repainted twice by Mulvany, reproduced as a color lithograph and used as the frontispiece to a popular history of the Western Indian wars, *Custer's Last Rally* won acclaim and wide exposure for its creator. Moreover, as Robert Taft remarked, it no doubt suggested the Custer theme to other artists.[60] Among these may well have been Edgar S. Paxson.

Paxson emigrated to Montana from his home in New York state in 1877, while reverberations from the Custer fight were still being felt. Shortly after his arrival the notion of painting the Last Stand apparently gripped his imagination, and it became his goal, according to one contemporary, to, "so far as was possible, depict with absolute faithfulness of detail that disastrous battle."[61]

Laborious research followed. On-the-spot investigations of the battle site and interviews with participants on both sides were supplemented through correspondence. An inquiry addressed to one of Benteen's officers, Edward S. Godfrey, was rewarded with a reply that provides as graphic a description as we have of the appearance of the field three days after the slaughter. Paxson had soon filled a notebook with pertinent data. The actual painting began early in the 1890's, and two decades of work finally culminated in 1899 with the completion of what has been variously titled *Custer's Last Stand*, *Custer's Last Fight* and *Custer's Last Battle on the Little Big Horn*.

Publicity releases claim that two hundred separate figures are crammed into the 6' x 10' oil, and no one familiar with the painting would care to disagree. "The canvas throbs with action, heroism and strength," one admirer wrote in 1915.[62] Designed like Mulvany's *Custer's Last Rally* to arouse interest in the artist's work, *Custer's Last Stand* toured the East for at least one year and apparently secured Paxson the national recognition that he was seeking.[63] Having served this purpose well, however, the painting eventually passed from the public eye.

Until 1960, *Custer's Last Stand* attracted dust and little else in an obscure corner of the University of Montana where, according to literary critic Leslie A. Fiedler, "the students of history were being taught facts that kept them from taking Custer for the innocent Victim, the symbolic figure of the white man betrayed by crafty redskins that he is elsewhere."[64] Then William E. Paxson's campaign to make his grandfather "immortal in spite of Montana's neglect" caught up with the huge painting and swept it back into a prominence that culminated in the fall of 1963 with the announcement that it had been sold to the Whitney Gallery of Western Art at Cody, Wyoming, for a sum in excess of $50,000.[65] In the estimation of the gallery's director, Paxson's *Custer's Last Stand* is not only the "best pictorial representation of ALL the paintings which have been created to immortalize that dramatic event," but "one of the most important paintings in Western history."[66] With its return to public display, each viewer may now judge for himself.

If Mulvany's *Last Rally* is the classic example of the soldiers at bay style,

William M. Cary, *THE BATTLE ON THE LITTLE BIG HORN RIVER— THE DEATH STRUGGLE OF GENERAL CUSTER* (1876). The very first Custer's Last Stand. Courtesy of the Library of Congress.

A.R. Waud, *CUSTER'S LAST FIGHT* (1876). Courtesy of Author's Collection.

Feodor Fuchs, *CUSTER'S LAST CHARGE* (1876) Lithograph. Courtesy of the Custer Battlefield National Monument Crow Agency, Montana.

H. Steinegger, *GENERAL CUSTER'S DEATH STRUGGLE: THE BATTLE OF THE LITTLE BIG HORN* (1878) Lithograph. Courtesy of the Custer Battlefield National Monument Crow Agency, Montana.

John Mulvany, *CUSTER'S LAST RALLY* (1881) Oil. Courtesy of the Custer Battlefield National Monument Crow Agency, Montana.

John A. Elder, *BATTLE OF THE LITTLE BIG HORN, JUNE 25, 1876* (1884) Oil. Courtesy of the Custer Battlefield National Monument Crow Agency, Montana.

O. Reich, *CUSTER'S LAST STAND AND DEATH* (1888). Courtesy of the Custer Battlefield National Monument Crow Agency, Montana.

Otto Becker, *CUSTER'S LAST FIGHT* (1896) Lithograph. Based on the oil by Cassilly Adams. Courtesy of Anheuser-Busch, Inc. St. Louis, Missouri.

E.S. Paxson, *CUSTER'S LAST STAND* (1889) Oil. Courtesy of William Edgar Paxson and the Whitney Gallery of Western Art, Cody, Wyoming.

L. Bettz, *THE CUSTER MASSACRE* (ca. 1907). An example of the flambouyant Last Stands in turn of the century school readers. Courtesy of Author's Collection.

W.R. Leigh, *CUSTER'S LAST FIGHT* (1939) Oil. From the original oil painting in Woolaroc Museum, Bartlesville, Oklahoma. Courtesy of Woolaroc Museum.

J.K. Ralston, *CUSTER'S LAST HOPE* (1959) Oil. Courtesy of Author's Collection.

CUSTER'S LAST FIGHT (1912). Francis Ford's Last Stand in a scene closely based on the Anheuser-Busch lithograph. Courtesy of Bison Film.

THE SCARLET WEST (1925). Custer goes off in a blaze of glory in an early Last Stand Sequence. Courtesy of Author's Collection.

THEY DIED WITH THEIR BOOTS ON (1941). Errol Flynn as Custer. Courtesy of Warner Brothers.

THEY DIED WITH THEIR BOOTS ON (1941). Errol Flynn's peerless Custer at his Last Stand. Courtesy of Cinerama Releasing Corporation.

SITTING BULL (1954). Douglas Kennedy's villainous Custer has his moment of glory. Courtesy of Author's Collection.

CUSTER OF THE WEST (1968). Robert Shaw as Custer leads his troops into the Indian trap at the Little Big Horn. Courtesy of Cinerama Releasing Corporation.

LITTLE BIG MAN (1970).
Richard Mulligan's Custer
conscientiously plays the
hero. Courtesy of Cinema
Center Films.

LITTLE BIG MAN Richard Mulligan's Custer goes mad. Courtesy of
Cinema Center Films.

The Indians came on regardless of the death-dealing bullets. It was the last stand of the cavalry, and no one knew it better than Wild. But he was going to do all he could before taking to the river.

Courtesy of the Edward T. LeBlanc dime novel collection.

THE FIVE CENT
WIDE AWAKE LIBRARY

Entered at the Post Office at New York, N. Y., as Second Class Matter.

No. 1196. {COMPLETE}   FRANK TOUSEY, PUBLISHER, 34 & 36 North Moore St., N.Y., New York, March 31, 1894.   ISSUED WEEKLY.   { PRICE } {5 CENTS.}   Vol. II.

Entered according to the Act of Congress, in the year 1894, by FRANK TOUSEY, in the office of the Librarian of Congress, at Washington, D. C.

Custer's Last Shot;
or, THE BOY TRAILER OF THE LITTLE HORN.

By COL. J. M. TRAVERS.

Wounds counted as nothing at this dread moment; so long as a man could keep his seat, he was in good luck; it was the death bullet that told. "My heavens! the general's shot!" shouted a soldier close to Pandy Ellis. Custer was reeling in his saddle.

Courtesy of the Edward T. LeBlanc dime novel collection.

Paxson's *Last Stand* is incontestably the most tangled of the compositions showing red and white locked together in mortal combat. While Custer is immediately recognizable, he does not stand out from his busy surroundings. Clutching at a wound on his left side, he is apparently going to fall fairly early in the struggle. The more dramatic poses, then, have been assumed by lesser figures — the General's brother Tom, for example, is performing the two-gun heroics, though he is about to be brained from behind by Rain-in-the-Face. So much is included as mounted Indians press in from all sides, literally crushing the little band of troopers underfoot, that the painting as a whole does not leave a distinct impression on the viewer's memory. Details merge and blur. Perhaps this partially explains its eclipse from popularity. Certainly no major Last Stand artist subsequently borrowed either its composition or its Custer. Yet if the impact of Paxson's *Custer's Last Stand* is diffused in a welter of detail, the very fact of this enormous picture and the attention it once attracted undoubtedly influenced other artists casting about for a stirring theme. Maybe its reputation as the only "true picture from a historical sense" — indeed, judged to be "historically accurate in every particular" by a retired colonel who should have known better — also offered a challenge that could not be ignored.[67]

Indirectly the most celebrated of all Last Stand paintings was another mammoth composition, Cassilly Adams' 9½' x 16½' *Custer's Last Fight* finished early in 1886.[68] Intended like the Mulvany and Paxson paintings for exhibition, Adams' oil eventually wound up on the wall of a St. Louis saloon. Anheuser-Busch, Inc., a brewing firm in the same city, acquired the picture in a claims settlement, had it repainted and lithographed in 1895 by F. Otto Becker (who made extensive departures from the original) and the next year began issuing copies as a promotional for Budweiser beer.

It would be superfluous to describe the Becker print. Since 1896, perhaps 200,000 copies have made their way into establishments and homes across the United States, and, as Robert Taft wrote, "it is probably safe to say that . . . [this print] has been viewed by a greater number of the lower-browed members of society — and by fewer art critics — than any other picture in American history."[69] To the extent that art critics take notice of Western American painting, even they should by now be acquainted with Becker's conception. It has appeared in Taft's *Artists and Illustrators of the Old West, 1850-1900* and in Harold McCracken's *Portrait of the Old West*. Indeed, *Custer's Last Fight* has never been more popular as an illustration. If its barroom days are largely finished; it has long since made its bow into the respectable society of nostalgic Americana, and color reproductions in several lavish popular histories are among the recent tributes to its peculiar charm.

Writers see the Anheuser-Busch lithograph as a mirror of American cultural values. For a student of the saloon, the print connotes the spirit of that masculine institution and everything it stood for in an earlier time.[70] Russell Lynes reproduced it as an example of the nation's lowbrow taste in the period from the 1870's through the 1890's.[71] John Ewers, in turn, assigned it a part in the process whereby the plains Indian, feather bonnet and all, has become the symbol for the American Indian, without regard to tribal diversity.[72] To expand on Ewers' thesis, the cavalry is essential to this plains Indian symbol, providing the necessary foe against whom the warrior tests his skill and daring and wins the public's begrudging admiration. Indian and cavalry fuse in combat to form a single American legend of what one historian has called "a world of bright and golden courage and endless space."[73] The Anheuser-Busch lithograph not only nourishes this legend, but also its most celebrated realization, Custer's Last Stand.

By now, the lithograph has become a vital part of the Custer myth, with a tradition of its own. Stewart Holbook relished a story about Silent Smith, the most garrulous old-timer he ever met and one of the multitude of pretenders to the distinction of being the sole survivor of Custer's Last Stand. Smith's tale was classic; he survived, "wounded but much alive," by lying under a dead horse for two days. Holbrook liked the yarn so much that he took Smith for a beer one day. In the bar he spotted the Budweiser *Last Fight*, and facetiously asked Smith to indicate exactly where he lay for the two days. "Certainly, young man," Smith said:

> With great briskness he stepped around and behind the bar, peered briefly at the great picture, then lifted his cane and placed the end smack on a felled horse in the right foreground. "I was right there," he said evenly, "right there under that hoss." Then he returned to his place in front of the bar and politely blew the collar off another beer.[74]

It is a story as irresistible as the picture itself.

So integral is the lithograph's role to the development of the Custer myth that Budweiser has been called "the beer that made the Seventh famous." Even an oblique reference to the print is enough to identify it and, through it, Custer's Last Stand. James Warner Bellah, in a story about "Major Owen Thursday's last stand," tipped his hand when he wrote:

> You have seen it so often in the Jonathan Redfield print. The powder-blue trace of Crazy Man Creek against the burnt yellow grass on the rising ground behind. The dead of Company A stripped naked and scalped, their heads looking like faces screaming in beards. Major Thursday, empty gun in hand, dying gloriously with what is left of Company B, in an attempt to rally and save the colors . . . [75]

It is equally certain that Dee Brown is referring to Custer and the Little Big Horn in his novel *Cavalry Scout* when John Singleterry, the sole survivor of "Colonel Charles Crawford Comstock's last stand," bitterly replies to a questioner who finds his version of the battle at variance with "all official accounts:"

> Singleterry smiled faintly. "The stories of how Comstock stood ringed by dead troopers and dead horses, firing his revolver bravely to the end? Comstock's Last Stand?"

"Yes, I'm thinking of Niles Christenson's great painting. Some historians have pointed out minor inaccuracies, but all seem to agree the painting is authentic in fact. The artist went out there, you know, and sketched the actual physical setting.[76]

As both writers imply, the heroic myth of Custer's Last Stand is embodied in the art that it has inspired, while the art, in turn, has fostered the myth. Poets have paid tribute to the Budweiser print ("drawn as from a photograph / of naked men sunrise pink / laid flat upon the prairie"), novelists have doted upon it and painters have been challenged by it.[77]

Twentieth-century writers confidently assume that their readers know the print and that even a casual reference will bring it springing into mind. Sitting Bull's biographer, Stanley Vestal, once likened the popular legend of the Sioux chief to the lithograph, both being "gaudy, but highly inaccurate."[78] Of course, Vestal was writing for an audience presumably interested in plains history. But *Time* magazine airily concluded a review of a novel by James Clavell with this comment:

It's all nonsense, of course. But there are worse literary crimes than that. Clavell's book can claim kinship to those wonderful lithographs of the Battle of the Little Bighorn that once decorated every barroom. It isn't art and it isn't truth. But its energy and scope command the eye.[79]

Occasionally writers of fiction have made searching use of the print in their work. Earl Thompson, for example, in his sensational first novel *A Garden of Sand*, helped establish the Depression milieu — as well as a young boy's fantasies of escape — by describing the interior of a "truck-stop-café-beer-joint" with flypaper draped from the overhead fans and "on the back wall above the jukebox . . . a big print of *Custer's Last Stand* distributed by the Anheuser-Busch Brewing Company:"

It was a great picture with ponies wild-eyed and frothing in the dust of battle, ridden by howling Indians in warpaint, dropping, dragging, dying like flies all over it. And Custer, his hair like golden flypapers, golden mustachios, great white hat, fringed buckskin jacket, supported dying troopers around his knees, his pearl-handled six-guns blazing, mowing down Indians as if they were wheat. That dusty golden land was of the world and the boy knew. He lived where Indians had walked. Where buffalo grazed. *Listen!* For the silent step. He could look at the picture for hours. Nuts to Western Union! When he grew up, he was going with the cavalry.[80]

Ernest Hemingway, who venerated the moment of truth whether in the bullring or on the battlefield, was also effusive about the print in *For Whom the Bell Tolls*:

"George Custer was not an intelligent leader of cavalry, Robert," his grandfather had said. "He was not even an intelligent man."

He remembered that when his grandfather said that he felt resentment that any one should speak against that figure in the buckskin shirt, the yellow curls blowing, that stood on that hill holding a service revolver as the Sioux closed in around him in the old Anheuser-Busch lithograph that hung on the poolroom wall in Red Lodge.

> "He just had great ability to get himself in and out of trouble," his grandfather went on, "and on the Little Big Horn he got into it but he couldn't get out."

The tension here, the annoyance that history should dare intrude upon a good story, however false, reflects contemporary ambivalence about Custer's Last Stand. Intellectually, Hemingway might form an antipathy for Custer, but emotionally he had always to admire the grand style Custer exhibited in dying. The Last Stand, after all, was the epitome of "grace under pressure."[81]

Another Nobel Prize-winning novelist, John Steinbeck, had a picture in mind when he visited the Custer Battlefield. "At Custer we made a side trip south to pay our respects to General Custer and Sitting Bull on the battlefield of Little Big Horn," he wrote in *Travels with Charley*. "I don't suppose there is an American who doesn't carry Remington's painting of the last defense of the center column of the 7th Cavalry in his head. I removed my hat in memory of brave men . . ."[82] It was the Becker lithograph, not a Remington painting, that Steinbeck was thinking of.

Homer Croy, who regarded *Custer's Last Fight* as the "greatest Wild West picture of all time," remarked that with the backing of Budweiser Beer Custer was eventually fighting "behind ten thousand bars. Men who had never paid the slightest attention to art, thirsted for more."[83] At least one imbiber, however, became disgruntled. Thomas Hart Benton, Missouri's iconoclastic delineator of Middle Border life, grew up entranced by the Anheuser-Busch lithograph. In his memoirs, published in 1937, he discussed his boyhood fascination with the wild Indians of popular legend. "I closed my eyes to what I knew and retreated into the ideal," he remembered:

> This ideal was composed of tomahawks, eagle feathers, bloody knives, and fierce expressions. My Indians were always victorious, slaughtering the white invaders left and right. The great work of this period, the picture on which I looked with the greatest admiration, was *Custer's Last Stand*, a large, colored lithograph which, as a barbershop and saloon masterpiece, survived all the efforts of imperialist patriotism to supplant it with the blowing up of the *Maine* and the charge up San Juan Hill.[84]

Appropriately, the Budweiser print was part of the saloon decor in Benton's 1939 depiction of the final act in the ill-starred romance of Frankie and Johnny. But by 1946 Benton claimed to have undergone a change of heart about the lithograph. "I've seen it in every saloon and pool hall in the southwest," he grumbled, and he had grown tired of what was "not much of a picture." So he painted his own version — a tribute, really, despite his strictures — titled *Custer's Last Stand: A Bar-Room Picture in the St. Louis Mode.* [85]

Obviously it was not on factual grounds that Benton had come to find the Budweiser print wanting, since only the year before he had defended the anachronisms in his historical murals with the remark "I paint the past through my own life experiences. I feel that an anachronism with life is better than any academically correct historical rehash." With Benton asserting the artist's prerogatives over factual purism, his *Custer's Last Stand* was a melodramatic conception every bit as improbable as the picture that inspired it. For Benton's "American image" consisted, as he said, of "what I have come across, of what was 'there' in the time of my experience — no more, no less."[86] It was an experience that encompassed not the battle of the Little Big Horn, fought almost thirteen years before Benton was born, but the myth of Custer's Last Stand embodied in the Anheuser-Busch lithograph. It was, in short, a thoroughly American experience.

V

A St. Louis journalist was doubtless right when he asserted that the Anheuser-Busch lithograph is "responsible for the vivid mental picture most Americans have of the tragedy on the Little Big Horn."[87] But it is equally true that the Last Stand paintings collectively have given form to an idea that was inherently spectacular. They have endowed the public with its image of Custer's Last Stand, and this image now thrives outside the context of the paintings. Static in itself, it gains flexibility through the interpretations made of it and the uses to which it is put.

For one thing, Custer's Last Stand is central to the larger concept of the Wild West. Both fuse romance and reality into an integrated whole, a cultural myth whose influence is pervasive and diffuse rather than specific. For example, an important artist like Walt Kuhn, who as secretary of the Association of American Painters and Sculptors played a major role in organizing the Armory Show of 1913, was addicted to the Western myth. Between 1918 and 1920 he completed a series of twenty-nine paintings "from memory" that have been grouped together as "An Imaginary History of the West." Two of these, *Wild West #1* and *Wild West #2*, are dream-like responses to Custer's heroic Last Stand.[88]

Andrew Wyeth, America's favorite realist painter, established a less obvious relationship between his work and the country's Western experience. Referring to his 1950 tempera *Young America*, in which an early-day "easy rider" pedals his bicycle furiously across an empty landscape, Wyeth said: "I was struck by the distances in this country, which are more imagined than suggested in the picture — by the plains of the Little Big Horn and Custer and Daniel Boone and a lot of other things in our history."[89] In the most elemental sense, the Wild West and such component parts of the myth as Custer's Last Stand are deeply embedded in the American consciousness.

Along with the painters, a few sculptors have also been inspired by the drama on the Little Big Horn, although their attempts at recreating the Last Stand in three dimensions have made no great impact on the public.[90] But Mary McCarthy found even the idea of such sculpture amusing enough to incorporate it in a tale of crooked art dealers. The story's narrator describes a "huge bronze" of Custer's Last Stand depicting "one tall American with a gun and a cowboy hat standing on a hill, surrounded by some dervish-like Indians. I could see that the work had a certain sporting character . . . But I could not imagine that it would be readily marketable. I was mistaken."[91] The narrator was indeed mistaken, for Custer's Last Stand has always been "readily marketable."

In fact, a reliable index to the popularity of Last Stand pictures might well be the commercial ends that they have served. The Anheuser-Busch lithograph, after all, was simply promotional material for Budweiser Beer — and a remarkably successful promotion at that. As the company history published in 1953 noted, "it was the sort of thing to stop passerby [sic] in their tracks, make them gasp, make them talk about Anheuser-Busch."[92] Sometime after 1900, H. J. Heinz acquired John Mulvany's *Custer's Last Rally*, and the oil hung for many years in the company's headquarters in Pittsburgh. Though the painting's ownership was well known, the Heinz people made no further use of it, apparently unable to establish a suitable correlation between the Custer disaster and their famous "fifty-seven varieties." However, Mulvany's masterpiece has received some exposure in advertisements for a Chicago savings and loan association, while Feodor Fuch's period piece *Custer's Last Charge* topped an advertisement in the *New York Times* advising readers who "need hard-to-find details on Custer's last stand" that they might locate them readily in back volumes of the *Times Index*.[93] Alfred Waud's 1876 drawing of the Last Stand has been altered so that the General's left hand now clutches a sack of McDonald's hamburgers instead of a trusty carbine — Custer left literally holding the bag![94]

Even Anheuser-Busch, recognizing the campy appeal of its *Custer's Last Fight* for the modern temperament, has spoofed the chromo in a color reproduction with an added balloon emanating from the mouth of one of the luckless troopers: "It's been a hair-raising day, General. How about a Budweiser?"[95] But perhaps the cleverest use made of the print was in an American Airlines advertisement. Beneath the words "I know it's your trip, General Custer, but as your travel agent, I'm only telling you," four cartoons and the Anheuser-Busch lithograph illustrated the sad outcome of Custer's failure to heed the advice of his travel agent.[96]

Some companies have commissioned Last Stand paintings specifically for advertising purposes. H. Charles McBarron's *Custer's Last Stand* was executed for the American Oil Company and included in a series of advertisements evoking America's colorful heritage. Many years earlier, the renowned illustrator N. C. Wyeth was commissioned to paint Custer's final moments to demonstrate the proposition that while "Nature *in the* raw is seldom *MILD*," Lucky Strikes were "the *mildest* cigarette you ever smoked." The result was a placid Last Stand scene that may have reflected this contention, but did nothing to advance Wyeth's reputation.[97]

Pictures of Custer's Last Stand have embellished advertising copy for products ranging from cap pistols through breakfast cereals. But more significantly, the concept itself, devoid of illustration, is serviceable. Among its many uses, the most pronounced is for purposes of dating a company or a service. The disaster on the Little Big Horn is remote in time and yet completely familiar to today's buying public. Thus the New York Life Insurance Company, Life of Virginia, the Hartford Group (Fire Insurance) and Levi's have all run advertisements referring to Custer's Last Stand in order to establish the venerability of their traditions in business, while one computer service used the same reference to the opposite effect: "If Custer had General Electric Computer Time-Sharing Service . . . it might have been Sitting Bull's Last Stand."[98]

VI

If a myth's lifespan is directly related to its currency, its relevance, then Custer's Last Stand is presently assured of a long future. Its flexibility is revitalizing. At the same time, it should be noted that this flexibility is contingent upon the continued viability of the central image of doomed heroism created by the Last Stand artists. That image is still at the heart of the myth, a point made most convincingly by reference to the humor of the Little Big Horn. For a stand-up comedian, the phrase "Custer's Last Stand" is equivalent to a one-line joke. Its mention brings an immediate response from the audience. The comedian can safely assume a shared mental picture of the Last Stand, and build a story around it with no further elaboration. In the discussion that follows, the reader might consider what sense could be made of most Custer jokes without a preconceived impression of how Custer's Last Stand looked.

Despite its variety, Custer humor falls into a limited number of categories. Several jokes revolve around the theme of Custer's last words, and all rely on a pre-existent image of the Last Stand. One version currently in vogue unconsciously echoes an exclamation attributed to Custer by the contemporary press. Upon seeing the Indian camp along the Little Big Horn, he reputedly doffed his hat, waved it in the air and shouted, "Hurrah, Custer's luck! the biggest Indian village on the American continent."[99] The modern equivalent, beloved in anti-Custer circles and especially among the Indians, has Custer, surrounded by warriors closing in for the kill, still hollering, "Take no prisoners, men!"[100]

Though other versions of the General's last words abound, there is one perennial favorite that is never told in polite company but seems to have universal appeal. I have heard it in one form or another everywhere I have gone in Canada and the United States, and several sightings have been reported from abroad. The details change in each telling, and a series of obscene embellishments are frequently tacked on. But the basic situation remains constant: an artist is approached to illustrate Custer's last words (or thoughts), and the story unfolds from that point. The version recounted by comedian Red Skelton can serve for all the rest. To paraphrase: Did you hear about the fellow who approached an old

Indian squaw and asked her to weave him a rug showing General Custer's last thoughts? When he went to pick the rug up a few weeks later, it showed a cow wearing a headdress standing in a cotton field. "Well, what's this supposed to represent?" the angry patron demanded. "I asked you to illustrate Custer's last thoughts." "I did," she replied: " 'Holy cow, look at all those cotton-pickin' Indians.' "[101] The joke is elaborate, somewhat obvious and not particularly funny. Yet it continues to enjoy unique popularity as the perfect verbalization of a pictorial concept.

Cartoonists naturally thrive on Custer's Last Stand. For one thing, its appeal cuts across all strata of readers. A cartoon in the literary weekly *Saturday Review* depicts a busty, formidable teacher dressing down a student: "No matter what you saw on television, General Custer, Daniel Boone and Abe Lincoln were not all in love with the same Indian girl!"[102] In turn, *Cavalier*, a men's magazine, carries a full-page Last Stand in color showing a lieutenant waving a white flag on the end of his sabre, and Custer snarling at him, "What the hell do you mean? 'Better Red than dead!' "[103] (Or, as *Playboy* would have it, "Who said that blondes have more fun?!")[104]

The *Playboy* punchline provides a natural transition from the jokes about Custer's last words to those concerned with his famous golden locks. With hair length a matter of continuing concern, Yellow Hair or Long Hair as he was known to the Indians is a figure of topical interest. Depending on one's sympathies, one might identify with him, particularly since he endured a figurative barbering on the Little Big Horn. His coiffure was affected as a mark of nonconformity in his own time, and we can understand the lament of one trooper in a *True* cartoon. "I don't see why Custer doesn't have to get a haircut," he mutters to a buddy as their hirsute commander struts past.[105] Gordon Bess in his Indian cartoon strip *Redeye* has worked in the occasional joke about Yellow Hair. In the best of these, Chief Redeye, caught in an eternal comic predictment when his wife demands that he "explain those blonde hairs" on his vest, limply asks, "I don't suppose you'd buy that Custer story again, would you?"[106]

Many cartoonists besides Bess enjoy looking at Custer's Last Stand from the Indian viewpoint. A few have purposely dwelt on the fact that Indian militants today regard Custer as the symbolic white man, "the Ugly American of the last century," and as such heap their scorn upon him. A blanket Indian squatting in front of his tipi disgustedly watching his son send up smoke signals, turns to his wife and comments: "Is that all Junior learned at college? . . . sending up smart-alecky 'graffiti' like 'Custer is a ratfink'?"[107] A cartoon in *Argosy* summed the situation up with gentle humor. A smiling Indian walking out of a theater showing *Custer's Last Stand* remarks to his companion: "It's nice, for a change, to see a movie with a happy ending."[108] (In fact, three young Canadian Sioux were expelled from a Manitoba theater for "cheering wildly" during the climax of *Custer of the West*.)[109]

Custer's Last Stand seems something out of the ancient past.

Consequently, it is often employed to suggest extreme age. Advertisers use it to establish the old-fashioned, time-tested quality of their products or services. Politicians from Arkansas and Texas, in arguing the point that their state constitutions were antiquated and badly in need of revision, noted that they dated back to the days of Custer's Last Stand.[110] In reporting the case of a woman confined in an Ohio mental institution for ninety-seven years, the New York Times observed that she completed her first year in care the very day Custer was dying out West, while an article on the dean of American historians, Samuel Eliot Morison, expressed awe not only at his continuing productivity, but the fact that he was born "only eleven years after the Battle of Little Big Horn."[111] Custer's Last Stand in fact is not as remote in years as in its emotional connotations. It seems older than a century, belonging to the epoch of a vastly different, simpler and more adventurous America. Dagwood Bumstead was made aware of how much things change when he chanced to ask his son what he was studying in history. "The democratic organization of the Greek city states as they relate to the intellectual concepts of the ancient philosophers," comes the reply, and an abashed Dagwood is left to confess: "And I never got past Custer's Last Stand."[112]

A number of Custer jokes involve a play on words. More than one rock group has called itself Custer's Last Band, while Custer's Last Stand has referred to a hot dog stand, a Kelloggs' Corn Flakes stand, a Budweiser Beer stand, a McDonald's hamburger stand and, in one representative version of this hoary gag, a buffaloburger stand. "Have you read about that famous guy out West who set up a string of buffaloburger stands, but lost his shirt on 'em?," a boy asks, and his father, picking up the joke, carries it on: "Yeah, lost his places, one after another, until he finally had to close up the one at Little Big Horn! Yep — that was Custer's Last Stand!"[113]

Needless to say, the most popular word play is "Custard's Last Stand." In the days of slapstick and pie-in-the-face comedy on the movie screen, it enjoyed a definite vogue. Colonel Custard's Last Stand, with Chief Standing Cowski leading his braves, appeared in 1914, while the basic pun, stripped of its historical connotations, provided the title for two 1920's comedies.[114] It still reappears occasionally. A cleaning product boasts that it can remove stains that no other detergents can — thus, "Frozen Custard's Last Stand" — and Jughead, the perpetual adolescent clown in the Archie comic strip, gets a frozen custard in each eye for his troubles when he comes up with the same gag.[115]

By far the most common type of Custer joke is also the most reliant on the public's mental image of Custer's Last Stand. The Last Stand is now a synonym for wholesale slaughter. Sportswriters depend on it to characterize lopsided contests, while political analysts fondly invoke it after a landslide election. As President Lyndon B. Johnson was entering the final, stormy months of his term in office, he quipped at a dinner meeting with the press, "I don't think any veteran could appreciate my feelings on this night — except General Custer. And I don't know of any chief, executive or otherwise, who has ever been surrounded by more Indians."[116]

Cartoonists have always delighted in this usage. "You need another birthday . . . like Custer needed more Indians," one greeting card advises the recipient.[117] Another bluntly asks, "Why couldn't you have been with Custer . . . when he got into all that trouble?" A cartoon Last Stand makes the implication explicit.[118] The king in *Wizard of Id*, having received assurances from his bumbling knight Sir Rodney that he can "sleep well, for your troops and I are ever vigilant," knows "how Custer felt."[119]

The poets had celebrated Custer's Last Stand as the American Charge of the Light Brigade. Today we can still appreciate the analogy, though we interpret it differently. Custer is the general who blundered, an inimitable and thus indispensable great American boob. Tom K. Ryan's popular strip *Tumbleweeds* features as a regular character a curly-headed officer, Colonel Fluster of the 4,187th Cavalry, commander of Fort Ridiculous, known to his Poohawk Indian enemies as Goldilocks. As his name implies, Colonel Fluster is a self-important peacock, fairly bursting with sound and fury but given to postponing Indian wars because his hair is still in curlers or his men are taking their naps.[120]

Bill Freyse in *Our Boarding House* frequently indulged in Custer one-liners. Major Hoople knew that to tangle with his Martha was tantamount to re-enacting Custer's Last Stand — with himself in the leading role. His improbable schemes were likened to "Custer's battle plan," and his belabored explanations were so slanted that "he'd describe Custer's Last Stand as a retirement party." One panel transcended the usual jokes to a humorous appreciation of the Custer myth. The Major is shown doing a slow burn as he valiantly struggles to ignore several pointed barbs about a "talking dog" he has bought. Two of the boarding house's roomers propose ludicrous names for the puppy before a third pipes in: "Never mind those wise-guys, Major! They just want to remind you of your blunder! But it's men who dare to be different who made this country great! I say name him Custer!"[121]

VI

Today the idea of Custer's Last Stand provokes more laughter than awed admiration. Yet when the layers of jokes are peeled away and their cores exposed, one is confronted with an old, heroic myth still going strong in our irreverent age. The artists in a line stretching back to Cary and Waud are responsible for what we see when we hear the words "Custer's Last Stand." They created a memorable image that has since assumed many forms. At bottom, however, it is always the same: a moment of American heroism, frozen in time, prepackaged and available for anyone to use as he sees fit.

Thus the heroic concept of Custer's Last Stand survives long after the nineteenth-century pietism that first inspired it has vanished. Custer's Last Stand is an accepted tradition, as common as pretzels, beer and the comic page. A genteel versifier was wiser than she knew when she solemnly lamented in 1876:

How sad, amid the festal days
Of our Memorial year,
A Nation all should turn to weep
Beside poor Custer's bier! [122]

Unwittingly, the poetess had caught the flavor of the modern Custer myth.

But Custer's Last Stand is something more than a moment divorced from time. It is the climactic incident in a series of events, and the image created by the artists is a picture framed by narrative. This narrative determines how we interpret the picture and, at the least, it involves movement and change. Thus Custer's Last Stand is also a tale that is being constantly retold. Advertisements and cartoons imply this. But tale-telling is really the province of the novelist, and for him the artists' image of Custer's Last Stand is a beginning, not an end. It is a departure point for story.

Chapter 4

"NO SURVIVORS:"
The Novelists and
Custer's Last Stand

[The villain] too cleared away formidable obstacles until the climactic duel in which he and the hero faced each other at point blank range while the universe, in suspension, held its breath. Here again, sharply and simply put, was the lost reality: destiny held tightly in one's hand. This was the attraction in every horse opera . . .

Leo Gurko, *Heroes, Highbrows and the Popular Mind.*

Captain Keogh's horse Comanche may indeed have been the only living thing found on the banks of the Little Big Horn "forty-eight hours" (as the books say) after Custer's last battle . . . [But] there was another survivor, though, to be sure, "forty eight hours later" found him riding far out and away from the stark windrows of tongueless dead. And riding far out and away from the remembered pages of history. I was that survivor.

From the Journal of Colonel John Buell Clayton, C.S.A.

Novelists who choose to write about Custer's Last Stand begin with their climactic scene decided for them. Their readers know where the story is heading and how it will end. Custer's Last Stand is utterly predictable. It can have only one conclusion. The Custer novelists' concern, then, is with character and plot — the infinite variations that can be worked on a single, well-defined theme. They work entirely within the realm of myth, modifying endlessly the narrative frame around that grand finale on the Little Big Horn.

Last Stand fiction is repetitive just as myth is repetitive. It consists of the ritualistic retelling of the same basic story. Thus the writers who have usually broached the subject are in one sense at least admirably equipped to handle it since most have been schooled in the ritualized conventions of the Western novel. Frank Gruber, a prolific writer and the author of two Custer books,[1] once observed that there were only seven basic Western plots. One was "Custer's Last Stand." "This is simply the Cavalry and Indian story," he explained, and "it may not have to do with Custer on the Little Big Horn."[2] The label Gruber selected for this type of story is significant, however, for it implies, correctly, that the bulk of Custer fiction constitutes a single twist on the formula Western.

I

"It must be admitted that good novels are much compromised by bad ones," Henry James wrote in 1884, "and that the field at large suffers discredit from overcrowding."[3] If the novel as an art form requires no justification today, several of its conventionalized subgenres including the Western, the mystery, the spy story and the science fiction story are still being defended before the bar of critical opinion. Elaborate and sometimes weighty analyses of the formulas have been advanced to elucidate content, function and cultural significance and to account for their mass appeal. Increasingly, such analysis has been empathetic and occasionally even rather querulous in its insistence on the intrinsic merit of the various formulas. But an acceptance of them on their own terms need not entail a total suspension of critical judgment. There are good and bad Westerns just as there are good and bad sonnets. Moreover, within the ranks of those who write them there has been a lively debate over the nature and purpose of the Western.

Two clear-cut schools have formed among Western writers, and they divide over a fundamental issue: Should the Western continue with the standard themes that have always attracted an uncritical mass audience, or should it strive to elevate its quality and thus the level of its appeal? This question is taken seriously if one may judge from the file of *The Roundup*, the official organ of Western Writers of America.

Frank Gruber, for one, belonged to the old school that measures success strictly by sales. "The ten Western novels I published have, as of this moment, earned me directly $156,250," he wrote in 1955. Gruber's pecuniary concern is understandable since he was addressing an audience interested in learning how to make money from writing.[4] But Tom Curry exhibited much the same preoccupation in an article published in *Saturday Review*. Working from the perfectly respectable premise that "it isn't shameful to amuse millions," he noted that "*The Virginian* didn't finish the Western," and went on to say: "Thousands of writers, generation after generation, have made and still make a living grinding out these yarns. I was one. I brought up my family and educated my children chiefly from the proceeds of 125 Western novels and innumerable novelettes and short stories." Naturally, Curry, too, has ground out a Custer novel.[5] Those who like their Westerns straight can be prickly in stating this preference. "The purpose is to create a distinct, individual character and pit him against a specific human problem and see how he meets it," one Western writer commented. "If he misses, the academic pinheads call it art, a complex human document full of ambiguities. Mine don't miss, because I make a living at it."[6] The tone perhaps belies the argument. Purveyors of the formula Western often sport a chip on their shoulders.

There is another side to the story, and many serious writers have dedicated themselves to the task of elevating the status of Western fiction. They take as their models men of the stature of A. B. Guthrie, Jr., Walter Van Tilburg Clark, Frederick Manfred, Wallace Stegner and, to represent the more popular school, Ernest Haycox. Like Henry James they feel that "good novels are much compromised by bad ones," and they have tried, through example, to lead the Western novel to the promised land of literary respectability.

Clifton Fadiman once remarked with evident disdain that Western novelists give their audiences "action, melodrama, easily recognized types, synthetic maleness, Sunday-school morality, vicarious escape into the wide-open spaces and a modicum of history-and-water."[7] Fadiman is close to right, but his blanket indictment implicates one of the Western's real strengths: a sensitive appreciation of the relationship between man and his natural environment. The finest Western writers today share in common an affinity with the land and a love for uncluttered vistas stretching out beneath the Big Sky. These are at the very heart of the American West's appeal. If an emphasis on the "wide-open spaces" leads to escapism, this is appropriate, for the West has always meant freedom from societal restraint and a world of infinite possibilities.

Michael Gold, who grew up in a New York ghetto around the turn of the century, remembered his boyhood yearning for escape to some shimmering never-never land far away to the West:

> On our East Side, suffocated with miles of tenements, an open space was a fairy-tale gift to children.

> Air, space, weeds, elbow room, one sickened for space on the East Side, any kind of marsh or wasteland to testify that the world was still young, and wild and free.

> My gang seized upon one of these Delancey Street lots, and turned it, with the power of imagination, into a vast western plain.

So Gold sustained himself, avidly consuming every dime novel Western he could lay his hands on and dreaming of a Jewish Messiah "who would look like Buffalo Bill, and who could annihilate our enemies."[8]

Escapism is a legitimate function of the Western, then, and is even more prominent in it than in the other formulas. But diluted history, as Fadiman suggested, is also too often an earmark of Western fiction. Certainly this is true of the majority of Custer novels, juvenile and adult alike. Cardboard figures staged against a backdrop of fact become part of a "sweeping panorama" or an "epic pageant" of history, to borrow favorite dust jacket blurbs. For the reader, one veteran writer ruefully admitted, the effect can be "like a dam busting."[9] Too much is offered too superficially, and characters struggle to keep from drowning in the flood of information dredged up through research. "A good historical novel," as A. B. Guthrie pointed out,

> has to be more than ghosts among the gimcracks. It has to be more than history faintly inhabited by figures. . . . It has to be people, it has to be personalities, set in a time and place subordinate to them. Perhaps the hardest lesson for us historical novelists. . . is that it isn't event that is important; it is human and individual involvement in and response to event.[10]

Guthrie's stricture aside, in using an event of the magnitude of the Little Big Horn, Western writers have tended to relegate character to a subordinate position. However, there has usually been one important exception: George Armstrong Custer himself.

II

Custer's character has usually been a matter of primary concern in Last Stand fiction, and the novelists have reflected with precision the basic historical reassessment that has made a villain or a fool of the former hero.[11]

The roots of the heroic Custer legend are easily traced. Though the rancor that saturated the press during the summer of 1876 extended to Custer personally, the poets rose above such acrimony and dispute to proclaim a higher truth, that of self-sacrificing heroism. The heroic Custer image that they wrought was most congenial to Americans of the time. Moreover, it was not without precedent.

Like the small town boy from the mid-West that he was, Custer had always been awed by the big city and the "talented and distinguished men" that his Civil War fame had brought within his social orbit. He also possessed a limitless appetite for flattery. At a dinner party he attended with twenty-five New York journalistic luminaries in 1871, Custer was sought out by the poet Edmund C. Stedman who, after arranging an introduction, proceeded to heap praise on him without stint or measure. Dazzled by this attention, Custer poured out his ecstasy in a letter to his Libbie: "Mr. Steadman [sic] . . . told me that during and since the war I had been to him, and, he believed, to most people, the beau ideal of the Chevalier Bayard, 'knight sans peur et sans reproche' and that I stood unrivaled as the 'young American hero.' " With characteristic ingenuousness, he cautioned, "I repeat this to you alone, as I know it will please you."[12] After Custer fell at the Little Big Horn and Stedman and his fellow poets had paid due tribute to a hero now perfectly enshrined in memory, Elizabeth Custer proceeded to make a small literary career out of recollecting details of her life with the General, thereby keeping his image polished and at the same time handsomely supplementing her meager army pension.

But even before Mrs. Custer set to work immortalizing the exploits of her husband, "the echo of whose voice has been my inspiration," Custer's posthumous career as an American hero was launched auspiciously in a worshipful biography rushed into print the autumn of the year he died. Confronted with Frederick Whittaker's bulky whitewash, A Complete Life of Gen. George A. Custer, one skeptical reviewer thought it "doubtful whether the American public takes sufficient interest in Custer to dispose it to welcome such a ponderous volume." But, everything considered, he had to admit that Whittaker "has probably done much to establish the fame of his beau sabreur."[13] This was an understatement of the first magnitude.

The whole burden of Whittaker's biography was compressed into a brief advertisement. Custer "was the best purely cavalry officer this country has ever seen," it asserted. "He was the ablest Indian fighter we have ever had. His life was a perfect romance. His name recalls nothing but brillant deeds of daring and romantic courage, and all that is noble and charming."[14] In short, Custer was a sure-fire inspiration for the nation's youth. Whittaker explored this theme directly not only in his poem on "Custer's Last Charge," which found its way into at least one school reader, but also in an 1882 dime novel, The Dashing Dragoon; or, The Story of Gen. George A. Custer from West Point to the Big Horn. "So ended the life of the flower of the American army, the brave, the gentle, the heroic, the people's idol, Cavalry Custer," it concluded. "God bless him, and may we see more like him."[15] The pattern was set.

On the whole, juvenile fiction about Custer has conformed faithfully to the Whittaker model, the Boy General, "as warm-hearted as he was daring," often serving as both friend and advisor to the boy hero of the book.[16] To accomplish this feat of illogical familiarity, authors are forced to cast their young protagonists as trumpeters, apprentice scouts, herders or messengers — anything to put them in close contact with the general. But though the boy hero will often idolize Custer, he never goes to the extreme of perishing with him at the Last Stand.

Teenager "Yellowstone Jack" Shelby escapes death by carrying Custer's eleventh-hour dispatch to Captain Benteen — as does Ned Fletcher, boy bugler and orderly.[17] Corporal Peter Shannon, a young trumpeter, performs the same feat, not realizing at the time "that the paper he clutched was his own reprieve from death."[18] Gabe Wilson, a fourteen-year-old distant relative of the General serving with the Seventh as a herder, survives as the bearer of a dispatch from Custer to the packtrain.[19] Jack Huntington, a sixteen-year-old assistant herder, and John Rand, a fifteen-year-old recruit, both muddle through with Reno's command, while the Stamford boys from Boston, Don and Hank, along with their trusty companion, a veteran scout named Washita Joe, miss the battle but are on hand aboard the steamer Far West to hear a Crow scout relate the first news of the destruction of Custer's whole command.[20] Oscar Stillwell, a youthful goldminer, rides with Custer, but is assigned to help get a message through to Reno. Stillwell makes it, but his companion is killed and scalped and the General's last orders are lost to posterity, inside the dead man's shirt.[21] A few juvenile heroes have outdone the average boy scout or herder by breaking through the circle of death around Custer Hill and riding to safety. "Boy trailer" Mason Pierrepont, who had come into intimate association with Custer while searching for a lost sister, and Young Wild West, the hero of his own dime novel series, both miraculously survive the Last Stand, while boy bugler Jim Peters not only escapes, but does so on the horse Comanche, hacking his way through the Indians with Custer's own sabre.[22]

Nothing compares for vicarious thrills, however, to the account of the battle in the anonymously-authored *Buffalo Bill Wild West Annual* (1950). The book's characters are three typical English schoolboys, Tom, Dick and Harry, and their mentor and guide, an amiable ghost named Gordon Gregory. Gordon takes his mortal friends on a tour of living Western history, including an eye-witness view of the Last Stand. So engrossed do the four become in the tragedy unfolding in front of them that they are unaware of the presence of Indians in their rear. The warriors are almost upon them before they realize their danger. Then, in a concluding scene touched with the fantasies of boyhood, Tom, Dick and Harry flee hand-in-hand with Gordon across the meadows of the Little Big Horn valley, the distance between them and their howling pursuers narrowing until, just in the nick of time, Gordon's powers prevail and they are spirited away to safety. As Gordon had forewarned his chums, "whilst we cannot alter history, we can *add* to history by you three being killed . . ."[23] Though the logic is not clear, the meaning is. Gordon's worst fears had very nearly come to pass.

Adult Custer fiction, too, has a stock hero: the former Seventh Cavalry officer who, cashiered on false charges, returns to his regiment in some lesser capacity in order to clear his name. Invariably, he accomplishes his mission at the Little Big Horn.[24] In one early novel, Randall Parrish's *Bob Hampton of Placer* (1906), the officer dies with honor restored on the field of battle. In another, Cyrus Townsend Brady's *Britton of the Seventh* (1914), he gains absolution as a civilian scout serving under Reno. Custer in both stories is still Whittaker's flawless hero, and Brady's Preface to *Britton of the Seventh* reveals just how consciously contrived this characterization was. A decade earlier, in his history *Indian Fights and Fighters*, Brady had reached the conclusion that Custer disobeyed the spirit if not the letter of his orders at the Little Big Horn. Now, feeling that he had been "possibly unduly severe, perhaps just a little harsh," Brady recanted: "Those who loved this brave man, this gallant gentleman, this ideal swordsman and cavalry leader may perhaps accept this as some *amende*. Certainly, he and his men died gloriously as they had lived bravely."[25]

However, the end of Custer's heroic career in adult fiction was in sight. The years after his death had produced a number of laudatory biographies, culminating in 1928 in Frazier Hunt's fulsome and virtually unresearched panegyric *Custer: The Last of the Cavaliers*. Embellished with an excellent wash drawing of the Last Stand by the Texas artist John W. Thomason, the book, in retrospect, can be seen as a final tribute to Custer at the peak of his popularity. The next year, the Roaring Twenties ended when the stock market's crash plunged the nation into depression. Hard times spawned a new bitterness and cynicism that rejected many of the heroes of happier times. Historical revisionism was the order of the day, and Custer, for one, fell victim.

Debunking was nothing new on the American scene. The word itself was coined in 1923, and it still connotes an attitude, an intellectual style that we customarily associate with H. L. Mencken and the *Smart Set* school of journalism. As for why Custer escaped unscathed in a decade of dedicated irreverence, one must assume that a lingering, nineteenth-century respect for his widow had must to do with it. Fred Huntington claimed to have been told by officers in the Philippines in 1898-99 that Mrs. Custer was "so beloved in the army of that day that by a sort of common consent . . . [her husband's] misdeeds were not given much publicity."[26] As late as 1930 one Custer writer confessed to a critical correspondent that "while not having intentions of 'covering up' anything, my admiration for Mrs. Custer in holding tenaciously to the well-known memories of her husband, is so great that I would not want to do anything to disturb her at this time of her life."[27] The waiting-for-Mrs.-Custer-to-die approach to Custer historiography has been scored for its insensitivity; but there is evidence for it, and it does possess an irresistible logic. Many of the General's severest critics refused to speak out during his widow's lifetime, and she survived to the age of ninety, outlasting most of them and winning a final victory for her beloved "Autie." The effect of her presence in stifling criticism can be gauged from the remarks of Captain Benteen, who was "only too proud" to say that he "despised" Custer, yet cautioned a correspondent seeking moral support for an article condemning Custer's leadership at the Little Big Horn: "As to taking any notice of what bereaved widows have to say, then I'm 'not in it.' The game isn't worth the candle."[28] Benteen died in June, 1898, and Mrs. Custer not until April, 1933. The very next year Frederic F. Van de Water's hostile biography *Glory-Hunter* appeared on the market.

Riding the crest of Depression iconoclasm, *Glory-Hunter* was a brilliant portrait of Custer as a perpetual adolescent, the Boy General driven by a consuming, almost monomaniacal passion for national recognition and adulation. In one stroke, Custer has been excluded from the company of deserving heroes. He was now fair game for sensationalists like E. V. Westrate, who in 1936 published *Those Fatal Generals,* "a parade of skeletons which everyone has the right to see." In it, Westrate developed the thesis that Americans have always been cursed with bad military leadership — and inordinately high battle casualties. Custer, naturally, was a case in point, a General who had needlessly sacrificed his men to an "insatiable glory-lust:"

> The Custer Myth is one of the most glamorous on America's pages.
> He is pictured — almost canonized — as the romantic, impetuous

warrior who died with lustrous nobility, giving his life for his country in a heroic battle with the Sioux Indians. The facts are somewhat different.[29]

Custer had entered the 1930's still "the hero of every boy" and, according to one crusading reformer who regarded American Indian policy as tantamount to a "massacre," "a true friend of the red man."[30] It was a very different Boy General who emerged from the Great Depression.

The success and immediate influence of *Glory-Hunter* has obscured the fact that Van de Water was not primarily a historian, but a novelist, and a popular one at that. Much of the impact of his biography can be traced to his skillful treatment of Custer's life as a story with a made-to-order plotline, a strong cast of characters and the single, dominant theme expressed in the book's title. Only a few Custer specialists are even aware that Van de Water anticipated the biography's interpretation by a year in his 1933 novel *Thunder Shield*, which also chipped away at the heroic Custer image.

Historical revisionism in the 1930's involved a basic reconsideration of traditional judgments on the relative merits of "civilized" and "savage" cultures. The rediscovery of the native American that had been underway at Taos and other Southwestern outposts throughout the 1920's reached fruition in the next decade in a mania for arts and crafts by Indians, books about Indians and a potentially revolutionary "New Deal" for Indians inaugurated in 1934. As Americans began to respond to the attractions of the First Americans, Custer became a repugnant figure to many. Charles J. Brill's 1938 history *Conquest of the Southern Plains: Uncensored Narrative of the Battle of the Washita and Custer's Southern Campaign* slashed away at the General's Achilles' heel, the Washita battle of 1868, implying that it, not the Little Big Horn, was the real Custer Massacre. In this climate of opinion, one that must seem quite familiar to an American of the 1970's, Van de Water was free to overturn the conventions of Custer fiction. In *Thunder Shield*, his juvenile hero, Hiram Shaw, prefers the Cheyennes who have adopted him to the white race and his ties of blood. Fittingly, then, Hiram is killed at the Little Big Horn while charging alongside Crazy Horse against Custer's troopers. His death seals forever his decision to remain loyal to his chosen people.

Frederick Whittaker had fostered the legend of Custer as a knight in shining armor in a poem, an article, a biography, and a dime novel. Frederick F. Van de Water, in turn, demolished Whittaker's Custer and replaced him with an unprincipled egotist through the vehicles of both fact and fiction. And, just as the writers of early Custer novels not only borrowed the Whittaker pattern but further embroidered it, so authors of more recent Westerns have frequently gone far beyond Van de Water in their vitriolic characterizations of Custer. Among the post-Van de Water novels dealing with the Little Big Horn, three stand out above the rest: Ernest Haycox's *Bugles in the Afternoon* (1944), Will Henry's *No Survivors* (1950) and Thomas Berger's *Little Big Man* (1964).

Bugles in the Afternoon is unquestionably the most successful of those novels utilizing the disgraced-officer-returns plot. The disgraced officer in this instance, Kern Shafter, is as handsome, strong, noble and tender as his name suggests, or as any reader of Westerns could desire. Too, his character is spiced with an evocative dash of bitters. The heroine is pretty and pure, the villain underhanded and cowardly. In short, it is a novel squarely within the time-honored conventions of the Western, with good and evil polarized and personified.

But Haycox was too dedicated a craftsman to be satisfied with just another wrinkle on the formula. Bugles in the Afternoon is fast-moving and yet faithful to its time and place, a rare combination in Custer fiction. More often, fact is subordinated to action, as Frank Gruber's Broken Lance and Bugles West attest. Hoffman Birney, who aptly described Bugles West as a "historical mishmash," himself wrote an interpretation of the Custer theme, The Dice of God, that for all of its evident sincerity of purpose erred in the opposite direction and sacrificed pace and clarity in a convoluted and murky attempt to parallel the separate stories of several characters whose lives culminate on the Little Big Horn.[31]

Blending action and history in a smooth concoction, Bugles in the Afternoon won a large audience as a Saturday Evening Post serial in 1943. When it appeared in book form the next year, one knowledgeable critic, John K. Hutchens, delivered a fair assessment: "Mr. Haycox is very far from having written the novel that an artist will some day find in the tragedy which reached its climax that fearful Sunday afternoon. But by the standards of his school this is a competent work, and seldom a slow one."[32] As the years passed and the great Custer novel envisioned by Hutchens remained unwritten, the reputation of Bugles in the Afternoon steadily appreciated. Thus we have a novel with the best of Western pedigrees — born in the slicks and faithful to the code of six-gun action — being acclaimed for a secondary quality, its authenticity. Frederick D. Glidden, better known under the pen-name Luke Short, insisted that in it Haycox had been "faithful to history and a damned sight more understanding, detailed, and perceptive than the recorded pedagogues."[33] Bernard De Voto, who made his mark as an accomplished Western historian rather than as the novelist he longed to be, expressed his opinion with a typical reservation: "Bugles in the Afternoon, which incidentally to its purpose is a sound history of the Little Bighorn campaign, is almost a good novel."[34] This was high praise indeed for De Voto, and yet fully justified.

In the denouement to Bugles in the Afternoon, Kern Shafter crushes the fair Josephine in his arms, and the reader knows that his bitterness has been washed away with the blood that flowed along the banks of the Little Big Horn, and the gnawing anger, nursed so long, is at last spent. A familiar cycle has been completed. The Western hero has been rescued from that lonely, single-minded pursuit of vengeance which borders on the deviant and restored to a normal range of human feelings through the love of a good woman. Symbolically, the lone wolf has been reclaimed for society. It is a classic Western situation. Frank Gruber for one utilized it to no great effect in *Broken Lance*. But in *Bugles in the Afternoon* there is something more.

Haycox has created a memorable Custer, a concentrated version of Van de Water's glory-hunter. The General's character is developed by means of omniscient description and, more tellingly, through the eyes of those who serve under him, admirers and detractors alike. Closely-observed domestic scenes show him to be a demanding child, devoted to his wife, but even more to her devotion to him. Having awakened her one night to listen as he reads a few pages of manuscript recounting his past exploits, he awaits her approval:

> "That's very good, Autie."
> "Is it?" he asked, like a small boy anxious for praise. "Is it any good?"
> "Nothing you put your hand to is not good."

So the bloated ego receives its ritualistic refueling, and the obsession grows in Custer's mind that the Seventh Cavalry, with him at its head, could easily route the whole Sioux nation.

On the eve of the Little Big Horn, then, determined to disobey General Terry's orders and strike out on his own, Custer muses over his prospects. "To himself he was a candid man," Haycox writes:

> He knew what he wanted, and what he would do to get what he wanted . . . He had no hypocrisy in him, no political caution and none of that mellowness whereby a man might smooth himself a pathway through other men. The egotism which lies in the tissues of all men was thicker in him than in others; the hunger for applause which is a thirst in all men was a greater craving in him. The sense of drama which made quieter men silently wish they had the stature and the daring to play great parts was in George Armstrong Custer so vivid that it gave him the stature and the daring. He created the color which other men shrank from, even as they wanted it. He played his part straight as would a great actor and believed in himself and in his part until the two were one . . . .

Haycox concludes this assessment with a masterly summation of the prosecution's case: "All these things he was — an elemental complex of emotions and hungers and dreams never cooled, never disciplined, never refined by maturity; for he had never grown up."[35]

Besides his forceful characterization of Custer, Haycox conveys to his reader the flavor of the fighting on Reno Hill. One's sense of probability is never offended despite the routine nature of the novel's plot. As a result, and because of the wide range of the book's appeal, from the reading masses to the eggheads, *Bugles in the Afternoon* remains an exceptional Custer novel.[36]

In first presenting Custer to his readers, Haycox observed, "There sat the man who was a living legend . . ."[37] This casual remark, tossed off in passing, is the crucial insight that serves as the focal point for *No Survivors* and *Little Big Man*. Both novels can be seen as studies in the Western myth. Thus while their concern with living legends extends beyond Custer, it is Custer's Last Stand, nevertheless, that immediately endows them with a mythic dimension and directly establishes their theme.

Will Henry's *No Survivors* is an interesting failure. The story's hero, Colonel John Buell Clayton, an unreconstructed Reb, goes to live with the Sioux soon after the Fetterman battle of December 21, 1866, and remains with them for nine years, "a 'red' Indian in fact and being," until the very eve of Custer's Last Stand.[38] Clayton is ubiquitous and indestructible, a super hero with all the potential for becoming a legend. But Henry does not hold a steady course. During much of the novel, Clayton is stranded in the nebulous middle ground between man and myth. As a normal being he is utterly unconvincing; his lack of probability is painfully evident, and he seems devoid of motive, logic and life. Clayton's sole reason for joining the Sioux is his love for the beautiful North Star (an obvious *deus ex machina*, since her role in the story thereafter is negligible). His abrupt departure is even less explicable. After living with the Sioux for almost a decade, he is suddenly and very conveniently convinced by the Rosebud battle that he is still a white man at heart. So Clayton deserts his Indian companions, and winds up with the soldiers at the Little Big Horn. In narrating the Last Stand, Henry reverts to the approach which, consistently followed, might have resulted in a distinguished Western novel. Clayton once more is an outsized hero who fights beside Custer until he is "killed" — only to rise again and on his equally indestructible horse Hussein ride off in search of the people he had forsaken, into the enfolding mists of legend like a modern El Cid.

Will Henry had the opportunity to write a great Custer novel within reach, but it finally eluded him. Fourteen years later, Thomas Berger finished the book that Henry might have written. *Little Big Man* is an extraordinary achievement which mines the same vein as *No Survivors*, but turns up all the gold. *No Survivors* is "based" on the journal of the late John Clayton; *Little Big Man* is the first-hand narrative of irascible, impossibly ancient Jack Crabb. Both men are super heroes, but Crabb does just twice as much as Clayton, and covers twice as much ground in doing it. The real superiority of *Little Big Man*, however, lies in Berger's flawless control of his theme. Though the novel is a rollicking satire, Berger never loses his wry appreciation of that which he is spoofing: "A small elite are picked by fate to crouch on that knoll above the Little Bighorn, and they provide examples for the many commonplace individuals whose challenge is only a flat tire on a deserted road, the insult of a bully at the beach, or a sneezing spell in the absence of one's nasal spray."[39]

In *Little Big Man*, Berger is not so much exploding the old legends as, in Granville Hicks' words, "creating a new legend."[40] Crabb, of course, is the new legend, and in himself encompasses most of the old ones. His story breaks off as it should just after Custer's Last Stand, that great American "legend of total annihilation" to which he, like Clayton before him, is the sole exception. By embodying a huge chunk of the Western experience within this "mythomaniac," Berger avoided the pitfall of making him subordinate to his setting. The historical background is not external to Crabb; he *is* that history.

A secondary but nonetheless remarkable facet of *Little Big Man* is the detailed account of the Custer disaster and its rich characterization of the General. Berger's Custer, down to such expert touches as a mad monologue delivered during his Last Stand — a pompous disquisition on the red man and the Indian problem lifted verbatim from the real Custer's opus *My Life on the Plains* — is a triumph, a subtly-shaded portrait of a personality usually rendered in broad strokes of black or white. Here is neither villain nor vacuous paragon, but something more: a balding former hero, entrapped in a legend largely of his own devising, who looked much older than his years on his last campaign, but showed the stuff of which legends are made when it came his time to die.

Finally, however, it is not the General, but Jack Crabb, the perfectly-conceived survivor-hero, who makes *Little Big Man* the best novel about Custer's Last Stand yet written. There are two time-honored traditions of sole survivors at the battle of the Little Big Horn, those in fiction and those who purported to be so in fact. Jack Crabb naturally belongs within the first; but in the context of *Little Big Man*, as a 111-year-old recollecting his youthful adventures, he belongs in the second as well. Thus he is both the fictional hero who alone survives Custer's Last Stand and the garrulous old claimant to that distinction: "From here on you have only my word for what happened to Custer and his five troops that Sunday afternoon, *for I am the only man what survived out of them 200-odd who rode down Medicine Tail Coulee towards the ford of the Little Bighorn River.*"[41] It is the ultimate Western boast, and it strikes to the very heart of that body of fiction built around Custer's Last Stand.

IV

When an editor was asked once why relatively few Indian-cavalry Westerns are published, he replied to the effect that "of this type of story that did cross his desk probably ninety percent had as a setting and background either the Custer-Sioux gambit or the Geronimo-Apache rat race, both tired old themes."[42] It is significant that the Little Big Horn should be regarded as a "tired old theme."

In point of fact, as Frank Gruber indicated, the Custer novel has usually been nothing more than the routine Indian-cavalry Western set in 1876 with its climax on the banks of the Little Big Horn River. The plot is not distinctive — after all, any officer falsely maligned by some former live rival and drummed out of the service in disgrace might return as an enlisted man to his old regiment in order to restore his tarnished reputation. The events at the Little Big Horn do not really impinge on this formula except for one inescapable fact, that of total annihilation. This alone has made an impression on the average Custer novelist: he must provide a hero who will somehow come out of a battle that is famous precisely because there were no survivors. The dilemma is obvious. If for historical purposes no man can survive, for fictional purposes the hero cannot be killed. Naturally there have been exceptions to both rules.

When someone who actually fell at the Little Big Horn is made the central character of a story, he must, in the end, die. In his novelette *Tragedy in the Great Sioux Camp* (1936), for example, Usher L. Burdick added an imaginary romance with a Sioux girl to the known facts about Sergeant James Butler, whose solitary grave has inspired a minor legend. Butler's tombstone marks the deepest penetration made toward Reno Hill by any member of Custer's immediate command, and some believe that Butler died bearing a final, desperate appeal for help. J. K. Ralston's oil painting *Custer's Last Hope* and Burdick's *Tragedy in the Great Sioux Camp* have immortalized this possibility. Since the real sergeant was killed at the Little Big Horn, of course, so also is Burdick's Butler.

More satisfying artistically as a solution to the problem of the survivor-hero are the fictitious, nonwhite protagonists of a few of the Custer novels. Writers of juveniles, with the greater latitude for invention permitted them, have occasionally made animals their central characters. Bigelow Neal's *The Last of the Thundering Herd* (1933) and Jane and Paul Annixter's *Buffalo Chief* (1958) follow the action at the Last Stand through the eyes of a buffalo bull, while David Appel's *Comanche* (1951) employs the fabled horse as its narrator. Barred from such convenient anthropomorphism, adult novelists as well as a growing number of juvenile writers have opted for Indian heroes.

In stories told from the Indian viewpoint, Custer's Last Stand is often treated as only another incident, and not the central event, in the hero's life. Custer's character is played down accordingly. Warren K. Moorehead, a reformer long active in Indian affairs, was respectful of Custer but not uncritical in the few efforts he made at giving him some character in his novel about a Sioux woman and her warrior husband, *Tonda* (1904). Though the Little Big Horn was in fact a pivotal point in Sitting Bull's career, Hamlin Garland made it an early and almost insignificant episode in his fictionalized biography of the Sioux leader, *The Silent Eaters*. It was the tragedy that befell Sitting Bull's people after the battle that preoccupied Garland — perhaps because the story was based in large part on material gathered on the Standing Rock Reservation in 1897, long after the glory of the Little Big Horn had faded for the Sioux. In John Neihardt's lyrical "tale of the old Sioux world," *When the Tree Flowered* (1951), Custer is no more than one among a faceless multitude of bluecoats who perish in the choking dust of battle, while the Washita and Little Big Horn merely serve as brackets around Dark Elk's quest for manhood and the Cheyenne girl he loves in Nathaniel Benchley's *Only Earth and Sky Last Forever* (1972).

Similarly, Frederick and Frank Goshe's story of the Plains Indians' doomed struggle for freedom and dignity in an alien world, *The Dauntless and the Dreamers* (1963), places slight emphasis on the Little Big Horn. But the authors do provide a novel slant on Custer's character when they imply that, fearing capture and torture at the hands of the Indians, he committed suicide.

This notion has persisted in the historiography of Custer's Last Stand, though it has never found wide acceptance. An army officer first proposed the possibility to the public in a popular history of the Western Indian wars published in 1882: "It is said that Custer's body was found unscalped and unmutilated. If so, my knowledge of Indians convinces me that he died by his own hand."[43] The suicide story was greatly elaborated by a self-styled Blackfoot named Chief Buffalo Child Long Lance, who in 1927 revealed "The Secret of the Sioux." Custer and Sitting Bull, it turned out, were old friends dating back to the General's West Point days. At the battle of the Little Big Horn, Sitting Bull ordered his braves to kill all but Yellow Hair. However, the attempt to spare his life was frustrated when Custer suddenly realized that "he alone was alive . . . [and] *put his gun against his body and pulled the trigger.*"[44] It was a tale that should have fooled no one, but a prominent historian swallowed it whole, and it occasionally resurfaces in altered form.[45]

When the Goshe brothers elected to support the suicide theory in *The Dauntless and the Dreamers*, they softened its impact in a verbal exchange between the book's educated Sioux hero, Chetanzi, and the war chief Crazy Horse:

> Chetanzi thought a moment. "Since we can never be sure let us do like Lance Chief. Let us believe that Custer died a hero's death, fighting to the last."
>
> "Aye," agreed Crazy Horse, his lean face softening. "Let it be so."[46]

Such a tender regard for Custer's heroic reputation did not inhibit D. Chief Eagle in *Winter Count* (1968). Here a warrior refuses to claim the General's pistols after the Last Stand, saying: "When he looked up and saw his forces crumbling all around him, there was terror on his face. He put a gun to his head with both hands and fired. When he did this thing, I knew I did not want his guns. I swear this is true."[47] Fully developed, Custer's suicide might well become an Indian convention, the perfect rebuttal to an American myth.

In striking contrast to the other Indian stories is Frederick Remington's *The Way of an Indian* (1906). For one thing, it is not in sympathy with its main character. For another, it seems to belie the contention that Custer's Last Stand plays a minor role in such fiction. Although only the sketchiest of historical detail is included as backdrop to the exploits of Fire Eater, the novel's bloodthirsty Cheyenne protagonist, the Custer battle, being just that much bloodier than the run-of-the-mill affair, provides the inevitable capstone to the Indian's sanguinary career. As his title suggests, Remington was interested in portraying a type, not an individual, and the novel's action is generalized in much the same fashion as his artistic depictions of various last stands.

Consequently, the Little Big Horn battle is not specifically identified as such, though the inference is unmistakable. Remington dwelt on the slaughter lovingly.

With the fighting over and all of the soldiers presumably dead, Fire Eater spotted a figure wrapped in a red blanket hastily departing from the battle area. The boot prints which trailed behind were a fatal give away. Following on horseback, Fire Eater soon overtook his enemy. When the terrified trooper threw his hands up in surrender, the Cheyenne responded by calmly shooting him through the thigh. Dismounting, and "chuckling while he advanced," Fire Eater "sat down a few yards from the stricken man." This is Remington's finest touch: the image of a fiend incarnate, squatting, studying his trapped victim, chatting with him awhile, building up his hopes. Then, still chuckling one imagines, Fire Eater stood up, walked over the cowering white man, "sank his three-pronged battle-ax into the soldier's skull and wiped it on his pony's shoulder . . ."[48] Fire Eater's triumph is predictably short-lived, and in the next chapter he is presented as a broken man, alone, forsaken by his gods, his medicine impotent and his young son killed, awaiting death at the hands of the elements or the troopers who have with stunning suddenness brought his people to their knees. The same bias manifest in Remington's Indian-cavalry art work dominates *The Way of an Indian*. While Remington produced graphic scenes of the Western wars as viewed through the soldier's eyes, he lacked insight into the Indian mind. Thus his book, despite its red "hero," is in fact a white novel.

With all of this said, we are left with the original dilemma: since most Custer novelists want their protagonists to be fictitious white men, not buffaloes or horses or Indians, the problem of the survivor-hero remains. Other than the unsatisfactory device of having the hero arrive first on the battlefield, where he discovers the bodies of Custer's slaughtered command, the writer has four alternatives. He can have his hero reside in the Indian camp either as a prisoner or a renegade; ride with Custer's subordinates, Major Reno and Captain Benteen; serve as Custer's final messenger; or, throwing the stipulation about historical plausibility aside, escape death in the Last Stand itself. Whatever else happens, the hero must survive.

Another factor that complicates the situation for the novelist is the very real challenge of trying to outdo the multitude of charlatans who have paraded themselves about as sole survivors of Custer's Last Stand. "It is astonishing the number of fakes who pose as 'heroes' as to Custer's last battle and campaign," an officer who had served under Benteen at the Little Big Horn remarked in 1918. "The plains and Rockies are full of them . . ."[49] By 1939 one writer had collected over seventy of their tales, and another was led to designate "The Survivor of the Custer Massacre" the major species of Northwestern "phony."[50] To this day survivor stories are foisted on the public, and the *Casper* (Wyoming) *Star-Tribune* saluted the ninetieth anniversary of the Little Big Horn with an article which not only had Custer outliving his Last Stand, but planning to attend the semicentennial observance in 1926![51] In short, the survivors of Custer fiction

76

must compete with an imposing crew of actual "survivors" whose inventiveness and resourcefulness were sometimes awesome.

To understand the difficulty, one might compare Buffalo Bill Cody's career in fiction with the wondrous tales that accumulated about Frank Tarbeaux, a shady international adventurer of French and Indian extraction, outlaw and Indian-fighter, gambler and monumental poseur, hob-nobber with European nobility and Hawaiian royalty, friend of several prominent literati and, in one way or another, a featured actor in the drama at the Little Big Horn.

To put the matter as succinctly as possible, the historical William F. (Buffalo Bill) Cody was active in the Sioux expedition of 1876, but he was in no way associated with Custer's command. However he was by that time already a celebrity, a popular stage personality and a dime novel hero.[52] The first deliberate fiction published about the Little Big Horn took the form of dime novels, six appearing in 1876 alone. Of these, the most renowned was *The Crimson Trail; or, On Custer's Last Warpath*, which ran in Street & Smith's *New York Weekly* between September 25 and October 30. Attributed variously to Prentiss Ingraham and Cody himself, *The Crimson Trail* claimed nothing less for Buffalo Bill than that he took "the first scalp for Custer" in an engagement fought three weeks after the Last Stand. The story had a definite basis in fact, and, re-enacted by Cody on the stage and fleshed out with fresh details in subsequent retellings, it satisfactorily accounted for Cody's whereabouts during the summer of 1876.

But Buffalo Bill was more than an ordinary mortal. As a dime novel character he was naturally ubiquitous. *The Crimson Trail* had linked him by name with Custer's Last Stand, and whether it was Ingraham or Cody himself who wrote that story, Ingraham was unable to let the matter rest. In 1887, under the pseudonym Dangerfield Burr, he published two tales which dealt peripherally with Custer — *Buffalo Bill's Secret Service Trail; or, Major Mephisto, the Soldier's Foe* and *Custer's Shadow; or, The Red Tomahawk* — and followed them up in 1901 with *Buffalo Bill's Unknown Ally; or, The Brand of the Red Arrow*. In each Custer is merely a name interjected to catch interest. *Buffalo Bill's Secret Service Trail*, for example, starts out on a promising note ("General Custer sat in his quarters reading his dispatches"), but quickly disintegrates into a complicated and purely fictional romance, chock-full of intrigue and heroics, with all of the latter being provided by "Custer's chief of scouts," Cody.[53] However, Ingraham did produce two Last Stand tales.

Buffalo Bill's Grip; or, Oath-Bound to Custer (1883) described Cody's arrival on the battlefield where "hardly yet had the thirsty ground drunk up the crimson tide that had flowed from death-wounds given to man and beast alike" — the first man to discover the bodies of Custer's troopers. On the spot Buffalo Bill swears to avenge the General, an oath he subsequently fulfills when he kills a Cheyenne warrior and takes the "first scalp for Custer." Here, at least, was a welcome concession to consistency in light of *The Crimson Trail*.

Two decades later, in the year before he died, Ingraham wrote his final words on the subject, *Buffalo Bill's Gallant Stand; or, The Indian's Last Victory* (1903). This time Cody marches with Custer, but fails to persuade the impetuous General of the danger ahead. His words of caution are met with the withering retort, "What, Cody, are you, too, going to turn croaker?" So, against his better judgment, he finds himself hip-deep in dead Indians and soldiers, fighting beside Custer at the Last Stand. Sabres in hand, they wreak havoc upon the savages until both finally fall on the field of battle. Cody, merely stunned, later regains consciousness. He is surrounded by the corpses of his comrades and a prisoner of the redskins, but at least he has survived to fight again another day.[54] In the person of Cody, Ingraham had utilized two of the hero types permitted by the tenets of Custer fiction: the first man on the field after the disaster and the survivor of the Last Stand itself.

The same two options were exercised by a man whose pretensions were legion, Frank Tarbeaux. In his autobiography, told to Donald Henderson Clarke, Tarbeaux recalled that Custer, a "favorite" of his, a "great fighter" and "a hell of a fellow," asked him to carry a message to General Terry "the day before the massacre." Unfortunately Tarbeaux did not see fit to divulge the contents of this historic dispatch, informing the reader only that by riding through the night he reached Terry in the morning. No matter. It was too late, as Tarbeaux subsequently ascertained when the advance guard he was accompanying came upon the corpses on Custer Hill.[55]

It was a good yarn, but nowhere near as exciting as the one with which Tarbeaux had regaled the popular British novelist Gilbert Parker several years before. Parker met Tarboe (as he spells it) about 1886 on a train near Fort Leavenworth, Kansas, when Tarboe, attracted by Parker's reading Mrs. Custer's *Boots and Saddles*, suddenly blurted out, "Rash — rash, in his last fight! He was caught in a trap." Only through prodding and time was Parker able to draw out the full story behind these Delphic mutterings, but it was well worth the waiting for. Tarboe, it turned out, had escaped from Custer's Last Stand:

> Custer was dead. I crawled to where was a dead Indian, got his war headdress and pantaloons, stripped myself to the waist, put myself into them, and mounted his pony. The Indians saw me riding hard, but thinking I was of their tribe, did not fire on me, and I escaped.

The only question left is how Tarboe got himself into such a predicament in the first place. In the Parker version, it was simply a matter of seeking diversion. Tarboe was traveling the theater circuit with Buffalo Bill, and had snapped at the chance for some real adventure out West. He enlisted in the army and Custer, recognizing his uncommon merit at a glance, instantly promoted him to sergeant. Thus, the Little Big Horn.[56]

The obvious problem with this story is that its contents can be checked out against the official record. A trooper who was with the Montana Column in 1876 and helped bury the Custer dead suggested in 1925 that "the next time somebody tries to tell you a Custer story, make him show his discharge papers."[57] Tarbeaux did not commit the same error twice. When he recounted the toned-down version of his Little Big Horn exploits for Clarke, he exhibited at least one skill of the experienced frontiersman he claimed to be by carefully covering his tracks. He was never a "duly accredited scout" with any of the commands he served, Tarbeaux conceded, and consequently "never drew a dollar of pay" in his life. Thus like Berger's Jack Crabb, whom he in many respects resembles, Tarbeaux suffers the fate that there can be no corroboration for his claims in the contemporary records. It is a disadvantage not without its compensations, of course, since there can be no refutation either.[58]

Tarbeaux is representative of the Custer novelist's competition. No matter what survivor-hero type the writer chooses and no matter how improbable the deeds he ascribes to him, someone, somewhere, sometime will have claimed as much or more in all apparent seriousness. Thus the weight of myth tests the author's imaginative faculties at the same time that it channels them in prescribed courses.

There is general consensus that Lieutenant James H. Bradley of the Montana Column was the first white man on the Custer battlefield. It was he who found the bloated corpses on the morning of June 27. Yet rivals for this strange honor were plentiful.

The autobiography of Frank Grouard, a highly regarded scout with General George Crook's command, describes how he stumbled onto the bodies of Custer's men during the night of June 25. Little credence need be given this tale, however, for the autobiograpy was dictated to newspaperman Joe DeBarthe, and between Grouard and DeBarthe history occasionally got lost.[59] Will Logan vividly remembered how he, as the first white man on the battleground, strolled among the trampled roses and the corpses from which "fresh blood . . . in many places . . . still oozed, bubbled and flowed from gaping wounds."[60] Not to be outdone, "old Indian scout" Bob Nixon in 1927 swore to the fact that it was he who actually discovered the mutilated remains of the General, with the "long dark hair" still on his severed head.[61] Besides modestly asserting that in his capacity as "official investigator of the Custer Massacre for the War Department" he rounded up the recalcitrant Sioux almost single-handedly, "Lone Star" Fred M. Hans also purported to have found the bodies of the Seventh Cavalry troopers,[26] while Captain Charles L. Von Berg, who carried dispatches to Custer from General Terry in one account, from General Crook in another, told how he discovered Custer's "heroic clay:" "Yah! he was bareheaded. One side of the hair was matted with blood from a wound but his scalp was untouched. That was a high tribute of the Sioux's respect . . ."[63]

Nor can one neglect the evidence that it was Calamity Jane herself who first chanced upon the gory corpses on the ridge above the Little Big Horn. "I went to the battlefield after Custers battle," Calamity supposedly wrote her daughter Janey in July, 1879,

> and I never want to see such a sight again in a horse which had been disemboweled was the carcass of a man apparently hidden there to escape the indians seeking revenge the squaws had cut legs and arms

from the dead soldiers their heads were chopped their eyes poked out. . . . Your Uncle Cy was in that battle Janey I found him hacked to pieces his head in one place and legs and arms scattered about. I dug a grave and put his poor old body in my saddle blanket and buried him I can never think of him without crying. Goodnight dear till next time.[64]

All Calamity's letter lacks is "pleasant dreams" at the end.

Such imaginative contenders for the title "First Man on the Custer Battlefield" have left scant operating room for fictitious claimants, though the avid dime novel reader had learned back in 1883 that it was none other than Buffalo Bill who discovered the General's body. (This fact was subsequently reaffirmed at many performances of Cody's Wild West, though it came into question in 1959 when several million television viewers saw *Have Gun — Will Travel's* gunfighter-hero Paladin chance upon the corpse of Custer.) Fiction, then, has generally avoided the "First Man" theme, and an exception such as squawman Ben Kane, hero of George Heinzman's *Only the Earth and the Mountains* (1964), is but a pale shadow of his historical prototype, Frank Grouard. Kane does not even discover the Seventh's remains, if one were being precise about it. He merely learns of the command's fate the night after the battle during an amiable conversation with an old Sioux Indian on the banks of the Little Big Horn — hardly very stirring stuff.[65]

To digress for a moment, the "First Man on the Battlefield" is but a variant of a type more common on the screen than in novels. Their mission: to warn Custer of impending disaster. Plot: through unavoidable complications, they are detained. Outcome: they arrive just too late to save the Seventh Cavalry from destruction. Several old-timers linked their names to the Little Big Horn battle by claiming such a tangential involvement in the disaster. Thomas Frost simply said he was a member of a relief expedition that was sent out to rescue Custer too late to do any good.[66] This is always the central motif: Too late! W. P. H. Peters, alias Bob Preston, was more imaginative than Frost. A Kansas buffalo hunter in 1876, he was contracted to carry a message to Captain Benteen personally warning him that the cavalry would be outnumbered on the Little Big Horn and must turn back. Frustrated by hostile Indians and white renegades who roamed the country, Peters was forced to skirt west until he wound up in Idaho. "Then," he stated, presumably poker-faced, "it was too late."[67] Harvey ("Arapahoe Harve") S. Faucett had a less ornate but strangely compelling tale to tell. Alerted to the concentration of hostiles along the Little Big Horn and the ambush being prepared for Custer, he made a frantic, 200-mile dash northward to warn the General, "but his pony dropped dead after galloping over the broken prairie of Wyoming twenty hours." And that, presumably, was that — a link to the Custer disaster that no one could possibly *prove* false.[68]

In the realm of pure fiction, scouts Buckskin Joe and Jerome B. James of Herbert Myrick's *Cache la Poudre* (1905) fit this pattern. Sent out by Custer a few weeks before his ill-fated attack to locate and determine the strength of the hostile Indians, the two thrash about in the brush long enough for the Seventh to get annihilated. Only then do they emerge, breathless from exhaustion, but not speechless. Before falling into the open arms of their respective girl friends, conveniently on hand for the occasion, they manage to gasp out their belated tidings. Buckskin Joe comes up with "Tell Custer — it was lie — thousands of Indians — beware . . . Oh, Milly." Moments later,

> an even more gaunt, bloody and bedraggled form staggered into camp from the brush, and clutching by the shoulder the first one he met, whispered hoarsely:
>
> "Where's Custer? Give him this dispatch!"

Too late. The General and his men were even then cold in death on a nearby hill, mercifully oblivious to the scene enacted when Jerome at last spotted his Gladys:

> "Sweetheart!" was all he said.
>
> "My Jerome" — and Gladys folded the weary frame to her strong, virgin bosom that rose and fell in mighty heartbeats.[69]

The reader can find some consolation in the fact that whenever Custer *is* warned, in films and in fiction, he either explodes in anger, accuses his informant of lying and places him under arrest as an Indian spy, or else he loftily dismisses the proferred advice as foolishness.[70] Another traditional type was the man who narrowly missed riding with Custer and ever after fondly recalled how "there, but for the grace of God, went I!" S.B. Clark, an old Indian scout who purported to be a friend of Custer and other frontier notables, can serve for all the rest. Shot while carrying a message from Custer to General Crook, he missed out on the Little Big Horn and thus survived to tell how had he not been "delegated to carry the message he would have been with Custer in the engagement."[71] It is not very inspiring stuff, and this survivor type does not make a particularly gripping fictional hero either. Wayne D. Overholser did create Patrick O'Hara, a *Chicago Herald* reporter who, eager to accompany Custer, was assigned instead to Crook's command. Disgruntled at his bad luck, O'Hara was more than mollified when he returned to civilization after the Rosebud battle and learned the news about the Little Big Horn. "A strange, electric prickle ran across his scalp. He took off his derby and touched his wiry red hair."[72] Better to live with the steady, plodding Crook than to die with the meteoric Custer!

Although the "First Man on the Battlefield" and others of his kind have garnered some notoriety, they are not in the same league with eyewitnesses to the Last Stand. Theirs was always the lion's share of fame, despite the transparent, even guileless, absurdity of many of their claims, and the blatantly derivative nature of the details that they lifted from the contemporary press which, anxious to milk the last drop of interest from a sensational story, printed the effluvia as well as the hard news of the Little Big Horn. "Custer shot three Indians with his pistol and killed three others with his sabre, when he fell shot through the head by 'Rain In The Face,'" one news account stated.[73] Its inexplicably exact dime novel details with their I-was-there immediacy were to reappear more than once in some wrinkled scout's personal reminiscences of the fighting on that June Sunday so long ago. . . .

While Tom Logan in Frank Gruber's bugles West and Dick Howard in Joseph A. Altsheler's The Last of the Chiefs (1909) caught glimpses of the action at Custer's Last Stand as captives in the Indian village, their tales are tepid beside those of D. H. Ridgeley, Walter Winnett and Willard J. Carlyle. Ridgeley, "an old Trapper," not only claimed to have seen Custer shot off his horse in the middle of the battle, but related how he was later forced to watch six prisoners being burned at the stake: "While the flames were torturing them to death the Indian boys fired red hot arrows into their quivering flesh . . ." Ridgeley enjoyed exactly seventeen days of notoriety before a former employer exposed him as an itinerant field hand possessed of "an imaginative mind."[74] In retrospect, Ridgeley was simply a man ahead of his time. With a little patience and the passage of a few years, his whereabouts that summer might have been forgotten, and possibly no former employer would have popped up to spoil his performance. Walter Winnett, for example, bided his time before revealing that he was once a captive of the Sioux for some four years. Sixteen or seventeen years old at the time of the Custer battle, he was discreetly absent during the fighting "hunting beaver in the hills," but he did remember seeing the corpses afterward.[75]

Perhaps no such story is quite so marvelous as Willard Carlyle's. At the age of sixteen, while mining gold in the Black Hills, he was shot in the mouth, taken captive by the Sioux and, after enduring a test of courage, made a full-fledged member of the tribe. Naturally he was present at the Little Big Horn.[76] "I am," he wrote Mrs. Custer in 1926, "the only living white man that saw that fight," and he went on to tell her of the General's demise:

> One sweep of his saber and an Indians head was split in two, one flash of his revolver, his last shot, and a red-skin got the bullet between the eyes, then he fell with a bullet in the breast, the last of that brave band.

> I saw him within 15 minutes after he was shot, and there was still a smile on his face. Perhaps he was thinking of his home, his beloved wife or Mother. Who can tell?[77]

Obviously just "one of them cranks who wrote letters to poor Mrs. Custer in later years, some of them still children in 1876," as Jack Crabb would have it.[78]

Alfred L. Chapman, born in 1842 and the self-proclaimed chief scout and interpreter with the Seventh Cavalry as well as an eyewitness to the

Last Stand, managed to combine three survivor types in one: Indian captive, belated messenger sent to warn Custer, and first man on the battlefield. On May 30, 1876, while "looking for Indians," he shot a mountain sheep and ended up with more than he had bargained for: Sioux Indians, who held him prisoner for eighteen days before he escaped and made his way back to Fort Lincoln, thirty miles distant. On June 20 he was ordered to rejoin the Seventh and warn Custer that the twelve hundred Indians he expected to encounter had been reinforced and now numbered between six thousand to seven thousand:

> Chapman arrived near the scene of battle about an hour and fifteen minutes before the battle begun, but could not get to Custer on account of the Indians. So hiding his horse in the brush, he crawled to the top of a hill overlooking the battlefield about three-fourths of a mile away where through a spy glass he witnessed the battle from beginning to end. The fight lasted about an hour and twenty minutes, . . . Custer being the last to fall.

Chapman shed additional light on history when he placed the Indian casualties at seven hundred and noted that, after it was safe to do so, he "went to see if there were any of the wounded that he could help." But none was left alive, and Chapman was "there on the field alone" when General Terry rode up. All this should have been glory enough for any man, but Chapman was not finished yet. After helping to bury the dead, he dispatched Captain Jack Crawford to Fort Buford with the terrible news, thereby scooping everyone else on the year's most sensational story. And, best of all, the old fraud had "papers and credentials to prove every statement" he made.[79] Chapman's fable was so preposterous that it takes on a majesty of its own. In 1914, it was made into a two-reel movie, *Custer's Last Scout* — "The Only narrative in film of the only living witness of the Custer massacre!" — starring Chapman himself as the "last scout."[80] The novelist who would outdo this imaginative charlatan had his work cut out for him.

A favorite plot of the Custer writers stations a renegade white man in the Indian camp. He may join Major Reno, and thus symbolically rejoin his own race, at some decisive point in the fighting (as does Jim Aherne in Leonard L. Foreman's *The Renegade* [1942]), or he may even have a change of heart in time to ride into the fray with Reno or Custer (for example, John Clayton in *No Survivors*). In contrast are Beau Mannix, artist and outcast, who has found a new life and a home among the Indians in Robert Steelman's superior Western *Winter of the Sioux* (1959), and Hiram Shaw, the adopted son of a Cheyenne chief in Frederic Van de Water's *Thunder Shield*. Both elect to stay with their Indian friends at the Little Big Horn. Bert Raynor, captured and adopted by a band of Oglala Sioux in William O. Stoddard's *Little Smoke* (1891), also witnesses Custer's Last Stand, but refrains from participating on either side. This leaves him with both options open: he is morally free to rejoin white society without having to repudiate the Indian cause. "Ke-o-na-wagh [Bert's Indian name] go to his own people," he tells his "brother,"

Little Smoke. "Not Ogalallah. White. Love Little Smoke. Good-by. Keep Pah-sap-pa [the Black Hills]."[81]

The historical question of renegades in the Indian village remains a moot one, muddled in part by Major Reno's assertion that he was battling every squawman in the country at the Little Big Horn.[82] The press at the time carried confirmatory reports. A bugler honorably discharged from the Second Infantry in 1869 was said to have been with the Indians and to have practiced his art on a captured trumpet, while one Indian shot by Reno's men turned out upon examination to be a long-bearded white man wearing an Indian mask — or so the story went.[83] William A. Graham, a sober, clear-headed Custer student, held the qualified opinion that Frank Huston, an embittered former Confederate officer and a squawman, was in or near the Sioux camp when Custer attacked. To further confuse matters, Huston has been a character in a novel whose half-Cheyenne hero, Jim Sundance, not only fights on the side of the Indians at the Little Big Horn, but personally kills his old enemy, Custer.[84] The real Huston denied that he took part in the battle, but did admit that, "as a matter of fact, there *were* white men there; *not* with the Sioux, but with other nations present." As Huston so aptly put it, in their place "would you, *then* or *now*, acknowledge it?"[85]

At least one man, Jack Cleybourne, was willing to do so. Allegedly captured by the Cheyennes in 1866 and named Chialla (White Cheyenne), Cleybourne witnessed several battles from the Indian side over the years. At the Washita in 1868 he tried to save some children as the Seventh Cavalry charged through their village, and he claimed to have seen Custer fall last at the Little Big Horn eight years later.[86]

Jack Crabb, John Clayton, Jack Cleybourne. The names blend, and the line between possible fact and intentional fiction becomes so indistinct that one can hardly be positive which is which. Caught in this dilemma, an English reader of a popular Western magazine inquired of the editors whether or not "a Captain or a Colonel S. [*sic*] Clayton, a former Confederate," was with the Indians at the Little Big Horn. Appropriately, no one at the magazine could say for certain.[87]

The most historically-tenable escape-hatch for the protagonist of a Custer novel is with Reno's command, and the majority of writers have chosen this solution to the problem of the survivor-hero: Elbridge S. Brooks' *The Master of the Strong Hearts* (1898), Cyrus Townsend Brady's *Britton of the Seventh*, Harry Sinclair Drago's *Montana Road* (1935), Zoa Grace Hawley's *A Boy Rides with Custer* (1938), Ernest Haycox's *Bugles in the Afternoon*, Charles N. Heckelmann's imitative *Trumpets in the Dawn* (1958) and Lewis B. Patten's *The Red Sabbath* (1968). However, it is a solution with a major drawback, for the story's action is thereby shut off from the main event — Custer's Last Stand. (Only John Clayton of *No Survivors* fully overcomes this limitation. He fights with Reno in the valley and on the hill, sallies out with the others to Weir Point, Reno's furthest advance towards Custer's position, and then gallops off to join the General in time for the Last Stand.)

An alternative solution especially favored in juvenile fiction is to have the boy hero carry Custer's last message to Reno or Benteen. Thus Ned Fletcher, "Yellowstone Jack" Shelby, Peter Shannon, Jim Peters and Gabe Wilson all traverse the same somewhat worn path.

Historically, while more than one trooper bore dispatches from Custer, Giovanni Martini (or, in its Americanized form, John Martin) is recognized as Custer's last courier, the man who bore the cryptic message to Captain Benteen, "Come on. Big village. Be quick. Bring packs." Among others, Theodore Goldin and Henry L. Benner aspired to the distinction of being the last messenger, but Colonel Graham demolished their pretensions.[88] Goldin's motives are intriguing since he was actually at the Little Big Horn as a private in Reno's battalion. The story told about William McGee was another matter. It popped up in conjunction with a murder charge against McGee for fatally stabbing a man in a New York boarding house in a dispute over the merits of a kidney stew. The papers played off the notion of a hero of the Custer battle having fallen to such a low estate, and printed McGee's tale of how he and a Dutchman named Wagner were sent by Custer to order Reno to "hold in for 20 minutes." Wagner was shot to pieces by the Indians, but McGee made it through with only a single wound. "Of course," he added, "the message was too damn late."[89] B. Jones ran a gauntlet of thousands of Indians to carry Custer's last message to Reno, while Thomas J. Callan, assigned to go for reinforcements, burst through the circle of hostiles and, ignoring Reno and Benteen, galloped to the nearest military post, then back to the Little Big Horn at the head of a relief force . . . "too late, however."[90]

The autobiographical account of John C. Lockwood first published in 1966 contended not only that he and scout "Lonesome Charley" Reynolds carried the final dispatches (" 'Yes,' said Custer, 'Jack has his horse Satan, and the whole Sioux tribe can't catch that horse,' and he handed the other dispatch to me"), but also that he witnessed enough of the subsequent fighting to see the General die first. The parallels between Lockwood's story and the average juvenile Custer novel are unmistakable. At the age of fourteen, boy hero Jack meets Boy General Custer in a chapter titled "The Little Cowboy Meets the General," and by 1873 they have become fast friends and hunting companions. Lockwood serves his apprenticeship as a scout under "Lonesome Charley," and at the Little Big Horn he carries Custer's last message. (Note that the General, in keeping with the motif of illogical familiarity, even knows the name of Jack's horse, Satan.) After the battle, Jack now a world-wise nineteen, decides to enlist in the Seventh Cavalry.[91] Not without cause, Lockwood's membership in the Veterans of the Indian Wars Association was suspended for "unsubstantiated pretensions" prior to his death in 1928.[92]

Survivors of the actual Last Stand would seem to fall exclusively within the province of novelists. Yet it is precisely here that the competition for the limelight has been most fierce. Though Curly, one of four Crow scouts with Custer's detachment, probably saw parts of the fight, he can hardly be termed a survivor of it. But a news-hungry press in 1876 dubbed him "in all human probability the only survivor of his command," and attributed to him a description of the sound of the concentrated, furious gunfire at the Little Big Horn — like "the snapping of the threads in the tearing of a blanket" — that was not only graphic, but also seemed to establish conclusively that he was there, that "he alone survived."[93] This distinction stuck, and Curly, a mere stripling of seventeen years at the time of the battle, suffered the misfortune of living out the rest of his days as the central figure in a controversy that has not abated with his passing in 1923: Was he, in truth, the sole survivor of Custer's Last Stand? The superb Indian photographer Edward S. Curtis astutely assessed the matter in 1906 when he wrote that Curly "has been so bullied, badgered, questioned, cross-questioned, leading-questioned, and called, by mouth and in type, a coward and a liar by an endless horde of the curious and knowledge seeking, that I doubt to-day, if his life depended on it, he could tell whether he was ever at or near the Custer fight."[94] In the public's mind, however, Curly has remained the "Sole Survivor of the Custer Massacre."

This fact never daunted a multitude of pretenders to the title. Two qualities, historian Edgar I. Stewart has pointed out, commonly distinguished each one's tale: "There was invariably a very ingenious explanation of how he happened to escape from the field of carnage and an equally ingenious reason for having remained silent so long."[95] Methods of escape ranged from hiding in a hollow log or in a tree[96] to lying under a dead horse[97] or curled up inside the carcass of a buffalo.[98] One inventive soul, a New Jersey farmer named Charles Hayward, stepped forward in 1923 to tell how, wounded and "half out of his mind," he was taken captive by the Indians at the Little Big Horn and spared because they considered him *wakan*, touched by the gods. Amnesia wiped out his memory of the next twenty-four years, but one day in 1900, while bent over a "bubbling spring" fetching water for his red masters, his mind suddenly cleared and he escaped, "still carrying with him the old headquarters flag of the Seventh Cavalry wound about his waist." The story convinced at least one gullible Congressman to support Hayward's claim for a pension based on his services under Custer.[99] Better yet was the tale of "Curley" Hicks. Eighty-nine years old, erect of step and with long silvery hair hanging to his shoulders, Hicks in 1930 demonstrated that he had an inventive mind of the sort only a jaded dime novelist could fully appreciate. There he was at Custer's Last Stand fighting for his life when the General motioned him over and ordered him to get a message through to General Terry. Hicks had not covered more than fifty paces before he saw Custer fall. Snatching up the bodies of two dead Indians to serve as shields, he made good his escape. It was too late to do anything for Custer, of course, but Hicks lived on to marry an Indian princess and tour with a side show or two. He declared all other sole survivors "fakes" and defended his own case with disarming logic: "Why should I say I have had these experiences if there is no truth behind my statements?"[100] That was the question, and apparently Hicks had found a satisfactory answer. In contrast, Frank Finkel, the man with perhaps the soundest case ever advanced by a "Sole Survivor" simply stated that he outran his pursuers to safety, and thus gained in credibility what he lost in drama.[101]

In comparison with such exploits, those of the fictional figures seem pedestrian. Buffalo Bill, John Clayton and Jack Crabb battle to the end with Custer, merely to be revived and rescued by Indian benefactors. Old scout Pandy Ellis fights his way clear of the circle of death and Young Wild West escapes down the Little Big Horn. Two other dime novel heroes, Mason Pierrepont and Tom Carleton, fall beside the General. Left for dead on the battlefield, they recover in time to dispatch looters engaged in robbing the corpses, and so make good their respective escapes.[102]

Belief in a survivor of Custer's Last Stand is a faith, built like most faiths on myth, not history. One begins with the certainty that there was a Custer survivor (or that Hitler is alive, that John F. Kennedy was killed by three snipers, that America was settled by one of the Ten Lost Tribes of Israel or by the citizens of the lost continents of Atlantis and Mu). This belief is not open to question. It is an article of faith, and may be demonstrated to the believer's satisfaction by a priori reasoning. Because it is gospel, one need only convince the already converted of its truth. It is a matter of the flat earth advocate unrolling his elaborate charts to discredit the findings of the astronauts — and succeeding, in an address delivered at a convention of the Flat Earth Society. The logic of such arguments is internally consistent once the initial premise, the creed, is accepted. Everything falls into place harmoniously, and the ridicule of establishmentarian pedants can be attributed to a monstrous international conspiracy to suppress the truth. A scorching refutation, by extension, is merely the scorn of the unbeliever that any true believer must learn to expect, to endure and to ignore.

In all likelihood, there were no survivors of Custer's Last Stand in the conventional sense of that phrase. But this assertion carries no absolute validity, for the glorious liars who claimed to have survived did not live in the world as we know it. People like Frank Tarbeaux, Captain Charles L. Von Berg and Fred M. Hans occupied worlds of their own, all-inclusive creations contained entirely within their minds. Though they filled these miniature globes to bursting, they were left to explain why their adventures made so little impress on the outside world, on history at large.

In his own recollections, the monumental liar was everywhere, met everyone and did everything. But no one else seems to remember him. "One name is missing from every index, every roster, every dossier," the "Editor" of Little Big Man confesses in his Epilogue: "In my library of three thousand volumes on the Old West, in the hundreds of clippings, letters, magazines, you will search in vain, as I have, for the most fleeting reference to one man, and not a commonplace individual by any means, but by his own account a participant in the pre-eminent events of the most colorful quarter-century on the American frontier. I refer, of course, to Jack Crabb."[103] Precisely! Tarbeaux by his own admission was never a "duly accredited scout," and that accounts for the omission in his case. When Captain Von Berg, a busy man in 1876, came to explain why the records offered no confirmation of the fact that he was General Crook's special emissary to the Sioux early in the year, a participant in the Rosebud battle in late June, a courier between Generals Terry and Custer and one of the first white men on the Little Big Horn battlefield, he pointed out that he was known under many different aliases (What army clerk could keep them all straight?), and, moreover, was a look alike for Buffalo Bill and often mistaken for him. Thus while Von Berg braved untold perils out West, Cody performed on the stage and continued to enjoy all the credit for the other scout's deeds.[104] Many seemingly irresolvable historical conundrums thus evaporate, contradictions are reconciled and a tale replete with elusive documentation becomes utterly true in the realm of the true believer.

The charlatans and liars who found their challenge in Custer's Last Stand dwelt finally in a universe not of history but of myth. This enabled them to maintain their pretensions or delusions undaunted in the face of a formidable array of evidence to the contrary marshaled by a world perversely intent on discrediting them. History lied, not them. In a sense, the universe they shared in common is a perfect mirror of that expansive adventureland of the Western, an escapist's paradise become more real than reality.

V

By the very limitations of their theme most Custer novelists have been perpetrators of myth. Their options are few, since they must work within the cherished tradition of a survivor of the Little Big Horn. Since most have also operated within the constricted confines of the Western formula, they have, through repetition, endowed Custer's Last Stand with a ritual of its own, a narrative that complements the artists' static image of doomed heroism. At the same time, the novelists have succeeded in clearly delineating the conflicting interpretations of Custer's character and, to a lesser degree, his Last Stand. Thus Custer fiction not only provides an exposition of the myth, but also an analysis of its content. It only remains to take the myth one step further. Through re-enactment, the wedding of narrative to imagery is consummated.

Chapter 5

"THEY DIED WITH THEIR BOOTS ON:" Re-enactments and Custer's Last Stand

While the last veterans of the old circus West were dying, the movies were born to make the American Sherwood Forest part of the world's great legends.

D.W. Brogan, *The American Character.*

Thrilling Charges . . . Sensational Hand-to-Hand Conflicts . . . The Indian "Circle of Death" . . . The Last Stand of Custer on the Hill . . . THE MOST THRILLING FILM EVER SEEN, COSTING MORE THAN $30,000.00.
Publicity for *Custer's Last Fight* (1912).

The Custer epic has been described as a "ritual drama."[1] Custer is eternal youth riding forth into the dawn of adventure, relishing a full noon of great deeds and public adoration and, finally, welcoming the sunset of a noble death. But through the dark night of sorrow there is solace in the certain knowledge of another dawn and another day. The ritual of cyclical re-enactment holds out the promise that there is really no Last Stand, for its perfect, self-sacrificing heroism assures that it will flourish ever green in memory, enjoying perpetual life. On a more mundane level, Custer's Last Stand has always lent itself to dramatic re-enactment. It played before packed arenas in the nineteenth century, and crowds jammed a bleacher in Montana to see it re-created every summer from 1964 to 1973. It has lighted up the screens in theaters and homes across the nation almost since the advent of motion pictures and television. In short, it has been repeatedly performed both live and on film before audiences whose numbers defy estimation. Thus the dramatic representation of Custer's Last Stand is one of the cornerstones of myth.

Since re-enactments fuse the visual and the narrative, they are often concentrated expressions of the whole myth within a single entertainment. For purposes of analysis, they may be approached with two criteria in mind: their presentation of the Custer character, which is key to the narrative portion of the myth; and their contribution to Last Stand imagery, that is, how they have extended the work of the artists.

With the possible exception of a few of the gargantuan nineteenth-century paintings, the re-enactments of Custer's Last Stand differ from the poetry, art and fiction chiefly in scale, in the ambitiousness and cost of their conception and execution. They are elaborate undertakings involving the individual skills of casts and crews numbering often enough in the hundreds, if not in the thousands that their publicity always claims. Consequently, re-enactments of the battle have been limited in number, and it is possible to comment individually upon them and the movies concerned with the Custer theme. Collectively, the movies have proven promiscuous, borrowing ideas freely from one another and, in a few instances, stock footage as well. Because of this, and to better appreciate the images of Custer and his Last Stand as they have evolved in the cinema, the films are most profitably considered in chronological sequence. But when one searches for the prototype of the successive Last Stand re-enactments on the screen, he is drawn back to a time before the first silent movies flickered in darkened theaters, to that source of so many of the Western traditions, Buffalo Bill Cody's Wild West.

I

During the intensive military campaigning that followed the debacle on the Little Big Horn, Buffalo Bill served as a scout with the Fifth Cavalry. On July 17, 1876, at the battle of War Bonnet Creek, a minor skirmish between the Fifth and some eight hundred Cheyennes, Cody and a warrior named Yellow Hand engaged in their controversial "duel." When this event is stripped to its essentials, we are left with the fact that Buffalo Bill faced and killed the Cheyenne in single-handed combat.[2]

Whatever its actual significance, the incident assumed major proportions when it was converted into the catch phrase "First Scalp for Custer." Lurid posters showed a handsome and unruffled Cody melodramatically displaying his bloody trophy. The Red Right Hand; or, Buffalo Bill's First Scalp for Custer, a five-act drama written by J. V. Arlington and based on The Crimson Trail, was quickly added to Cody's repertoire. It was not the first "sensation play" to exploit the disaster — on August 14 Sitting Bull; or, Custer's Last Charge opened at Wood's Museum in New York City to a "good audience"[3] — but The Red Right Hand had something none of its rivals could boast, Buffalo Bill himself, and by the fall of 1876 the scout was relieving Yellow Hand of his braids almost nightly. This new drama, Cody later recalled, "afforded us . . . ample opportunity to give a noisy, rattling, gun-powder entertainment, and to present a procession of scenes in the late Indian war." Since it capitalized on the public's interest in the Custer battle as well as in the Yellow Hand duel, *The Red Right Hand* attracted large crowds, and Cody was doubtlessly justified in feeling that it gave his audiences "general satisfaction."[4] By 1887, when Buffalo Bill's Wild West toured England, a re-enactment of the Last Stand itself was one of the show's highlights.[5] The Wild West's 1893 program, standard for nearly a decade, listed nineteen acts, of which #18 was *"The Battle of the Little Big Horn,* Showing with Historical Accuracy the scene of CUSTER'S LAST CHARGE!"[6] The scenario began in a log fort with Custer receiving news from his scouts concerning the whereabouts of the hostile Sioux. Acting on this intelligence, he led his men out of the fort and off to the next setting, the Indian camp on the Little Big Horn, where the Seventh was promptly ambushed and wiped out.[7]

At that point, the star made his entrance:

> When Custer's whole army was slaughtered, Buffalo Bill rode in, the spotlight on his majestic figure. He saw the carnage and on a screen appeared the simple words, "Too late!" The great scout reverently took off his Stetson and bowed his head. The lights dimmed. . . .[8]

It must have been a sight to see. The anonymous author of an 1898 promotional booklet four times described the Wild West's "Custer's Last Charge" as "indescribable," even in the middle of his one sentence masterpiece: "Actual death and carnage could alone add a single touch to the vivid truthfulness of this stupendous, animate, indescribable reflex of surprise, savage onslaught, desperate defense, murderous combat and annihilation." He went on to note that "there is not, never has been, and will never again be anything in a spectacular and reproductive way to remotely compare" with Buffalo Bill's version of the Custer fight.[9] Nevertheless, re-enactments of Custer's Last Stand have become familiar entertainment.

The major anniversaries of the Little Big Horn battle have usually been observed in a manner befitting the nature of the occasion. Full-scale re-enactments, with their attendant sensationalism, have been eschewed in favor of solemn ceremonies honoring the dead and reaffirming peace and brotherhood. Back in the nineteenth century, it was deemed inadvisable to remind either side of the past record of violence. Certainly while soldiers and Indians intermingled freely at a gathering to mark the tenth anniversary of the battle, no one seriously suggested re-creating it in any form more vivid than words. When it is remembered that the Ghost Dance war and Wounded Knee were yet four years in the future, the wisdom behind such discretion is obvious. The summer after Wounded Knee Crow Indians, as part of their July Fourth celebration, did stage a sham battle that was supposed to represent the Last Stand within a mile of the Custer Monument. But Indian fought Indian, since the United

States troops were played by a company of Crow cavalry, while officers and their ladies from Fort Custer and civilians from Billings participated only as spectators.[10]

By 1916, however, Indian resistance was a fading memory, and a re-enactment of Custer's Last Stand could no longer be inflammatory. The editor of *The Teepee Book*, a little magazine of Western lore dedicated to promoting tourism in the Sheridan, Wyoming, area, wrote historian Grace Raymond Hebard on May 16 of that year: "It is hoped that a large village of Indians will be on the ground where the Indians were camped at the time of the battle, and the movements of the battle may be reproduced in pantomime."[11] Instead, the organizers of the fortieth anniversary observance settled for a program "of a purely memorial nature" — a peace parley in the Indian camp and speeches by such dignitaries as General Edward S. Godfrey, who stood up in an automobile to address the crowd; White-Man-Runs-Him and Two Moons, participants in the Custer fight representing, respectively, the soldiers, the Indian scouts and the hostiles. Between four thousand and six thousand people turned out for the simple commemorative activities, and two movie companies filmed them for weekly news features.[12] So successful was the whole affair that the *Billings Gazette* urged some similar observance every five years as just tribute to Custer, as good publicity for the area and, presumably, as good business.[13] Though "pageants and exercises" were held on the battlefield in 1921, the highlight of the forty-fifth anniversary commemoration was the unveiling of a small stone marker with a bas-relief bust of the General in Custer Park in Hardin, Montana.[14]

The semi-centennial exercises in 1926 were appropriately elaborate as some fifty thousand spectators watched units of the modern Seventh Cavalry retrace Custer's probable route along the ridge above the Little Big Horn River. Down on the river bottom an estimated three thousand Sioux and Cheyenne and an additional one thousand Crow were camped. At the approach of the Seventh, the warriors charged out of their village and the lines of red and blue drew near — only to halt facing one another and exchange not bullets and arrows but greetings and tokens of friendship. "There were many present, no doubt, who hoped for a mimic or sham battle portraying in some fashion the tragic events which took place there 50 years before," one observer wrote. "They misunderstood the spirit and intent of the occasion, however, since the events of the day were intended to portray in unmistakable terms, the friendly relations and long continued peace between the red and the white."[15] The next day, in an impressive ceremony, services were held for the unknown trooper of the Little Big Horn, and a tomahawk was symbolically buried. This concluded the three-day fete, but its unqualified success and the national interest it had attracted ensured that others would follow.

The very next year, President Calvin Coolidge doffed his ten-gallon hat and donned a headdress instead for his adoption into the Sioux tribe at the Deadwood, South Dakota, Days of '76 celebration. Afterwards, the newly-named "Leading Eagle" (the Sioux council had rejected "Still Waters" and "Solemn Warrior" as too undignified) watched a re-creation of Custer's Last Stand.[16] Through such politicking Coolidge helped blaze the way West for a second conquest, this one by the newly-mobile generation of American tourists who were packing their Model T's and hitting the trail to vacation wonderlands beyond the Mississippi.

With tourism an increasingly important economic consideration, it was natural for business-oriented groups in the Custer Battlefield region to push for another major commemoration in 1936. The Hardin Lions Club and several American Legion posts sponsored a sixtieth-anniversary program that, it was hoped, would match the 1926 observance in attracting dignitaries, national coverage and hordes of tourists who, in depression times, would provide a welcome stimulus to the local economy. Perhaps General J. J. Pershing would consent to deliver the principal address, and maybe the Seventh Cavalry would again participate in the activities. In the end, the governor of Montana was the featured speaker, and a troop of Fourth Cavalrymen from Fort Meade, South Dakota, put on a display of marching formations, a demonstration of armament and a modern sham battle. Though hundreds of Indians were encamped in the Little Big Horn valley, there was no re-enactment of the Last Stand. Instead, the cavalry maneuvered, the speakers orated and bands played in a festive pageant that attracted several thousand spectators despite the "terrific heat."[17]

The repeated congregation of large crowds at the National Cemetery and on the battlefield proper could permanently deface the site and reduce its historical value for future generations. Foreseeing this danger, officials after 1936 prohibited further commemorative spectacles on the actual battleground. Thus the seventy-fifth anniversary was marked only with speeches. The promoters in 1936 had stressed as their anniversary theme a "last great call" of survivors from the exciting days of the Sioux wars.[18] The seventy-fifth anniversary would be too late, they argued, and, in fact, the living link with the past had become perilously thin by 1951. But the relatively spartan observance that year was made memorable by the presence of two wrinkled Sioux Indians, Dewey Beard and High Eagle. As children they had been in the camp on the Little Big Horn when Custer attacked. Now they were old men, bent by the years and perhaps slightly uncomfortable in the buckskin outfits and flowing feather bonnets that popular taste dictated they wear. Yet they stood with regal dignity on Custer Hill, poignant reminders of the plains Indians' former power.[19]

If the official anniversary commemorations have settled for expressions of red-white friendship in lieu of re-enactments of the battle, no such sense of decorum has ever hampered the promoters of unofficial observances. The tourist appeal of the Custer myth was always evident. By the turn of the century both the Northern Pacific and the Burlington Route were advertising the Custer Battlefield as a major attraction on their lines. "Traveler, visit this spot!," the Northern Pacific commanded. "It is worthy a pilgrimage from a distance."[20] The Burlington, in turn, was involved in "a somewhat elaborate programme" to commemorate the twenty-fifth anniversary of the fight. The plan eventually collapsed for want of the necessary cars to run special excursions from Billings and Sheridan.[21] But in 1909 the Burlington did run a special excursion train to the Crow Agency from Billings to accommodate those who wanted to watch a re-enactment of the battle.[22]

In 1919, with automobile tourism (or "auto-gypsying," as one writer called it) steadily growing in economic importance, a Sheridan businessman successfully campaigned to have a 1,500-mile stretch of highway between Omaha, Nebraska, and Glacier National Park named the Custer Battlefield Highway. Presumably it was the name's drawing power he was after, since little use was made of the Custer affiliation in subsequent advertising.[23] But some regional promoters recognized that the Last Stand could also serve as a direct means of luring tourists.

John J. Harris, an optimistic booster of the sleepy little town of Hardin, had prophesied in 1922 that the modest celebration planned at the Custer Battlefield for that year was but a presage of greater things to come. "It will be one of the big publicity agents for this eastern slope of the Rockies," he proclaimed, "and will grow in importance each year."[24] Accepting such predictions at face value, the state of Montana officially blessed the semi-centennial commemoration four years later in an opportunistic brochure. "Custer's sacrifice was not in vain, as 47,000 Montana farmers will testify," one paragraph replete with statistics on the state's agricultural productivity began. Another pitch was launched with Custer's last dispatch to Captain Benteen, "Come on. Big Village. Be quick. Bring Packs." The hard sell followed:

> General Custer's last command rings out through the vista of fifty years with prophetic accent. "COME ON" might well be the watchword of the Great Sovereign State of Montana. . . .
>
> "COME ON" — Montana will welcome you.[25]

Today's promoters of the Billings-Hardin-Sheridan area, while not eclipsing this 1920's boosterism, have issued numerous leaflets and press releases expounding on the virtues of "Custer country" or "Custer land." In 1965, almost 190,000 tourists visited the Custer Battlefield, and it was being estimated that by 1970 the figure for all of "Custer country" would swell to 500,000.[26] The economic implications of such a flood of tourists have not been lost on the local citizens. Myth can be converted into gold, and the alchemists who effect this transformation are fully aware of the commercial advantages of Custer's Last Stand re-enactments.

Montana, to celebrate its territorial centennial and the silver anniversary of its statehood, in 1964 sponsored a historical drama, *The Montana Story*, which was scheduled to tour twelve major centers in the state from July through September. "One of the most colorful scenes" of this spectacular, its advertising noted, was to be the nightly re-enactment of Custer's Last Stand: "Nearly three hundred people will appear in this scene to give it the dramatic impact of one of Montana's and the nation's darkest hours."[27]

Simultaneously, Crow tribesmen were staging their own re-creation of The Last Stand "from the Indian point of view." Sitting Bull, not Custer, was the star, and the audience was treated to a rare geographical authenticity since the actual Custer Battlefield is on the Crow Reservation, within view of the bleacher seats erected for the spectacle. Historical irony is always implicit whenever the descendants of Custer's scouts perform as their ancestral foes, the Sioux. However, some ten thousand spectators were attracted to the show, paying from one to three dollars each into the tribal treasury. So, with the double-edged slogan "America's Greatest Moment of Living History" heading its publicity, the Crow version of Custer's Last Stand became an annual affair, running for ten years until consecutive losses coupled with the threat of severe gasoline shortages and a consequent reduction in tourism forced its cancellation in 1974.[28]

Other states besides Montana have vied for a slice of the Custer pie, and annual "historical outdoor dramas" have been staged in both Dakotas. In 1964, in a natural amphitheater on the Fall River five miles from Hot Springs, South Dakota, a cast of 212 persons and up to 100 horses was re-creating Custer's defeat four nights weekly throughout the summer as the high point of the Crazy Horse Pageant.[29] At Mandan, North Dakota, the same scene played five nights a week on a 110-foot wide stage. The two-hour pageant, called *Trails West*, featured seventy actors and forty horses doing their respective duties.[30] The proliferation of re-enactments during the summer of 1964 meant that several Last Stands were being fought each day. But this was fitting. To borrow the words of one of Buffalo Bill's copy writers, such performances raise, "as it were, a daily monument, in addition to the storm blown one," to Custer's Last Stand.[31] Their continued popularity is promise that the last Last Stand will never be fought, and the Custer myth will be perpetually revitalized.

Though the commercial exploitation of the Custer myth is hardly a recent phenomenon, there is something in the earnest competition of the different chambers of commerce that makes one yearn for the presumably simpler days of the past. Back in 1902, when rivalry over the tourist dollar was relatively slight and an Indian was still more warrior than thespian, a Sheridan dentist, Will Frackelton, masterminded a re-enactment of the Custer battle to kick off the county fair. Having struggled through the usual tangle of red tape to procure permission for his scheme, he induced some one thousand Crows to play the Sioux and Cheyennes. In turn, four companies of the Wyoming National Guard plus a contingent of enthusiastic amateur actors were persuaded to take the part of the Seventh Cavalry. All went smoothly until the dress rehearsal was held "out in a natural amphitheater of the hills of Prairie Dog Creek." Blue Bead, an influential Crow, chose that moment to insist that he be allowed to capture the cavalry's flag during the fighting. Otherwise, he would not participate. The guardsmen, understandably, would not hear of such a thing. Displaying a natural genius for diplomacy,

Frackelton assured the "cavalry" that their colors were safe, and promised Blue Bead that he would have his way. To ensure that his duplicity would go off as planned, Frackelton decided to ride with the Indians. The rest of the story is best told in his own words:

> The big day arrived. Folks drove in from all over Johnson county and even down from Montana to see the doings. Must have been night [sic] a thousand out there by Prairie Dog creek when we staged the sham battle . . .

> Man, that was the thrillin'est fight ever! . . . We had those spectators standing on the seats of their buckboards, with their eyes hanging out. One by one the guardsmen dropped dead. There was a final rush for the big white man with the yellow curls who was Custer. I, of course, went in with the Indians, Blue Bead right at my elbow. I sat down on the color sergeant's head while Blue Bead started off with the colors — the sergeant was cursing me something awful — a dead private rose up and shot point blank at the Crow chief. The slug from his blank cartridge [sic] burned Blue Bead — proper. There's where the spectators got their money's worth. Every guardsman came to life and slugged the nearest Crow. It was a knock-down and drag-out all over these hills.

> Mister man, Custer was avenged!

The aftermath of the incident, in the best tradition of warfare, included reparations. It took ten dollars and a quarter of a beef to pacify Blue Bead — a settlement that was far too generous, apparently, for the delighted brave promptly volunteered to be shot again.[32]

II

The tens of thousands of spectators who have enjoyed live re-enactments over the years since Custer made his Last Stand are but a tiny fraction of the multitude who have seen that event brought to life on the movie screen.

There is an image engraved on the American memory that excels even the Anheuser-Busch lithograph in its flamboyantly absurd heroics. A man dressed in a buckskin jacket stands on the crest of a hill — alone, though the ground about him is littered with corpses, Indian and white alike. Alone, his legs spread to brace himself for the imminent ordeal of death. His arms hang limply at his sides; his empty pistols have been cast away; only a sabre remains in his hand, a futile weapon in a futile defense against hopeless odds. Yet there is nothing of defeat in this scene. The man's head turns, blond hair spraying out behind, and with a glance his experienced eyes takes in the field of carnage. Now the audience can see the handsome face, brow furrowed, teeth clenched, jaw jutting out in determination. It is Custer, monumental, indomitable to the end, making his Last Stand not in despair nor even resignation but in defiance of the fate that has brought him here to die. Rather, it is not Custer at all, but Errol Flynn earning his pay from Warner Brothers in the 1941 movie *They Died With Their Boots On*, though today the distinction no longer seems of pressing importance.

Legend and controversy, dozens of bad paintings and worse poems have obscured the grim reality of death in battle and converted Custer's Last Stand into a triumphant saga. Errol Flynn is George Custer reincarnated and at the height of his heroism. Confronted by that solitary figure on the hill, a viewer can thrill to the superb defiance of its stance, the pointed rejection of the fears that haunt ordinary mortals. A hand reaching for popcorn in the darkened theater might even pause, suspended between carton and mouth, in anticipation of the climactic moment, dreadful and yet perfect, when Custer passes into immortality. There will be no faint blast of a trumpet sounding "Charge!," no rescuing thunder of advancing hooves, no welcome line of blue suddenly surging over a nearby ridge, no warriors lashing their ponies to a froth and emitting howls of disappointment as they effect a speedy retreat. Instead, in one great wave the Indians sweep over Custer, and the bright sword that flashed destruction for countless foes is stilled at last. No cinéaste would alter a frame of it.

The climactic scene of *They Died With Their Boots On* remains the cinematic equivalent of the Budweiser Beer print. But if Flynn's Last Stand set the standard against which the others are still measured, it was by no means the first to appear on the screen. That honor belongs to a 1909 film titled *On the Little Big Horn; or Custer's Last Stand*, a William Selin production that featured footage of a re-enactment staged earlier that year out West. The movie's historical action centers on three characters — Custer, Major Reno, whose animosity towards the General has cost him the confidence of his fellow officers, and Rain-in-the-Face, the savage arch-villain eager for revenge on Yellow Hair. The romantic plot is simple. Dollie, Colonel Godfrey's daughter, requests Custer to order her beau, Lieutenant Glenn, to take charge of the supply train once the hostiles have been encountered. Custer complies, and Glenn is spared the fate awaiting the rest of the command as "over the bluff they go, and the sight that meets their gaze freezes the blood, for stretched away as far as the eye can reach, upright and naked on their ponies they sit, three thousand Sioux warriors, waiting for the handful of white soldiers to be brought to the slaughter." The "brave little band" makes a gallant defence, but "the red circle of death closes in about them," and Rain-in-the-Face gets his revenge.[33]

The Last Stand sequence is the heart of the film. Selig had been planning a movie about the Custer battle by the end of 1908, and a band of Sioux, three of whom were "more than 70 years old, having actually been participants in the tragedy" on the Little Big Horn, were camped in Chicago through January, 1909, preparatory to shooting at the studio. Apparently "unfavorable weather" forced Selig to put the idea into deep freeze over the summer.[34]

That September, as the highlight of the annual Crow Indian fair, a company of the Montana National Guard from Billings along with forty civilian volunteers refought the Last Stand against a contingent of Crows on the actual battlefield. The re-enactment exhibited an unusual realism for the pained expressions on the faces of combatants stung by the wax plugs from some twenty thousand rounds of blank ammunition provided for the battle were genuine. Curley, the famous "Sole Survivor," was to reproduce his escape from the hill but, according to an eyewitness, "was unable to get past his Indian friends and lay rolling on the ground with the smart of a parafine plug landed just where his breech clout ended."[35] Selig's camera crew was present with exclusive rights to capture all the action on film.[36]

It would seem certain that this was the battle footage subsequently incorporated in *Custer's Last Stand*. But the Montana re-enactment had concluded on a startlingly iconoclastic note when Captain Paul McCormick, Jr., who played Custer, found himself the only soldier still alive:

> McCormick had previously thrown aside his sword, and revolver in either hand, faced some 500 Crows alone; a half a dozen shots he threw into their ranks and then his right hand fell helpless to his side and the revolver dropped; another shot with the left and he placed it to his head, but he failed to get it past his ear and when the report came, it fairly lifted him off the ground. His fall could not be improved upon for it landed him almost on his head and between ringing ear drums and dizzy brain, he imagined his was the real kind of a demise.[37]

Since a contemporary review of the film did not mention what would have been, to say the least, a surprise ending, there is the possibility that footage of another Last Stand re-enactment was also used. A visitor to the Selig studio in Chicago in November, 1909, watched while a few "detail scenes" were shot for an "Indian war drama, the main scenes of which were taken weeks ago in western South Dakota, . . . with real Indians in their war paint and feathers and several companies of U. S. soldiers participating."[38]

Custer's Last Stand was re-enacted daily from October 4 to 9 at the Pierre, South Dakota, Third Gas Belt Exposition. Camera crews from Chicago and Denver were on hand all week and secured "a complete set of films of the event," the National Guardsman who portrayed Custer reported.[39] Posters promoting the Exposition had promised that three hundred Sioux and Cheyenne would participate in the sham battle. Two hundred Sioux, as it turned out, as well as two companies of the State National Guard took part, while another two thousand "non-combatant" Indians were in camp, "adding greatly to the picturesque effect."[40] Newspaper coverage of the first performance of the Last Stand described "a hundred armed Indians charging down on the troops horseback":

> The troops knelt to meet the charge and poured out their "blanks"
> into the advancing enemy, only a few of who were willing to drop from

their horses and not be in at the finish. It was not long until the "fight" was over, and the braves gathered for a dance of victory, while the squaws and children swooped down on the "dead" and gathered in the spoils.[41]

None of these early re-enactments would have been complete without some incident to show how recently it was that the West had been tamed. The Pierre Last Stand was performed without casualty until the final engagement, when Eagleman was "seriously wounded in the leg by a close discharge of a blank cartridge." He became "unruly," and the mood of the Indians ugly. "The military officers felt much apprehension for a few minutes," but matters were soon adjusted and all parties — including the spectators, no doubt — departed happy.[42]

At any rate, Selig's *Custer's Last Stand* combined footage of one or both of these re-enactments with scenes shot in the Chicago studio. The result was the first recorded presentation of an American epic on the silver screen. It was followed three years later by Thomas H. Ince's ambitious *Custer's Last Fight*, a spectacular featuring a thousand soldiers and a thousand Indians, many of whom allegedly took part in "the original battle." A poster that accompanied a later release called it "The Greatest Wild West Feature Ever Filmed." Its original advertising was even more extravagant. An eight-page illustrated brochure declared *Custer's Last Fight* "the most colossal & sensational War Picture in the Entire History of Motion Pictures" — which, in 1912, was quite possibly true. A review by Louis Reeves Harrison was reprinted, and he pronounced the film "more sensible and less sentimental" than Longfellow's "The Revenge of Rain-in-the-Face," adding: "I have often wished that we could send all the poets, producers and pseudo-playwrights of the phony photodrama out to fight the Noble Redman or worse — to live with him." The brochure's clincher followed: "Every boy and girl in America should see this picture, as well as every man and woman with a spark of patriotism, as it is a perfect reproduction of the most heroic incident in the nation's history, eclipsing by far the famous English charge of the Light Brigade."[43]

All this ballyhoo was over an expensive three-reel reconstruction of the battle of the Little Big Horn. *Custer's Last Fight* was history as allegory, a plain tale of valor and goodness struck down in full flower by the forces of barbarism. Specifically, it was the valiant, blond-haired Custer versus the fiendish, red-skinned Rain-in-the-Face who, even "as he approached the hill on which stood the gallant commander," knew that while he "might belittle, degrade, destroy that proud figure . . . the enforming personality he could not reach. It was beyond his insults, beyond the sting of his bullet, the thrust of his knife."[44] Custer, the man, might perish; the cultural virtues he stood for were immortal.

Two years later, in 1914, Biograph released *The Massacre* for American viewing. The notion persists that this two-reel Western was about the Custer battle. While it ends with a dramatic last stand sequence, a wagon train of settlers and its cavalry escort are the victims of

Indian reprisal, not Custer's Seventh. Reinforcements are riding hard to the rescue, but "in the valley of death" (as the caption would have it) the Indians close in for the kill. The cavalry arrive too late to save the day, but from the pile of white corpses a hand protrudes — a mother, still sheltering her infant, both spared by the sacrifice of the men who had formed a living shield about them and in death concealed them with their corpses until help could reach the scene. Directed by David W. Griffith, *The Massacre* is usually remembered as a warm-up for his 1915 masterpiece *The Birth of a Nation*. In its own right, however, *The Massacre* was a major picture, exhibiting technical virtuosity in mounting the battle scenes, and leaving a strong impression of men at bay surrendering their lives bravely in a fight against hopeless odds that could only suggest Custer's Last Stand to the casual viewer.[45]

By 1920 the movies had achieved such sophistication and polish that directors were prepared to tackle fairly complicated story lines even in unpretentious commercial fare. Thus Randall Parrish's version of the disgraced-officer-returns-to-clear-his-name plot, *Bob Hampton of Placer* (1910), was brought to the screen under the same title by Marshall Neilan in 1921. Feilan treated the melodramatic tale of a father's quest for honor and a daughter's for love with realistic flair and lavished care on the climactic battle sequence. "Mr. Neilan went to Montana to make his scenes and employed real Indians and white actors costumed and mannered to suit the occasion," a reviewer noted. Though he was skeptical of the story and some of the performances, the critic considered "the staging of the famous last rally of General Custer and his troop . . . a remarkable piece of work."[46]

The Scarlet West, a 1925 film distributed by First National Pictures, inserted the Last Stand into another conventional situation, a romantic triangle made novel by its interracial composition. Miriam Kinnard, daughter of a general, is torn between her two suitors, Lieutenant Parkman and Captain Cardelanche, an educated Indian. Custer's Last Stand is a convenient vehicle for, by implicating all red men in a common guilt, it rescues Miriam from the throes of indecision and permits her to make the racially-correct choice and marry Parkman. Though Clara Bow, the "It" girl and archetypal flapper of the 1920's, played Miriam, the movie's outstanding feature from the standpoint of boxoffice draw was the sequence "depicting in realistic manner the last stand of General Custer."[47] It is possible that this footage was lifted from *Bob Hampton of Placer* since both were First National releases.

The semi-centennial anniversary of the Little Big Horn in 1926 made a new Custer spectacular almost mandatory, and no one was disappointed, for Universal Pictures rose to the occasion. *The Flaming Frontier* starred Hoot Gibson and Dustin Farnum — idols of a generation of Western fans — along with "a great cast of thousands."[48] Hoot played Bob Langdon, a former Pony Express rider who resigns from West Point under a cloud of innuendo in order to protect the reputation of the brother of the girl he loves. Bob serves as a scout with Custer and, during the Last Stand, gallops off to Major Reno for reinforcements. Despite his heroics,

Custer's command is annihilated, the General falling last, but Bob is rewarded with his sweetheart's devotion and reinstatement at the Point. The plot was routine, but *The Flaming Frontier* featured expert stunt riding, almost continuous action and a major Last Stand scene staged on ground that one officer declared "an exact duplicate" of the real site.[49]

As an early and expensive epic, *The Flaming Frontier* was much ballyhooed by Universal Pictures and its distributors. One hundred thousand letters extolling the patriotic and historical virtues of the film were circulated among educators across the nation, and in Cleveland the public library was persuaded to mount a display of movie stills, books and artifacts to illustrate the theme "Flaming Frontier in fact and fiction."[50] Brigadier-General Edward S. Godfrey, a distinguished survivor of the fighting on the Little Big Horn, was a special guest at the movie's midnight premiere in New York's Colony Theater in early April, 1926. He provided a "stirring moment" when he rose to take a bow, a living link between history and its legendary distillation on the screen.[51] However, nowhere else was *The Flaming Frontier* accorded a more enthusiastic reception than it received in the little town of Sheridan, one of the three official Custer semi-centennial centers. "Forty Chieftains and Scores of Tribes Reported Mobilized at 'Little Big Horn,' " the *Sheridan Post* for June 23 trumpeted:

> All Available Army Troops Being Rushed to Aid of
> Seventh Cavalry.
>
> Greatest Battle in History of "Flaming Frontier"
> Imminent.
>
> All of Sheridan Warned of Invasion — "Flaming
> Frontier" Agog at Repetition of Wars.
>
> (Relayed to Sheridan by Scout Hoot Gibson of the
> Command of General George Custer.)

Sheridan's own Orpheum Theatre was holding the first showing of this major motion picture at, the local paper announced, regular prices, "whereas in all other cities of the nation, a minimum of one dollar will be charged."[52]

The honor conferred on Sheridan took an unexpected turn when Charles E. Lounsbury (accurately described as belonging to the "exploitation staff, Universal Pictures") published an interview with a Sioux named Red Horse. Red Horse, it seems, "struck Custer last" with his tomahawk at the Little Big Horn. He did *not* claim to be the General's slayer, but told instead how a despairing Custer took his own life. Red Horse's veracity was beyond question since Cunning Deer, "an erect, young and well-educated Sioux of Sheridan," had served as interpreter.[53] Thus *The Flaming Frontier* had wider significance than one might at first suppose since it gave the public the real lowdown on the end of Custer.

As for the movie's authenticity, a study of the Western notes that "the political and historical backgrounds were sketched in with general accuracy."[54] This statement must be challenged on the basis of a partial plot summary provided by the *Sheridan Post*. Apparently the Indians were incited to take the warpath by renegade whites greedy for their lands. President Grant, duped by his political advisers, was unable to extricate himself from the web of intrigue and corruption they had woven around his administration. Left to his own devices, and hoping to prevent an Indian war, Custer set out after the hostiles. He found them, and in numbers that even he, for all of his legendary rashness, should have known enough to avoid. For, according to *The Flaming Frontier*, every Indian tribe in North America was represented in the camp on the Little Big Horn. Sitting Bull alone commanded a following of ten thousand.[55] With only a touch of imagination, one can picture the scene: Indians lined up 100-deep along the entire length of the Little Big Horn, waiting turn for a shot at Custer. But one does well to keep in mind historian Leonard Jennewein's advice: "It is better to look at Western movies for recreation than for historical edification."[56]

With its high-power cast and sure-fire theme, *The Flaming Frontier* was a financial as well as critical success, earning "bushels of money" for Universal.[57] But it was not the only Custer movie released in the semi-centennial year. *With General Custer at Little Big Horn*, one in a series of six "historical" Westerns produced by Anthony J. Xydias for Sunset Productions, also appeared in 1926. One review service described it as "a thrilling account of Custer's fatal advance into the Indian trap, and of his tragic last stand," noting that a romance added to give the picture "more sentimental story value" did not unduly impede its retelling of history.[58] But as a typical six-reel Western made by an independent company on limited capital, *With General Custer at Little Big Horn* simply did without an elaborate concluding battle sequence.

Ten years passed before the Last Stand returned to the screen, in a fifteen-episode serial titled *Custer's Last Stand*. This was something of a misnomer, covering a bewildering array of concurrent plots about a lost Indian medicine arrow, a duplicitous renegade playing red and white off against each other, a search for a lost Indian cave of gold, an interracial love affair and a discredited officer seeking to restore his reputation — each moving turgidly towards a resolution of sorts on the Little Big Horn. But since the serial, like Xydias' movie, was produced "on a shoestring budget," its climax turned out to be "little more than a mild skirmish between several dozen horsemen."[59] Though scout Kit Cardigan fails to warn Custer in time of impending disaster, the renegade pays for his treachery with his life. The dime novel had made it to the screen in a small way; the next year, 1937, it would achieve epic recognition in Cecil B. DeMille's *The Plainsman*.

The Plainsman is best understood in the context of depression America. With the advent of hard times, the Western's popularity had steadily slipped, and the heroes of the Golden West who had dominated the screen in the 1920's mounted their stallions and rode off into the sunset of an apparently dying genre. By 1935, the back of the Depression seemed broken; at least, the New Deal had revived hope in the future, and that optimism so fundamental to the Western myth was back in fashion. If the formula Western had lost some of its appeal, the epic Western would more than fill the void.[60] *The Plainsman*, released on New Year's Day, 1937, was DeMille's overblown tribute to the enduring values of a pioneering race.

DeMille's cast of characters was drawn, seemingly promiscuously, from the pantheon of Western heroes. Wild Bill Hickok, Calamity Jane and Buffalo Bill Cody, played by Gary Cooper, Jean Arthur and James Ellison, were brought together for the proceedings. Nor was General Custer forgotten. A series of brief cameo appearances establish the fact that he is, though indubitably heroic, a trifle rigid. He chastizes Calamity for divulging the route taken by a cavalry patrol rushing ammunition through to a besieged post — information that she yielded to the Cheyenne chief Yellow Hand only under the extremest duress, when she could no longer bear the sight of her beloved Wild Bill slowly roasting over an Indian fire. Too, when Hickok shoots down three corrupt troopers who are in league with a scoundrel peddling rifles to the hostiles, Custer sends Buffalo Bill after him with orders to bring the fugitive Hickok back dead or alive. These are not endearing qualities, but Custer redeems himself, as he always does, by dying nobly. DeMille managed to work the Last Stand in rather ingeniously. Cody has caught up with Hickok in the Black Hills and the two are about to square off when Anthony Quinn shows up as a Cheyenne warrior returning from the victory on the Little Big Horn. Taken captive, he provides voice-over narration for a glimpse of the Last Stand in which Custer, clutching at a fatal wound in his chest, wraps his arm around the American flag in a thwarted salute, a final patriotic gesture . . . and expires.

The Plainsman is unblushing melodrama, in the proven tradition of the Buffalo Bill dime novels. The author of a recent history of the Western movie thought there was "an air of contrivance" about *The Plainsman's* "great Round Up of favourite Western characters."[61] Surprisingly, this "Round Up" was not as preposterous as the rest of DeMille's "history" might suggest. The crowded years after the Civil War produced an abundance of Western heroes and would-be heroes on the high plains. Sometimes their histories as well as their legends intertwined.

Tradition has it that Hickok, Cody and Calamity all "scouted for Custer." In fact, the Custers did know Hickok on the Southern plains, and Mrs. Custer later wrote that Wild Bill and her husband were "fast friends." For her part, the General's wife adored the "Prince of Pistoleers," describing him as "a delight to look upon," the epitome of "physical perfection." "Wild Bill reminded me of a thorough-bred horse," she went on innocently, concluding that "the days of the Greeks are slowly returning to us, when the human form will be so cared for that no development it is capable of will be neglected."[62] What triggered this rhapsodic recollection, no doubt, was the thought that Wild Bill was so like her George, handsome gallant — and cut down in the prime of life. Besides scouting for Custer, the real Wild Bill took a turn on the stage with Buffalo Bill during the 1873-74 season in *Scouts of the Plains*. In legend, he then married Martha Jane Cannary, "Calamity Jane," and sired a daughter by her before he was gunned down from behind on August 2, 1876, while playing poker in a Deadwood, Dakota Territory, saloon. Carved on one of Wild Bill's early monuments were the enigmatic words "Custer was lonely without him."

It is a matter of record that Cody's and Custer's paths also crossed. For one thing, both took part in the Western buffalo hunt staged for the benefit of the Grand Duke Alexis, third son of the Russian czar, in 1872. Calamity Jane's link to Custer is another matter. Of the foursome, her reputation is the least substantial. Though her name flits in and out of history, she impinged only tangentially on the men. Yet the legends about her know no bounds, and one of the more persistent of these has the manly Calamity working as a muleskinner or scout for the Seventh Cavalry. A writer in 1922 had her carrying dispatches for General Crook. After crossing a river and riding ninety miles she became ill and was hospitalized at Fort Fetterman. "This probably saved her from being present at the massacre of the Little Big Horn," he solemnly averred, thereby adding her to the list of putative survivors belonging to the "there but for the grace of God" category.[63] And, of course, there is always Calamity's own letter placing her on the field shortly after the battle.

One might better understand the complex interrelationships among the Western heroes in fact and in fiction by considering the case of Captain Jack Crawford, "The Poet Scout."[64] A legitimate Western character, a "close friend" of Wild Bill, a onetime actor with Buffalo Bill, a Wild West show performer and the author of three Western melodramas and several volumes of tortured verse, Crawford spent his adult life in a single-minded quest for fame and popularity. They proved elusive, however, and he remained a minor celebrity who never quite attained heroic stature. As one of the many who were not chosen, Captain Jack nursed deep and abiding resentments towards those who were. His particular target was Buffalo Bill. During their theatrical days together, and totally inebriated at the time, Cody had accidentally wounded the Poet Scout in a knife fight on stage. Crawford could never forget this, nor forgive the hard-drinking Buffalo Bill for being a national idol while he, a teetotaler who had dedicated himself to motherhood and clean-living, was left standing in the shadows. Captain Jack never seemed to realize that temperance was simply not the stuff of Western heroes. The nation needed only one Carrie. Its Custers and Codys, its Calamities and Wild Bills, were cut from an altogether different piece of cloth.

All that remained for the Poet Scout was the dream of earning an imperishable reputation by composing verse that would resound through future time, and link him to the paramount events of his own time. Back in the days of '76, while he and Buffalo Bill were still on the best of terms and both active in the field against the Sioux, Crawford described his reaction to Custer's death in rhyme. "Did I hear the news from Custer? / Well, I reckon I did, old pard," he wrote Cody:

> It came like a streak of lightin'[*sic*]
>> And, you bet, it hit me hard.
> I ain't no hand to blubber,
>> And the briny ain't run for years;
> But chalk me down for a lubber,
>> If I didn't shed regular tears.

While Crawford was earnestly trying to scribble his way to immortality, however, the others were performing the deeds that captured the popular imagination. He was reduced to the role of recorder, playing Boswell to their Johnson. Thus while he labored over "The Death of Custer," Cody was grabbing headlines by taking the "first scalp" in revenge. A few weeks later a slug passed through Hickok's skull and pairs of aces and eights became forever after the "deadman's hand." It was left to Crawford to write a verse on "Wild Bill's Grave" and provide the inscription for the Hickok marker:

> Oh, Charity! come fling your mantle about him;
>> Judge him not harshly — he sleeps 'neath the sod.
> Custer — brave Custer! — was lonely without him.
>> Even with God.[65]

While Crawford lectured on the evils of strong spirits, Calamity Jane continued to imbibe them in quantity, accept the occasional donation for her favors and, all unknowingly, contribute to her legend when one of those guardian angels who watch over such heroes placed her on the Custer battlefield for a stroll among the mutilated corpses. While Captain Jack urged moral rectitude and filial obedience upon the nation's youth, a dissipated Calamity went on exhibition for a dime as "The Famous Woman Scout of the Wild West . . . The Comrade of Buffalo Bill and Wild Bill," and, before dying, was heard to mumble, "Bury me next to Bill." Today she and Hickok lie closeby in Mount Moriah Cemetery overlooking Deadwood, their legends mutually secure. And while Captain Jack castigated dime novels for their pernicious influence on the younger generation and fretted over his own slender fame, that preeminent dime novel hero, Buffalo Bill, toured the world with his Wild West, one year featuring "Custer's Conqueror," Sitting Bull, and in many others re-enacting the Last Stand before rapt audiences. No one would ever dislodge him from his position as the supreme Western hero.

Whatever its other merits, then, *The Plainsman* had made an uncanny choice of celebrated Western characters. Exceptionally popular in its own time, its success inspired a 1941 reunion of Wild Bill, Calamity and Custer called *Badlands of Dakota*, and it still makes the occasional well-publicized appearance on late night television.[66] Indeed, a new version of *The Plainsman*, in color but without a comparable cast, debuted in 1966. Though the critics had few kind words for it, the remake was an impressive tribute to the indestructible reputation of the 1937 original.

If *The Plainsman* indicated a renewed interest in the Custer theme, there was decided activity by 1940. That year *Wyoming*, a typical Wallace

Beery vehicle, portrayed Custer as the rather stiff purveyor of law and order on the frontier, though he was flexible enough to appreciate Beery's antics and turn the other way when duty dictated a stern reprimand. In *Santa Fe Trail*, released the same year, Hollywood brought several big guns into action. Errol Flynn starred as a dashing Jeb Stuart and Ronald Reagan as a short-haired George Custer, recent West Point classmates in a pre-Civil War epic that united the flowers of Southern and Northern chivalry against a fanatical John Brown and his abolitionist followers.[67] Olivia de Havilland provided Flynn's love interest, a fortunate pairing since the very next year she was Mrs. George A. Custer in *They Died With Their Boots On*, the big-budget cinematic biography that marked the high point of Custer's career on the screen.

They Died With Their Boots On is unquestionably the most influential version of the Custer story ever filmed.[68] In attempting to account for this fact, astute casting is the obvious explanation. Errol Flynn brought to his portrayal of the Boy General his own mystique as a handsome, reckless, romantic swashbuckler, chafing under restraints and forever at odds with authority. His Custer is a fusion of two men and two legends ideally matched to one another.[69] Too, the manner in which Flynn-Custer went down to death left an indelible picture in the mind of every impressionable viewer. Thus *They Died With Their Boots On* still marks the zenith of Custer's heroic image in the movies.

For one thing, after Errol Flynn's Last Stand there was really nothing more to say on the subject. For another, *They Died With Their Boots On's* heroic interpretation of Custer was anachronistic even in 1941, postdating Frederic Van de Water's *Glory-Hunter* by seven years. Moreover, this interpretation represented a calculated decision on the part of the studio, not ignorance of recent historical opinion. The original script, co-authored by Aeneas MacKenzie and Wally Kline, had been critical of Custer. It did not ignore the Washita battle, as the finished movie did, and it blamed the Last Stand on Custer's "greed for glory." But with war raging in Europe and patriotic ardor on the rise in the States, Warner's chose to paint Custer in pristine hues with, MacKenzie sardonically observed, "an eye more to generosity than to fact."[70] In the Golden Age of Hollywood, the major studios were rarely pathbreakers in historical revisionism. Only after the novelists had absorbed and begun to popularize the Custerphobic viewpoint did the General's image darken on the screen. Even then it happened slowly.

The opening volley in Hollywood's desultory war on Custer's reputation was fired in 1948, but it was muffled to the point of being inaudible. *Fort Apache*, loosely modelled on James Warner Bellah's iconoclastic short story "Massacre," provided John Ford with the opportunity to present his personal assessment of Custer and the responsibility for the debacle on the Little Big Horn without having directly to encounter the limitations of historical fact. Fort Lincoln becomes Fort Apache, and Custer, Lieutenant-Colonel Thursday, leaving Ford free to etch the General's portrait in acid and depict the Apaches (read Sioux) as victims of white mendacity and avarice. Thursday emerges as an obdurate, unbending martinet, demanding absolute obedience from his men and contemptuous of his foes. French critic Jean-Louis Rieupeyrout, who considered *Fort Apache* an "admirable character study," marvelled at Ford's boldness in assigning the responsibility for the Little Big Horn to "one of the most renowned American Army officers of the second half of the nineteenth century."[71] The naivety of such a judgment is symptomatic of a congenital reluctance on the part of those who make movies and those who review them to accept the fact that Custer has long been a hero out of favor. Moreover, it misses the point that Ford undercuts his own interpretation and permits Thursday a measure of redemption though self-sacrifice. In the original Bellah story, Thursday survives the Last Stand but, unable to face the censure of the nation for leading his troops into slaughter despite ample warning from his subordinates, returns to the hill after the battle is over — and commits suicide.[72] In the movie, Thursday is critically wounded but spurns the chance to escape and instead rides off to die with the remnant of his command. The action scenes were up to Ford's standard, but made no contribution to the tradition of cinematic Last Stands since the contemporary reviewers — and presumably the majority of the audience — were unaware that *Fort Apache* was a veiled retelling of the Custer saga.[73]

Though John Ford's name became synonymous with the cavalry Western, he failed to redefine the Custer type on the screen because his viewpoint was fundamentally sentimental and romantic. Thus *Fort Apache* concludes on a revealing note when John Wayne's Captain York, now commander at Fort Apache, fields reporters' questions about the martyred Thursday. "No man," York says, "died more gallantly, nor won more honor for his regiment." There is supposed to be some irony in this, but Ford believed in his own dictum about protecting legends, and as York delivers his tribute to the guts of men like Thursday a ghostly column fades into the sky — just as it did at the end of *They Died With Their Boots On* — and martial valor is reaffirmed. Some things are more important than truth. Ford seemed more at home in his follow-up Western *She Wore a Yellow Ribbon* (1949) which was set immediately after the Custer battle and opened with these words: "Custer is dead, and around the bloody guidon of the immortal Seventh Cavalry lie the bodies of 212 officers and men." The spell of Custer's heroism had not yet been broken on the screen.

Movies about the Custer battle appeared with some frequency in the 1950's, but most were low budget affairs and the epic climax on the Little Big Horn was more talked about than seen. This was true even in 1951 when *Little Big Horn* or *The Fighting 7th* was released to the accompaniment of tabloid heralds and posters reproducing the Anheuser-Busch print, and a pressbook that advised exhibitors: "EX-PLOIT IT . . . June 25th Is the 75th Anniversary of the Little Big Horn." Perhaps local newspapers could be encouraged to publish an article commemorating the disaster or an editorial "drawing a parallel to the current Korean fracas." Maybe the theater owner could "dig up an old

Indian fighter" for press interviews and the movie's opening. Whatever, "PLUG THE 75th." [74] It all made good boxoffice sense, though the viewer who went to *Little Big Horn* expecting to see a depiction of Custer's Last Stand was in for a disappointment, since the story actually dealt with a small patrol of cavalrymen traveling through Indian country in an attempt to warn Custer that he is badly outnumbered and must turn back. They never make it. "Sacrifice a few to save many" is their commander's philosophy, and casualties deplete their ranks throughout their perilous mission. At the Little Big Horn, the few who remain offer up their lives in a diversionary strike against the Sioux designed to buy time for Custer to extricate his troops from the jaws of destruction. With the blast of a bugle and their lieutenant's ringing cry, "Make it loud, Stevie, for the ones we left behind!," they charge to their deaths in style. Only a cluster of graves found near the battlefield honors the heroism of the doomed patrol.

While the idea of a man or group of men struggling to reach the Seventh before it perishes has always been popular, it is without historical justification. Naturally, this has not discouraged a grizzled charlatan or two from claiming credit for such a rescue attempt. Besides Thomas Frost, W.P.H.Peters (alias Bob Preston) and "Arapahoe Harve" Faucett, "Uncle Billy" Boutwell, a Confederate veteran, had quite a tale with which he regaled visitors to the old soldier's home in Austin, Texas. It seems that Uncle Billy was a member of a nine-man party prospecting for gold in the Black Hills in 1876. When they learned that Sitting Bull was on the warpath, they sought out Custer's force for protection, locating it just in time to witness the commencement of the fatal attack on the Indian village. Pinned down by Sioux, the group made a desperate defence that ended for Uncle Billy when he was struck with a war club and rendered unconscious. He recovered his senses only to find his companions all dead save one, who asked for a drink of water, then promptly expired. Custer's men were all dead too, of course, and Uncle Billy, with several bones in his neck dislocated by the blow he had received, crawled to his old pack ox Tony, hidden in a deep canyon nearby, and made good his escape by riding nights and hiding during the day. [75]

Hollywood never did it as well, though *Little Big Horn* was a decent Western with a strong cast. The same cannot be said of another, more elaborate 1951 Custer movie, *Warpath*, which was based on Frank Gruber's inept novel *Broken Lance*. Its release, too, was timed to coincide with the seventy-fifth anniversary, and it had the added distinction of being filmed in its entirety in Montana. Its premiere in Billings garnered considerable publicity in the local press, and once again a movie was the occasion for the "authentic Indian version" of Custer's Last Stand to be "revealed." [76] A Great Falls writer expressed appreciation for the fact that *Warpath*'s locales were authentic. "Beautiful as it is, who isn't getting a bit tired of seeing all the Western epics filmed in Monument Valley?," he asked, in backhanded recognition of John Ford's dominant influence on the genre. [77] But the finished product was unworthy of even qualified praise. *Warpath*'s plot, like *Little Big Horn*'s, involves a frustrated attempt to head off the Seventh short of disaster.

Held captive by the Sioux and threatened with torture in a fiendish effort to make them reveal Custer's battle plans — "Where Long Hair? . . . Long Hair come. How many soldiers he bring?" — the hero and the heroine escape just too late to save the General, though they do manage to reach Reno's beleaguered command and weather the battle in comparative comfort.

Both *Little Big Horn* and *Warpath* successfully skirted Custer's character and his Last Stand. *Bugles in the Afternoon*, brought to the screen in 1952 by Warner Brothers, also managed to avoid any controversy in its depiction of Custer despite the obvious lead provided by Ernest Haycox's novel. The General does not even appear in the movie until the Seventh sets out on its final campaign, and apart from his long hair and buckskin suit he is characterless. The only hint of criticism comes during a cursory Last Stand when hero Kern Shafter, perched on a bluff high above the battlefield like a football spectator with a seat on the fifty-yard line, follows the action through his binoculars and offers this terse commentary, the grumbles of a fan watching his side lose: "Custer doesn't have a chance. He shouldn't have split the command." All the audience sees of the action is "a distant and muddy-colored glimpse" through Shaftner's binoculars — and even this, it should be noted, is lifted from the climactic sequence of *They Died With Their Boots On.*[78] A decade had elapsed without effacing the memory of Errol Flynn's cavalier hero or updating the imagery of his Last Stand.

The transition from hero to villain was finally accomplished in a trite, 1954 B-Western, *Sitting Bull*. In this, Custer is a buckskin-clad scoundrel, unfeeling and irresponsible, who stands tall only once, during a Little Big Horn sequence shot in Mexico and remarkable mainly for its inappropriately grandiose heroics. With a sabre in his hand and an arrow in his breast, Custer remains on his feet swaying like a mighty tree through a blizzard of arrows before he topples over and crashes to the ground — the last of his command to fall. Though he is not denied a spectacular end in *Sitting Bull*, clearly the General's star had plummeted since the day Flynn-Custer stood on that hill for Warner Brothers "like a sheaf of corn with all the ears fallen around him."[79] The double-meaning of this line, taken from Sitting Bull's own solemn account of Custer's death, is ours to savor in a spirit of cynicism that had no part in Warner's tribute to the Boy General. In 1941, Custer could still be played as the unblemished hero, without a smirk or a self-conscious giggle. It was appropriate that when this phase of his cinematic career terminated it should be in a film about his Indian nemesis.

To succeed as entertainment, movies must be attuned to and rather closely reflect the public's changing moods and interests. The Custer films always have. *They Died With Their Boots On* was one among several big-budget Westerns produced as the Depression neared its end. Conceived in a rising spirit of patriotism and released just a few weeks before Pearl Harbor was bombed, *They Died With Their Boots On* exemplifies the apotheosis of the soldier-hero that preceded direct American involvement in World War II. Flynn's character, the *National*

Board of Review Magazine commented at the time, "has been aimed at presenting occasional moral lessons regarding warfare and conduct which, together with the historical reconstructions, should make the film enjoyable to younger boys especially."[80] After the war was over and Americans had resumed their normal peacetime activities, an emotional letdown followed, intensified by an awareness of man's new destructive capabilities. The movies reflected this sombre, introspective mood, and the upbeat dramas of the war years yielded to a succession of "problem pictures." The Western was not immune, and "three new elements" emerged according to the standard history of the genre: "sex, neuroses, and a racial conscience."[81] The influence of presentism on the Western is nowhere more evident than in the spate of pro-Indian films that, beginning with *Fort Apache* and crystallizing in *Broken Arrow* two years later, paralleled the burgeoning Negro civil rights movement and its own well-meaning translation in cinematic terms (*Home of the Brave, Lost Boundaries, Pinky, Intruder in the Dust*). Faithful to Helen Hunt Jackson's moral indignation over a "century of dishonor" in American dealings with the Indians, Hollywood repented its shabby treatment of the red man and began to turn out movies sympathetic to its favorite targets of yesteryear. *Sitting Bull* was one melancholy result of this spurt of interest in the First Americans. Indebted to *Fort Apache* for its basic approach, *Sitting Bull* managed to trivialize the idea of a patriarchal Indian chief and his obnoxious counterpart in blue by reducing the entire problem of Indian-white conflict to a matter of personalities. Thus once Custer is eliminated at the Little Big Horn, Sitting Bull and President Grant, men of wisdom and good faith, are quickly able to come to terms. Custer's death has magically abolished all animosity between the races; a spirit of harmony and cooperation hovers over the land. "To peace," Grant says; "To friendship," Sitting Bull replies. Then the two statesmen part, presumably to live happily ever after. The *New York Times* critic deplored "this outrageously phoney climax:"

> One could work up a pique at this picture for playing so loosely with facts merely to be on the currently popular side of a racial theme. Such a happy and easy solution — while it may have been most desirable — is a wicked deception of youngsters, who are likely to be the principal partons of this film.[82]

Yet, for all its blatant absurdities, *Sitting Bull* had chosen wisely in making Custer its villain. It had singled out for opprobrium the man whom Indians themselves have since elevated to the status of supreme white anti-hero.

What it had done to Sitting Bull, Hollywood could do to others. In 1955, another pearl was added to the string of Indian movies with the release of *Chief Crazy Horse*. If Victor Mature and his five o'clock shadow made for a disconcerting Sioux war chief, a more serious defect in the film was the absence of Custer's Last Stand, the apogee of Crazy Horse's martial career. "He Hurled the Lance That Smashed Custer that Historic

Day at Little Big Horn!," a lobby poster exclaimed. If so, the movie's audience never saw him do it. Instead, the camera took in the clouds overhead (*war* clouds?) while the roar of the battle taking place below blared out of the speakers. In a different movie, this amazing lapse may have slid by as a misguided attempt at artistic effect, but *Chief Crazy Horse*'s reviewers were not fooled: "By the time [Crazy Horse] . . . wins a couple of cavalry skirmishes, there were apparently not enough extras left to stage Custer's last stand . . ."[83] After it was finished and the soldiers were all dead, Crazy Horse did consent to give the audience an inkling of what the fighting had been like that day. "Yes," he comments, "General Custer's men died bravely — but foolishly." The viewer had no choice but to take his word for it. Together, *Sitting Bull* and *Chief Crazy Horse* should have been enough to make an Indian yearn for the good old days when red men were merely faceless targets for the white hero's bullets, not feather-sprouting, pseudo-poetic caricatures devised, as one reviewer of *Crazy Horse* noted, to pay "a Technicolor installment on Hollywood's mountain of debt to the American Indian."[84]

While timidly planting the tradition of a villainous Custer in the movie-going public's mind, Westerns have occasionally paused to look back. For example, the dead General's memory was treated tenderly in *7th Cavalry* (1956). The story was set after the Little Big Horn and centered on the efforts of Randolph Scott's granite-faced Captain Tom Benson, described as "Custer's closest friend," to prove himself innocent of the innuendo of cowardice arising from his failure to die with the others on the Little Big Horn. As "one who will always be remembered as the man who wasn't there," Benson sees no alternative but to clear his name by leading a burial detail into Sioux country to recover the slain officers' remains. Apparently the Code of the West will justify sheer idiocy so long as it is valiant. After braving many perils, Benson's contingent reaches the Custer battlefield but is surrounded by the Sioux before it can complete its mission. The Indians superstitiously refuse to permit Custer's remains to be removed lest they be deprived of the General's "bravery and wisdom," the chief fruits of their victory. Fortunately their superstitiousness cuts both ways, and when Custer's horse Dandy suddenly gallops into the picture, the Sioux are so awed that they lift their siege and allow Benson's men to ride away. The spirit of Yellow Hair had spoken; even dead he was more than a match for the Indians.

Early in *7th Cavalry*, one disenchanted officer curtly told Captain Benson that Custer "thought he was God Almighty and couldn't lose in any situation." This blunt assessment aptly characterizes the General portrayed in Walt Disney's backhanded salute to the Custer legend, *Tonka* (1958). Typically, Disney approached the subject from the standpoint of its animal interest, the horse Comanche. Comanche had previously enjoyed a few moments of cinematic glory in Ince's 1912 *Custer's Last Fight*. As the only creature on Custer's side to escape death at the Little Big Horn, he wandered back to Fort Lincoln where his numerous wounds gave the anxiously-waiting army wives their first intimation of impending widowhood. Forty-six years later "the silent messenger" of disaster had a movie of his own. "In One Great Blaze of Action a Legend Was Born!," *Tonka*'s advertising claimed. Confirmation was soon provided when the question-and-answer department of a popular men's magazine printed the query, "Was a horse named Tonka sole survivor of the Custer Massacre?"[85]

Based on David Appel's juvenile novel *Comanche*, *Tonka* went well beyond its source in depicting Custer as a harsh, blustering Indian-hater, capable of any cruelty in his pursuit of glory. On the question of Indian rights, he holds that "there is no way to separate the good from the bad. They burn — massacre — pillage — they're all bad." Sporting a ludicrous bleach-blond coiffure, Custer seems more a shrewish Old West barmaid than a cavalry officer, and he even has the temerity to rough up the movie's principal character, *Tonka*'s young Indian master White Bull played by teenage star Sal Mineo "in a different kind of role." At the Little Big Horn, then, the bully merely gets his just desserts. When a special pleader for Custer informed Disney that *Tonka* would constitute a willful distortion of history, he received the ultimate rejoinder: it would be "entertaining to the masses."[86] The movie's Last Stand made no pretension to geographical accuracy. Filmed on the Warm Springs Reservation in Oregon, it pitted between four hundred and five hundred local Indians against three hundred whites — odds that Custer could have used on that fatal June Sunday.[87] Though one critic dismissed the big scene as "the most routine sort of Western carnage," it, along with the finale in *Sitting Bull*, represented the only serious attempt to re-create the Last Stand on film between 1941 and the middle 1960's.[88] And the battle sequence in *Tonka* had something else in its favor that the comparable scene in *Sitting Bull* could not boast: consistency with its interpretation of Custer's character. Here the General makes his Last Stand sitting down, and he is disposed of early so that *Tonka*'s white master, Captain Keogh, can perform the customary heroics.

After *Tonka*, Hollywood gave the Custer battle a temporary respite. A wretched 1961 movie about the North-West Mounted Police, *The Canadians*, claimed "Theirs Was the Courage that Stood against the Killers Custer Couldn't Stop!," and opened with a view of the field of carnage after the Last Stand taken from *Sitting Bull*. There was talk in 1964 of a Western to be made by Dino de Laurentiis in California with the title *General Custer's Trumpeter*,[89] and stories began circulating the next year about a major Twentieth-Century Fox production to be called *The Day Custer Fell*. Occasional publicity releases appeared through 1966, but the movie never did. Indications were, however, that it would have been vehemently anti-Custer in viewpoint. Instead, the public had to settle for another interpretation of the Custer type in the person of General Fred McCabe, commander of the Fourth Cavalry in *The Glory Guys* (1965). Pushing his troops to the breaking point in his zeal to smash the Indians ("I have an appointment to keep — whether it's on horseback or foot"), McCabe, like Colonel Thursday before him, pays for his ambition with the lives of his men. "Well," a veteran sergeant remarks as he surveys the battlefield, "that's one way to get written up in the paper." *The Glory*

Guys is noteworthy chiefly because Sam Peckinpah, a talented and controversial director in his own right, wrote the screenplay based on Hoffman Birney's novel *The Dice of God*. To round out the picture, Paramount's low-budget 1967 release *Red Tomahawk* opened with its hero, a special agent for the United States Army, intently studying the field of slaughter through his binoculars one day after the battle of the Little Big Horn. Things had not advanced much since *The Canadians*.

Custer's Last Stand did receive direct attention in a 1965 potboiler that was released the following year. *The Great Sioux Massacre*, like most of its predecessors, was billed as "The True Story of Custer's Last Stand!" However, it did its utmost to surpass the others in belying this claim. Only the names of the characters come from history (and not all of them, since Captain Benteen is unaccountably called Benton); chronology, personalities and incidents are invented at will. The story unfolds in the words of Captain Benton, who is testifying at the "court martial" of Major Reno for cowardice and desertion at the Little Big Horn. Interestingly, two distinct Custers emerge from Benton's narration as the movie flashes back to a time when the General was a high-minded, sincere and idealistic soldier, while Reno was a lush and Benton, it would appear from his own testimony, a blundering incompetent. Then things begin to change, and about the time Benton decides to marry Reno's daughter (!), the hero and villain roles are reversed. Reno reforms, while Custer, his high-minded, sincere idealism having brought him nothing but grief in the corrupt world of Washington politics, jumps at the chance to salvage his military career — and perhaps initiate a political one — by killing a few Indians. A new man, bullheaded and brutal, he sets out to pave his way to the White House with the corpses of dead Sioux. He has made a fair start before his gains are nullified on the Little Big Horn where, one confused advertisement insisted, "the waters still run red . . . with Indian blood . . . and white men's infamy!"

For such a low-grade movie, *The Great Sioux Massacre*'s Last Stand scenes seem surprisingly large-scale, and madman though he is, Custer is once again accorded the dignity of a heroic end. As the ring of Sioux relentlessly closes in, the General, buckskins and golden hair shining in the sun, pistol blazing and sabre swinging, fights by the Seventh's guidon until an arrow cuts him down. The viewer should be prepared for a sense of *déjà-vu* at this point, because he *has* seen this Last Stand before. Sidney Salkow, who made *Sitting Bull* a decade earlier, wrote and directed *The Great Sioux Massacre*. Both films play havoc with history. Plot elements from the one reappear in the other. And both feature preposterously heroic, utterly inappropriate Last Stand sequences that completely undercut the negative interpretation of Custer's character till then advanced in each movie. "Whatever his mistakes, George Armstrong Custer died a brave man," Captain Benton concludes his testimony in court. "I have nothing more to add." By dying well, Custer has wiped his slate clean. Only *Tonka* had eschewed such sophistry. As for the mystery of *The Great Sioux Massacre*'s impressively large-scale Last Stand, most of the footage was simply borrowed from *Sitting Bull*.

The Great Sioux Massacre's ambivalence is revealing. Custer could not be simply a flawed hero or an occasionally sympathetic villain. Instead, he is first a perfect hero and then an absolute villain. In 1968, a foreign import, *Custer of the West*, attempted to explore the neglected middleground between these two extremes. In so doing, however, it brushed away two decades of accumulated criticism only to uncover a modern version of the old, heroic Boy General. Like its interpretations, *Custer of the West* came out of nowhere as it were. A thoroughly cosmopolitan affair, it was filmed in Spain and Sweden, featured a musical score by a Brazilian, and had English and American actors in the leading roles. When it first charged onto American screens a year after its release abroad, a handbill explained its viewpoint in a phrase: "A Man Too Big for Legend."[90]

Hollywood has had a large part in creating the mythical West that is the real West for most of the world. The Western, that most American of genres, has found a receptive audience around the globe, inspiring not only admiration but emulation as well. The Japanese, for example, have translated the Western formula into Samurai movies, with the gunfighter-hero metamorphosed into a devastating swordsman. These, in turn, have been converted back into Westerns by Italian moviemakers who, beginning with *A Fistful of Dollars*, have evolved a genre of their own, the ultra-violent Western wallowing in blood. In such foreign productions, the influence of successive films on one another and thus on the Western tradition is evident, for the West is conceived of in purely cinematic (that is, mythical) terms. Consequently, *Custer of the West* harkens back to its most celebrated predecessor, *They Died With Their Boots On*, and the changes wrought in Custer's image in the intervening years are quietly ignored. *Custer of the West*'s indebtedness to Warner Brothers is obvious during the Last Stand scene.

Not since 1941 has Custer expired with such theatrical flair. Alone, his troopers slaughtered to a man, he stands in his buckskins facing a grim circle of Indians who have pulled back as if to observe a moment's silence in honor of a worthy foe. Then Custer roars out his defiance, and the circle converges on him with an answering roar. As he again goes down under a tidal wave of screaming warriors, a viewer might well ponder the critical observation that no movie has yet offered "a very realistic picture of Custer the man."[91]

In *Custer of the West*, it is not for want of trying. The film constantly borders on complexity, particularly in presenting Custer as that most compelling of Western heroes, the man who is inadvertently destroying the only setting in which he can function, the raw, lawless frontier. Custer is preparing the way for civilization by conquering the Indians, the last of the free-spirited warriors. To the East, creeping ever-Westward in the wake of his victories, is technology. "Trains — steel — guns that kill by thousands," he explains to a party of hostile chiefs. "Our kind of fighting is done." War for Custer is more than just killing. It is the immemorial test of manhood. It is flags and trumpets and personal courage. It is "honor, duty, loyalty — everything a soldier lives by . . ." Custer realizes that his tragedy is to be trapped in a changing world with which he is out of sympathy but for which he is more than a little responsible. His Last Stand, then, is a ceremonial ritual from the days of King Arthur. Choreographed as carefully as a ballet, it took a month and a half to flim.[92] But its implausibility undermines the attempt at a balanced portrayal of a real man. Though the distinguished actor Robert Shaw manages to convey a certain world-weariness and a definite trace of the martinet in his Custer, any negative attributes finally yield to bravery, commitment and an incorruptible, if tactless, honesty. Shaw's Custer, for all of his soliloquizing about the meaning of a soldier's life, resembles in the end nothing so much as a hard-edged version of Errol Flynn's romantic cavalier.

For those who prefer the customary taste of bile to *Custer of the West*'s cup of honey, a major Western appeared in 1970 that finally provided a memorable anti-heroic Custer: Arthur Penn's adaptation of the Thomas Berger novel *Little Big Man*. No Custer film since *They Died With Their Boots On* attracted as much attention in advance. For one thing, the vehicle was well-chosen. Penn's previous films about Billy the Kid and Bonnie and Clyde had already established his fascination with American folk legends and his expertise in handling them. Thus Berger's picaresque tale of the travels and travails of Jack Crabb, sole survivor of Custer's Last Stand, seemed a natural for him. No expense was spared to create that aura of verisimilitude in which Penn always cloaks his legends. The Last Stand, for example, was partially shot in the vicinity of the actual battle site, and some five hundred Crows galloped against Custer's men in a major battle scene.[93] Much of the advance publicity focused on *Little Big Man*'s "now generation" stars, Dustin Hoffman and Faye Dunaway.[94] When interest began to fade after the movie's release, it was revived with the emergence into prominence of a Canadian Indian, Dan George, who had given a wistful, memorable performance as a Cheyenne patriarch, and received an Academy Award nomination for his effort. All told, prospects were favorable for an influential retelling of the Custer story that would fully capture on the screen the other side of an American myth.

In making *Little Big Man*, Penn departed from Berger's novel principally in pounding home his conviction that America's conquest of the Indian was tantamount to genocide. Custer is the "hero of absurd mythology," Penn insisted, but in depicting him this way, he sacrificed the precarious balance between man and legend, hero and villain, so skillfully maintained by Berger.[95] Custer's entry is promising. Jack Crabb and his wife, wiped out by mismanagement, are despondently watching the auction of their general store. Custer happens to be passing through town at the time, and pauses to comment on this domestic tragedy. He advises the Crabbs to go West to recoup their fortunes, and personally guarantees them safety from any hostile Indians. The episode is highly effective, for Richard Mulligan's Custer bears a startling physical resemblance to the figure made familiar in the Matthew Brady Civil War portraits. Crabb is awestruck. As he stares up at Custer towering above on his horse, he loses him against the blinding sun. Momentarily, the General becomes an incandescent image, a bundle of raw energy or "electric life," as Walt Whitman put it. But nothing follows in the rest of *Little Big Man* to justify Crabb's stunning first impression. Far from being larger than life, a living legend with flaws as monumental as his fame, Custer proves a small man made all the smaller by his overpowering ego, his vanity, his bluster, his shallow conceit. He is too ordinary to matter.

At the Last Stand, Custer sports a crisp white shirt, a red tie and a white buckskin suit. He still cuts a dazzling figure, his impeccable attire in striking contrast to the sweat-and-dust-begrimed uniforms of the troopers he has led to early graves. But this outward radiance no longer reflects the inner glow of legend, however corrupt. His appearance is entirely superficial, a manner of dressing, a parody. Custer is simply the so-called "good guy" in a Wild West show. His tone rarely modulates. He brays out his orders and carries on conversations in the same booming, theatrical voice — a man forever playing to the gallery. Nearing his end, but supremely contemptuous of that fact, he preens, postures and struts about, waving two pistols in the air, rambling on in a ceaseless, incoherent monologue, occasionally pausing to aim with infinite precision down the barrel of his revolver at nonexistent targets. He is an actor relishing his greatest role.

Lost opportunities hover above this Last Stand. The myth is almost palpable. General Custer, in his madness, is an island of tranquility, the stable center of a raging chaos, untouched as clouds of arrows whiz by and men and horses drop all around him. Spinning out his paranoia and his delusions of grandeur, coolly leveling his revolver for one shot more, he is oblivious to the furious struggle outside of him, unaware even that his time has come and that his world, indeed all creation, is collapsing about him. It is in exceeding the absurdity of the white man's lot — to dwell eternally in a universe without a center — and surpassing the insanity of existence that Custer achieves a larger than life dimension. Perhaps that is what it means to be the hero of absurd mythology.

But the Custer legend eluded Arthur Penn. In shackling his General to a relevant message, he crossed the line into caricature. Mulligan plays Custer as pure villain — an insufferable egomaniac, a swaggering braggart who will brook no contradiction from his subalterns. He is a man without a redeeming virtue, not even real bravery. Thus the squaw-killer of the Washita bears down on the Indian camp along the Little Big Horn screaming "The hour of victory is at hand!" and (repeating the now-tired joke) "We have them on the run, men! Take no prisoners!" Stripped of every nuance, Mulligan's Custer is not just a villain, but a rather commonplace villain at that. No one would be surprised if he suddenly reached up, gave his moustache a twist and curled his lip in a sinister sneer. *Little Big Man* might have offered a chilling rebuttal to Errol Flynn's charming hero. Instead it settled for the flip side of the same old coin.

It would seem that *Little Big Man* provided the ultimate ugly Custer. Since he has no virtues, he has nothing left to lose. Nevertheless, Marcello Mastoianni's Custer in Marco Ferreri's 1974 farce *Touche pas la femme blanche (Custer Had It Coming)* added another negative dimension to the General's image. In Ferreri's didactic reading, Custer becomes the representative of global imperialism and oppression — as well as a victim. Filmed in Paris on the site of the recently-demolished markets, Les Halles, *Touche pas la femme blanche* employed Vietnamese refugees to play the Sioux, and translated the Last Stand, here fought in a gaping excavation pit, into a parable for the ceaseless war waged by the forces of capitalism against downtrodden peoples everywhere. Ferrari found it "laughable" that "the conquerors are eventually wiped out too. That's what happened at Little Big Horn and what will happen tomorrow, I hope, everywhere." Militarism carried within it the seeds of its own destruction, and Custer — portrayed as a "milksop braggart and dandy infatuated with his own success," spouting on about peace and prosperity while dreaming of slaughter — was intended to illustrate this premise.[96] But *Touche pas la femme blanche* aroused mixed emotions among reviewers abroad, and appears unlikely to leave a profound impression on Custer's screen image.

Since 1909 the Custer movies have been concerned with the General's character and the reasons for his Last Stand. Usually the two, character and causation, have been closely linked..Errol Flynn represents all those heroic Custers who, through the fault of others, have met splendid death on the Little Big Horn. Robert Shaw uneasily occupies the middle position, his Custer a tragic hero whose flaws are commensurate with his stature and impel him with classic inevitability to a splendid death on the Little Big Horn. Richard Mulligan and all the villainous Custers like him are marked for extinction because they richly deserve it, and their glory lust generally concludes in splendid death on the Little Big Horn. Though the exposition leading up to each Last Stand varies, the climactic scenes repeat one another with ritualistic fidelity.

The cinematic Last Stands differ not so much in the images they offer of Custer's final moments as in scope and spectacle, and these differ in proportion to the money and care lavished on them by the studios. When one company began scouting locations for a proposed Custer film in 1965, a delegation from Billings argued the reasonable case that southeastern Montana was the logical site. But studio economists had no trouble in building a case of their own against geographical accuracy. To make the picture in Montana instead of in New Mexico, where the very mesas of Monument Valley have been hallowed by John Ford's cameras, would simply double its production cost. As Mrs. J. K. Ralston, the wife of the Billings artist, pointedly remarked, "the movie people wanted a blacktop highway leading up to the locale on one side of the hill, while on the other they wanted land as virgin as the day Jim Bridger first saw it."[97] This is a fitting comment on the Hollywood process: modern technology impinges on the Custer myth, reshaping it to the demands of convenience, economy and shifting sentiment, but at the same time preserving its essentials. Less successful have been the numerous attempts to tell the Custer story on the most influential medium of all, television.

Perhaps the technical problem of projecting a larger than life image on a smaller than life screen accounts for television's failure to do justice to the Custer theme. Certainly the question of economics has been a dominant one. A television series must allocate its funds evenly over its scheduled run; re-creating the Last Stand would be prohibitively expensive. Unable to depict Custer's grand finale except by borrowing footage from the movies, television has had to resort to indirection. It has approached the subject obliquely, working various plots around an unseen Last Stand and relying on the public's imagination to fill in the gaps. Consequently, the Custer segments of popular Western shows have never been memorable in visual terms.

Gunsmoke, an enormously successful series set in Dodge City with Marshal Matt Dillon keeping a tight grip on the reins of law and order for twenty years, talked about Custer, Reno and the gallant Seventh back in 1958, but avoided a showdown with the Last Stand. Instead, the marshal, having arrested a Seventh Cavalry trooper for murder, is forced to release him to the army. The viewer, however, has the satisfaction of knowing that the guilty party is heading off to the Little Big Horn and will shortly pay for his crime in kind. Captain Benteen appeared in two episodes of *Wyatt Earp*, while *Cheyenne* screened a two-part story that planted its half-Indian hero, "Cheyenne" Brodie, in the hostile camp disguised as a warrior but actually working for the government. From his vantage point, Cheyenne observes a Last Stand spliced together from scenes out of *They Died With Their Boots On*. Later he appears before the Court of Inquiry convened at Major Reno's request to testify that, despite his personal aversion to Reno and earlier allegations to the contrary, the Major had been no coward at the Little Big Horn. There were just too many Indians. *Have Gun — Will Travel*, in turn, had its gunfighter-hero Paladin roaming over the battlefield right after Custer's Last Stand. He got there in typical Paladin fashion. Hired by a worried mother to locate her son, a deserter from the Seventh, Paladin is just in the process of escorting the boy and his new wife out of Indian country when a "kind of trembling, rumbling — like the sound of distant thunder" alerts him that there is trouble afoot. Just then a clayback gelding wanders in. It is Keogh's horse Comanche, wounded on both sides as though he had been caught in the crossfire of an ambush. Things are getting tense, but the party pushes on in the direction of the noise. At last they top a rise, and the viewer catches a glimpse of the battlefield. A hush falls over the scene. As Paladin walks among the corpses, absorbing the grisly sight, an officer rides up from behind and calls out heartily, "Hello, I'm Lieutenant Bradley, chief of scouts for Colonel Gibbon . . ." His voice trails off in mid-sentence as he, too, notices the carnage spread out before him.

In 1966, as the battle's ninetieth anniversary drew near, *Branded* featured a three-part Custer story, "Call for Glory." Jason McCord, hero of the series and a former cavalry officer drummed out of the service on trumped-up charges, is a close friend of President Grant and works under his personal orders. Custer is presented as a boisterous, likable officer who has been made the unwitting dupe of corrupt politicos. Through Jason's exertions he is brought to see the light, and the tale fades out on a forced happy note when the two friends dash out of Fort Lincoln in a burst of exuberance that carries them, after a thirty-second ride, to a ridge overlooking the Little Big Horn. (It took the real Custer from May 17 to June 25, with several layovers, to cover the same distance.) As they bid one another farewell, Custer, suddenly grown solemn, indicates the river valley with a sweep of his arm and predicts that one day soon a great Indian war will be fought here. If an impressionable youngster will not gather from such goings-on that "General Custer, Daniel Boone and Abe Lincoln were all in love with the same Indian girl," he should still get some unique insights into the American past from his television viewing. Another Western series had failed to respond to the "Call for Glory." Deprived of the Last Stand, it turns out, the Custer epic is thoroughly routine fare.

The Twilight Zone and Time Tunnel both included Custer stories, thus wedding two major pop culture genres, science fiction and the Western, in a single program. In fact, a tale employing Custer's Last Stand and a time-traveler device had been published as early as 1895. Its narrator, his curiosity aroused by a portal leading off the street into a little room containing four viewing instruments and nothing else, soon finds himself peering into the past by courtesy of the legendary charlatan Comte de Cagliostro, who "died" exactly one hundred years before and now wishes to barter for life itself, one year of the narrator's normal span for each ten years of the future unveiled to him. But the narrator is satisfied with the eight "visions" he has already been permitted, four of "delectable dances" and four of famous combats from romance and history. The last of these was the Custer battle:

> . . . after an interval the light once more returned and I saw a sadder scene than any yet. In a hollow of the bare mountains a little knot of men in dark blue uniforms were centered about their commander, whose long locks floated from beneath his broad hat. Around this small band of no more than a score of soldiers, thousands of red Indians were raging, with exultant hate in their eyes . . . They stood at bay, valiant and defiant, despite their many wounds; but the line of their implacable foeman was drawn tighter and tighter about them, and one after another they fell forward dying or dead, until at last only the long-haired commander was left, sore wounded but unconquered in spirit.
>
> . . . this picture of brave men facing death fearlessly was at last dissolved into darkness like the others . . . [98]

Such a passive role would never do for television's time-travelers. They want to be participants, not spectators, at the Last Stand.

In The Twilight Zone story, "The 7th is Made Up of Phantoms" (1963), three National Guardsmen, inexplicably trapped back in time but armed with modern weaponry — even a tank — charge into the Custer fray never to return. Their commanding officer, the epitome of *sang-froid*, accepts their fate with no great surprise when he finds their names carved on the monument honoring the dead at the Custer Battlefield. In a *Time Tunnel* episode titled "Massacre" (1966), the obdurate General on the eve of disaster angrily refuses to heed the warnings of two sojourners from the twentieth-century who are offering him not your run-of-the-mill prophecies of doom, but a *bona fide* historical hindsight. With a scornful chuckle and the remark "You must be daft," he dismisses the first warning; when the two persist, he has them put under close guard as renegades and promises that after he has "settled some Sioux hash," he will have them "tried and executed." Custer pays for his obduracy, of course — off-screen. There is one action scene, a mid-stream collision between charging cavalry and Indians that is supposed to represent Reno's fight in the valley, which should be familiar to Western movie buffs: it is taken from the 1944 epic *Buffalo Bill*.

Despite an unimpressive record, television producers remain convinced that Custer's magic will lure a respectable viewing audience. On this assumption, the ABC network in the fall of 1967 launched a new series called simply *Custer*. The show created a minor furor at the outset when certain Indian rights groups objected to the glorification of their favorite enemy. After a few episodes had established conclusively that *Custer* was something less than just another Western, it passed into obscurity and was cancelled by year's end. Given the climate of heightened ethnic awareness and prevailing opinion about the Boy General, *Custer* was a veritable masterpiece of mistiming. Certainly it entitles ABC to join company with Richard Lingeman's "Unwithit Press," whose current list of titles includes *George Custer: Indian Fighter*, the biography of the "gallant, swashbuckling cavalryman" who dealt fair payment out to the "savages" for "atrocities . . . described in all their sickening detail."[99]

As played by Wayne Maunder, Custer was typecast as a hero with minor blemishes resulting from an excess of zeal. Whatever his faults, he was infinitely preferable to Major Reno, a mouthpiece for his detractors. Since deeds speak louder than words, Custer always redeemed himself in action, silencing the backbiters with enviable decisiveness. Indeed, since its net result was always victory, rashness became a virtue in *Custer*. Following each of Custer's indiscretions, a stony-faced General Terry would dress down his unruly subordinate and then, upon dismissing him with a stern reprimand, turn away with a twinkle in his eyes to indulge in a secret smile. After all, boys — even Boy Generals — will be boys, and Terry can only dote paternalistically on his daring young protégé and await his next escapade with anticipation.

Custer confined itself to the period 1868-75 for the usual reason — to avoid the problem of re-fighting the Last Stand — and perhaps even in the faint hope that the series might catch on and have further need of its hero. There were also strategic considerations relating to plot and character development. Each segment was structured to pit Custer against his admirable arch-rival Crazy Horse. The Last Stand would render their tenuous mutual respect pointless. More importantly, it would transform General Terry's permissiveness into criminal folly, and demolish the show's underlying premise that discipline and discretion are considerations decidedly secondary to success.

In answer to initial charges that *Custer* was a wholesale misrepresentation of history, the series' producers took shelter in the word "legend." Originally the show was to have been called *The Legend of Custer*, and one beleaguered spokesman for ABC argued that "the program clearly is identified as a fictionalized series based on a legend."[100] But semantic distinctions could not save *Custer* from the Nielsen ratings, and its epitaph was inadvertently framed in advance by a producer when he remarked: "[Custer] lends himself to the TV medium."[101] That is one contention that remains to be proven.

Though the formula shows will never yield the visual equivalent of a major movie, television has given several of the Custer films exposure to a vast new audience and, in a number of documentaries, has far outdone Hollywood's nominal attempts at historical reconstruction. Public television has explored the Reno Court of Inquiry, and a ten-part series produced at the University of Michigan, *The Western Way*, opened with a show on "The Persistent Myth." "The Custer battle provides an indication of how Western fact and Western myth go hand-in-hand," its narrator maintained. "It shows how an insignificant and inglorious frontier event can become one of the most glorious and heroic legends in our national history."[102]

Commerical television too has made some notable contributions. In 1965, ABC screened a highly-regarded documentary in its "Saga of Western Man" series, *Custer to the Little Big Horn*. One-half of the hour-long show was devoted to background, carefully establishing the context of rapid expansion and Indian resistance within which Custer's Last Stand took place. A sophisticated voice-over narration, on-the-scene photography and small-scale, carefully staged re-enactments of certain events leading up to the battle produced an aura of verisimilitude. At the Last Stand, the troopers — played by the Westernaires 1st Cavalry Platoon of Golden, Colorado — are shown crouching and firing from a sagebrush-covered slope under their billowing stars and stripes guidon, until the noise of battle finally fades away and only the wind is left. *Custer to the Little Big Horn* was history told with unusual restraint.

A strong point of view is ordinarily the television documentary's hallmark, for good and ill. A 1961 "special" narrated by Gary Cooper attempted to present a balanced picture of *The Real West*. Cooper, for one, thought it might be "the first time the real west will be seen on television."[103] His presence was sufficient to attract a sizable audience, and the show did handle the Custer battle with a minimum of distortion. As a matter of course, *The Real West* debunked some of the more egregious fables about Custer's Last Stand, but it was not self-consciously iconoclastic, unlike a *Discovery* program three years later which set out to "explode" the myths about such popular Western heroes as Buffalo Bill, Bat Masterson and General Custer, revealing them "in their true and often not-so-noble colors."[104]

121

End of the Trail, a 1967 NBC special, compressed the sweep of plains Indian history into a single hour. The title was not fortuitous to begin with since it brings to mind James E. Fraser's equestrian statue of a warrior, his head bowed in defeat, his eagle plume drooping, his spear pointing at the ground — the soul of dejection as he contemplates the extinction of his people and a way of life. The idea is fine for an allegorical period piece, but it is a less than satisfactory basis for historical interpretation. What followed was in keeping with the title. *End of the Trail*'s script, by Philip Reisman, Jr., established an ingenious dialogue between Indian and white based on actual quotations. But the Indians got all the good lines. Thus they appeared philosophical; the whites, merely greedy. Models of a Job-like patience, the red men ignored one provocation after another until, the limits of their endurance reached, they took to the warpath. Custer's Last Stand followed, providing the climax, and was imaginatively visualized through Indian drawings of the fight and footage shot on the battlefield. But the narration was finally too strident in its outrage, too wearying in its earnestness and its arch ironies. Moreover, the concluding scene showing a line of warriors riding along a distant bluff, silhouetted against a fiery sunset, came uncomfortably close to parody. If it is unobjectionable to cast the past into the form of a morality play, it is nevertheless a disservice to the Indians to fade out on that convenient cliche', the Vanishing American.

As for the characterization of Custer in the *End of the Trail*, truly, he never had a chance. Reisman conceded that it was his intention to counter "the Beau Sabreur image," the Custer legend fostered in large part by "the barroom paintings of the Last Stand."[105] One is reminded of General Nelson A. Miles indignantly denouncing Custer's critics as men primarily adept at kicking a dead lion. By 1967, however, scoring points off Custer had become more nearly a case of beating a dead horse. Within the context of *End of the Trail*, the General was judged guilty before he made his first appearance on the screen, in a photograph showing him at work in his study at Fort Lincoln "under," narrator Walter Brennan snorted, "a protrait of his favorite person" — George Armstrong Custer.

The debunking of Custer has itself wound down into a ritual wherein a straw man, the heroic Custer supposedly still worshipped by the American public, is set up to be demolished with santimonious and biting sarcasm — is set up *repeatedly*, to be repeatedly demolished. It sometimes seems as though the only people left who believe Custer is a popular hero today are the writers and directors poising to slaughter him. In wave after wave they attack, hoping to outshine Errol Flynn's flashing sword with their own rapier-like wit as they slash away frantically at a phantom hero who no longer exists. Caught up in their iconociasm, they share in common the unshakable conviction that their views are as fresh in the 1970's as Frederic Van de Water's were when he first trimmed the "flower of the American Army" down to size more than forty years ago. Thus five years after Walter Brennan consigned Custer to infamy in *End of the Trail*, he was back on television narrating a portion of another

122

documentary, *The American Experience*, in which Custer, still lusting after glory, "rode off to lasting fame — and utter disaster." The timidity Hollywood exhibited in challenging Custer's heroic credentials before 1958 has been matched since by television's unwillingness to reconsider the glory-hunter interpretation it now finds so comfortable. In fairness, one should keep in mind what one television writer, referring to Bicentennial programming, has described as "the difficulty of popularizing anything complex:"

> The trick in a television broadcast is to do a job that is light enough to attract a large audience, but with weight enough to satisfy the experts. It is always difficult and often impossible. The historians are never going to be happy with any . . . programs done by television writers; and if they are done by historians, no one, including other historians, is going to watch them.[106]

Custer, it seems, will always be either hero or villain on the screen. Right now he is in his villain phase.

In the long run, historical debunking offers diminishing returns. By nature it is uncreative. It has to borrow life in order to thrive, and its very existence is a tribute of sorts to the durability of the legends and myths it preys upon. Whenever television forgets about the voices crying out for social significance and historical accuracy, it replaces its disapproving frown with a tolerant smile. Westerns, after all, have been good business, and Western heroes have more than paid their keep. Perhaps Vietnam has changed that situation; but nothing else can account for such a misguided venture as the *Custer* series. Indeed, television's tolerant smile has occasionally broadened into a grin. In 1964, for example, the viewer was threatened with a proposed situation comedy, *Who Goes There?*, that would have combined elements of the ghost story (then all the rage) and the Western in a series about Custer and his Indian lackey, who have returned as spectres to "gambol with a 'typical' American family."[107] Though this program never materialized, *F Troop*, a situation comedy about the cavalry and Indians, did, and during its run gave several musty Custer jokes an airing out. Both shows would suggest how willing television has been to back off its hard line on the glory-hunter in order to accommodate conventional taste. As the butt of endless jokes, a self-centered military buffoon, the General is more exploitable than as a murderous villain. *Custer* may seem an impossibly long leap from *End of the Trail*; but it was only a small step from *F Troop*.

IV

The successive re-enactments of Custer's Last Stand have tended to a natural repetitiveness. The same event is involved, and it is re-created in accordance with set rules. Instead of a single image, the audience is confronted with a series of images, a sequence that begins once Custer is trapped on the hill by encircling Indians. The exposition leading up to

123

this moment has already accounted for why he is there; anyway, the reasons no longer matter very much. Now the myth is dominant, and until the last shot is fired and the Boy General has crumpled to the ground the audience is witness to a ritual drama. Explicitly and covertly, Custer's Last Stand re-enactments draw upon their own pool of tradition. The sensation of déjà vu is expected, even encouraged.

Then it is all over. The narrative resumes. A stark figure in gunfighter's black, looking for all the world like Jack Palance's menacing, cold-blooded killer in *Shane*, stands frozen at the sight of the battlefield. His shoulders slump under the weight of the tragedy so recently concluded here. Then the homely, pock-marked face glances up, and it is Paladin, "soldier of fortune in a savage land," his eyes filled with the consummate horror of it all. Before he can whisper a word, one's mind flashes back to the image of Buffalo Bill grandly sweeping the Stetson off his bowed head in tribute to the gallant men of the Seventh, and the inescapable phrase blots out the television screen: "Too late!"

Chapter 6

THE HEROIC STANCE AND THE ENDURING MYTH

A hero is one who looks like a hero.
Robert Warshow, "The Westerner."

The health of a people depends largely on their ability to question their inherited symbols in light of contemporary actualities, to keep them fluid, vibrant, and responsive.

Alfred North Whitehead.

The movies are perhaps the most sensitive barometers of the public's shifting attitudes towards Custer. Moreover, at the same time that they reflect popular opinion, they also mould it, and a successful film will often attract a train of imitators, thus amplifying its original influence. Since Custer's personal reputation has never been blacker than it is in movies today, one can assume with reasonable certainty that Custer has reached his nadir in the public's estimation.

Despite this fact, the myth of Custer's Last Stand remains relatively untouched. That is to say, the imagery associated with the phrase has not been substantially modified by current evaluations of the General. A modern viewer, upon studying the Anheuser-Busch lithograph, is likely to blurt: "Wow, what a fool Custer was! Got all his men killed!" The imagery — indeed, the whole concept expressed in that print — is still accepted unquestioningly, but its meaning is subject to a radically different interpretation.

Frederic F. Van de Water once characterized a Custer subaltern as exhibiting a "clear, unwavering, beautiful loyalty" to his dead commander's memory.[1] In an ironic sense, the same might be said of the public, not in relation to Custer, but to Custer's Last Stand. The static image of the Last Stand is cut off from the narrative exposition framing it, and divorced from history. Custer's personal legend is irrelevant to it. This fact is manifest in what might be termed the "Heroic Stance." Whether Custer be hero, villain or simply fool, and in whatever medium, when it comes time for him to die he is, with few exceptions, magnificent.

125

I

General Custer's first biographer, Frederick Whittaker, related the version of the Last Stand told by (or for) Crow scout Curly. His rhetoric was as florid as the incident itself:

> ... When [Curly] saw that the party with the General was to be overwhelmed, he went to the General and begged him to let him show him a way to escape. General Custer dropped his head on his breast in thought for a moment, in a way he had of doing. There was a lull in the fight after a charge, the encircling Indians gathering for a fresh attack. In that moment, Custer looked at Curly, waved him away and rode back to the little group of men, to die with them. How many thoughts must have crossed that noble soul in that brief moment. There was no hope of victory if he stayed, nothing but certain death. With the scout he was nearly certain to escape. His horse was a thoroughbred and his way sure. He might have balanced the value of a leader's life against those of his men, and sought his safety. Why did he go back to certain death?
>
> Because he felt that such a death as that which that little band of heroes was about to die, was worth the lives of all the general officers in the world ... He weighed, in that brief moment of reflection, all the consequences to America of the lesson of life and the lesson of heroic death, and he chose death.[2]

Subsequent nineteenth-century popularizers so closely adhered to this reverent tone that one student of the Custer legend classified their works as "branches from the Whittaker trunk."[3] Matters continued much the same through the first three decades of the twentieth century, and though recent pro-Custer biographies have depicted the Last Stand more realistically, vestiges of the old, gushing prose are still to be found in books intended for young readers.

James E. West, one-time Chief Executive of the Boy Scouts of America, in an introduction to a juvenile Custer novel wrote that "the needful thing" in children's literature "is to find stories in which the heroes have the characteristics boys so much admire — unquenchable courage, immense resourcefulness, absolute fidelity, conspicuous greatness."[4] Custer and his Last Stand were tailor-made to West's specifications, and Quentin Reynolds was nothing averse to exploiting their appeal in a 1951 biography. "We'll have to fight it out here," Custer tells his brother Tom:

> "This is our last stand. And we'll take lots of Sioux with us" . . . Custer was surrounded on all sides. His men were twenty against a thousand. They were ten now, and finally only two. Autie Custer [George's pet name] and his brother Tom knelt side by side, pouring lead into the screaming braves.
>
> Two bullets hit Autie at the same time. He wheeled toward Tom and reached out a hand. Tom was hit at the same moment. He swerved toward Autie. They died as they had lived — together.[5]

126

Even when one turns from obvious juvenilia to the Last Stand in *Glory-Hunter*, however, the transition is surprisingly smooth. Frederic Van de Water did not concern himself with the Last Stand's details in his biography, but the implications of an earlier statement ("No command that Custer ever held esteemed him until it had followed him into battle") were important. The Little Big Horn was Custer's hardest battle, the occasion of his spectacular blood sacrifice, and Van de Water's closing sentences do nothing to minimize the consequences of that death on a hilltop: "George Armstrong Custer may well have lain content. Glory, sought all his stormy life, was his at last and forever."[6] Van de Water might judge such heroism pointless and inexcusable, but there was no denying that it was of the sort certain to hold the public's attention and secure for Custer the fame he had ever coveted. As an earlier boy's writer had put it, "Custer's unguarded advance and reckless charge were, perhaps, unwise generalship, but they were the chief ingredients of heroism and a dauntless courage and as such have given him an immortality that will ever make him the typical Indian fighter of the nineteenth century. Much is forgiven to valor; a brave man's death covers all mistakes."[7]

The nineteenth-century poets chose to celebrate the Last Stand in a flood of glowing phrases. Laura Webb and Ella Wilcox pictured the gallant General fighting to the end while tears coursed down his cheeks. These welled up not in fright or self-pity, of course, but in sorrow for his Elizabeth, so soon to be widowed. A tower of strength in the hour of ultimate peril, Whittaker's Custer yelled out "words of encouragement glowing: — / 'We can but die once, boys, but sell your lives dear.'"[8] Then, as one black poet, born a slave, wrote at the time:

> No more their leader calls,
> Pierced 'mid his men he falls,
> But sinks breathing, "Stand!"
> And where the hero lies,
> Each soldier till he dies,
> Fights hand to hand.[9]

A twentieth-century versifier was similarly reluctant to make the Last Stand final:

> The charm of his life is broken at last!
> Brave Custer fell as a bullet passed
> And cleaved a pathway through his breast,
> Fell like an oak, by storms hard-pressed.
>
> . . .
>
> So Custer fell upon the plain,
> But rising partly up again,
> Just as reacting branches may,
> Struck down three Indians more that day,
> Then shattered his sword on the barrel of a gun,

127

That was held in the hands of another one;
With his empty pistol and useless blade,
He still was dauntless and unafraid,
And fell amid the battle's sounds,
The victim of a dozen wounds.
The last to succumb to death, he won,
The glory of duty itself well done . . .[10]

A glance at the Anheuser-Busch lithograph will establish the authority for this description. But it is a latter-day Walt Whitman, Robert P. Tristram Coffin, who has fashioned the most memorable bardic tribute to the Heroic Stance in this century. Coffin's Custer, "the last cavalier," stands proud, "with bullets singing in his hair:"

And to the last the golden flower
Waved within the wall of dead,
When the sun burst, dark came downward,
The flower lay broken at its head.

But Custer rode by old Prince Rupert
And the long-curled Cavaliers
Off the earth in lace and laughter,
Safe from the safe and sober years.[11]

Most poets have been favorably disposed to Custer and naturally have treated his Last Stand as a heroic episode in American history. So also have the artists. Since they invested the concept with form, we picture the Last Stand as they have shown it. From such nineteenth-century Custers as William M. Cary's fearsome, sword-wielding, pistol-firing General and A. R. Waud's sombre, buckskin-clad frontier hero one turns to the twentieth-century Custers with no sense of abrupt transition. Indeed, the conceptions of artists like Harold von Schmidt and H. Charles McBarron for sheer drama have no peers.

This is not to suggest that painters have been insensitive to the times. Obviously, art styles have changed, and with them the Last Stands, though most painters who essay the subject today are still strict representationalists specializing in Western Americana. The recent stress on technical accuracy bespeaks a more critical approach to the Custer battle, however. Too, Custer no longer stares out from the exact center of every canvas. He has been shuffled around, usually to some less conspicuous spot near the top or to the side of the picture, where his costume and stance and the composition as a whole still make him the cynosure of every eye. For in the end, the artist's best efforts at restraint are inconsequential. He wishes to freeze the Last Stand at some decisive point in the fighting and to preserve its drama in one all-encompassing image. For his purposes, contemporary disenchantment with Custer is irrelevant, and he embraces the myth as both source and inspiration. Thus even in an age dubious of heroes, the Heroic Stance has lost none of its visual appeal.

128

The revisionists themselves succumb to the magic of the Last Stand. J. K. Ralston's many Custers are gaunt, tired-looking men, yet they snap into variations on the traditional heroic posture when the trumpet summons them to the grand finale. Nicholas Eggenhofer, after producing several epic Custer figures, was called upon to paint the General as he might actually have looked during the battle. If not as glamorous as before, Eggenhofer's Custer still calmly faced the foe, his two pistols raised in anticipation. In 1953 sculptor Dwight Franklin consciously set out to avoid the old heroic clichés and depict Custer as a man confronted by imminent death, not glory. His first model of the General, part of a grouping assembled in 1934, had been traditional in every respect. Custer stood solidly planted in front of a battle flag, hat on, one arm crooked and his revolver at the ready as he awaited the climactic Indian charge. Twenty years later Franklin was commissioned to sculpt a model of Custer at the instant of his death, "a weary, dirty, unkempt man who, fighting desperately for life, had reached the limit of vitality and strength, and whose drawn and haggard features made him appear older than his age by many years."[12] Yet *The Passing of the Yellow Hair* does not deny Custer a measure of heroism. Shabby and care-worn though he is, hatless and contorted in the agony of a mortal wound, the impression persists: "There Was a Man: Custer's Last Stand — The Massacre that Will Never Be Forgotten."

The triumph of the Heroic Stance over critical judgment is even more apparent in the work of the Custer novelists. "However daring the pen," Randall Parrish observed in *Bob Hampton of Placer*, "it cannot but falter when attempting to picture the events of those hours of victorious defeat." Yet the pens wrote on. Parrish's own Last Stand scene can represent several pre-Van de Water versions. His description of the Seventh Cavalry at bay sets the heroic tone, though it reduces Custer to an uncommonly passive role:

> They turned their loyal eyes toward him they loved and followed for the last time, and when he uttered one final word of undaunted courage, they cheered him faintly, with parched and fevered lips.

> . . . Shoulder to shoulder, in ever-contracting circle, officers and men stood shielding their commander to the last. Foot by foot, they were forced back, treading on their wounded, stumbling over their dead; they were choked in the stifling smoke, scorched by the flaming guns, clutched at by red hands, beaten down by horses' hoofs. Twenty or thirty made a despairing dash, in a vain endeavor to burst through the red enveloping lines, only to be tomahawked or shot; but the most remained, a thin struggling ring, with Custer in its centre. Then came the inevitable end. The red waves surged completely across the crest, no white man left alive upon the field. They had fought a good fight; they had kept the faith.[13]

From an open critic of Custer like Will Henry, one would expect a rather different rendering of the same scene. Thus the climax of John Clayton's narrative comes as a surprise:

> Custer had the time it takes a racing Indian pony to cover fifty yards, to prepare his last defense. All any man could do, he did — kept levering shells into his carbine and firing them. I can hear his last given orders as clearly as though he were calling them as I write. "Stay together, men. Don't break. Fire low. We'll make it." His unforgettable voice carried over the panic disorder which had seized our men at the appearance of Crazy Horse. They actually pulled together and stood to take the Oglala charge. This was bravery in its highest hour. But like so much of bravery, futile, senseless, pointless. . . .
>
> How history or the legend-makers will draw that death, God alone knows. Probably with yellow curls streaming, a gun blazing in either hand, a defiant burst of laughter on the smiling, boyish lips, a last-second, heroic flinging of the empty guns in the snarling faces of the enemy.
>
> Well, if so, they won't be too far amiss.[14]

Once again, the Heroic Stance prevailed.

Thomas Berger has realized most fully the dichotomy between Custer the fallible human being and Custer the legend. *Little Big Man*'s hero, Jack Crabb, is simultaneously attracted to and repelled by the General until the moment of truth. During his Last Stand, Custer recovers from a spell of madness induced by the fury of battle and the shattering of great dreams. He stands erect and unwounded, firing a pistol with one hand and grasping a company guidon with the other:

> So we fought on and no help came and one by one the remaining guns fell silent, but the Indians still didn't make no overrunning charge, just surged ever closer so that we was as if upon a diminishing island in a river at flood . . . I had stopped worrying about [Custer] standing erect: it didn't matter much now whether he was hit, and then too it did provide some inspiration even for me . . . the General stayed intact because he was Custer, better than anyone else, basically invulnerable even in defeat, and always right. You got to admire that type of conviction, even when you resent it. And I did both . . . He smiled through the dirt . . . as if in serene resignation. Then he fired several rounds from his pistol at what seemed, from his stance and firm aim, to be aprticular targets, still holding that battle guidon, now tattered, on its broken staff in his left hand.
>
> He was hit then, just once, a tear in his shirt directly over the heart. He turned some to favor the force, dropped the banner, clutched at the wound as if rather in courtesy than anguish. Onto his back he fell, arms outflung as though crucified, but his closed mouth still showing the traces of a smile. He might have went to sleep at a picnic. I couldn't see he was bleeding at all, but he must have been, somewhere. I had finally accepted that fact that he was great — and he sure was, don't let anybody ever tell you different, and if you don't agree, then maybe

something is queer about your definition of greatness — but it stands to reason he had blood.[15]

It was indeed a man of flesh and blood who fell on that hot June Sunday in 1876. But for one perfect moment he had been more than human, more than life-size. Custer of the Last Stand, Custer of the Heroic Stance, was the legendary hero of an enduring myth.

In putting Custer on the screen, the movies have usually accepted the artists' image of the Last Stand, without regard to the character interpretation they are advancing. A still from the 1912 film *Custer's Last Fight* showing "The Massacre" might almost be a living tableau of the Anheuser-Busch lithograph, so closely does the disposition of the actors approximate that of the figures in the print. The brief, dramatic demise of Custer in *The Plainsman* begins with the General in a pose right out of A. R. Waud's drawing, leaning on his rifle, firing a pistol with his right hand, before he receives a fatal wound and, clutching the American flag in his arm, falls to the ground. When Warner Brothers released *They Died With Their Boots On*, studio publicity noted that the climactic scene was based on the original Cassilly Adams painting — which, *Time* scoffed, was considered by everyone to be "all wrong."[16] A quarter of a century later, an anti-Custer movie, *The Day Custer Fell*, was scheduled to appear which included among its promotional materials copies of E. S. Paxson's *Custer's Last Stand*.[17] Even Arthur Penn's *Little Big Man*, which utilized the 1876 Waud drawing in its advertising, seems indebted to that classic Last Stand for the idea of a white-suited Custer in bold relief against the swarm of dark-uniformed troopers and darker Indians, a source of radiant light in the storm of battle. Because the movie was in fact burlesquing the traditional Last Stand, its Custer does *look* the hero, striking a series of appropriate poses in parody of all those two-dimensional Custers who, preserved forever by the painter's brush, linger on in our time.

The Last Stand sequence of any Custer movie demonstrates the extent of the Heroic Stance's victory over considerations of character consistency. On the one hand, there is Errol Flynn's super-heroic Custer awaiting the Indian rush that will allow him to join his men in glorious death in *They Died With Their Boots On*; on the other is Douglas Kennedy's despicable, villainous Custer paying fair price for his own obdurate egotism in *Sitting Bull*. Yet where is the visible difference? In knee-high boots and buckskin jacket, with a sabre, golden locks and a moustache, by a guidon planted in defiance of the foe, Custer makes his eternal, heroic Last Stand in both:

> He stayed with [his men] to the utmost hour,
> In letters of blood he wrote his name —
> His saber fell with its final power,
> And Custer died into deathless fame.[18]

His was, in short, a stance that transcended time itself.

131

II

Whether the myth of Custer's Last Stand be regarded as heroic or anti-heroic today, its relevance rests ultimately on the bedrock of tradition. The image of doomed heroism could feasibly be altered — Custer could be shown as a blubbering coward begging for his life — but what is left would not be Custer's Last Stand. The myth would be lost in the process of revising it. It can be used to positive or negative ends with equal effectiveness, but both usages must begin with the familiar concept of the Heroic Stance.

For sixty years Custer's Last Stand served as an American parallel to Thermopylae and the Charge of the Light Brigade, a matchless example of courage and daring. Now its most common reference value is as the American Waterloo, and Custer has taken on the qualities of a small-time Napoleon, a stereotyped megalomaniac haunted by visions of grandeur. The erstwhile emperor of all Europe stands scowling beneath his tri-cornered hat, hand tucked inside his waistcoat, while the aspiring presidential candidate, hoping to charge into office on the strength of a crushing victory over the Sioux, stands with his arms folded across his chest, imperiously peering at the world of lesser beings down his aquiline nose. Each will sacrifice an army to realize his mad ambitions.

The late nineteenth-century propensity for sentimentalizing disaster and enshrining martyred heroes was perhaps in itself enough to make a national myth of Custer's Last Stand in 1876. But there was something more. At the time, such an epic defeat filled a deep-felt need. Even as Americans were celebrating the Centennial Fourth and burdening the air with patriotic platitudes on past achievements and future prospects, the fact remained that the Year of a Hundred Years had in many respects been a disappointing one. Complex problems between North and South remained unsettled, and though military Reconstruction was nearing its end, national reconciliation was still an ideal, not a reality. The movement for Negro rights was losing momentum rapidly, and before another year had passed the black man would be sacrificed to political reunion, while the plains Indians, their victory over Custer having fatally compromised Grant's Peace Policy, would be whipped into submission. Change was everywhere and welcome, yet anxiety was also a natural reaction to the industrial developments that were transforming the nation's economic and social patterns.

The tone of political life had degenerated, it seemed, and the upcoming presidential election was an occasion more for resignation than expectation. The Belknap scandal, coming hard on the heels of the Whiskey Ring's exposure, was only the latest manifestation of what the *Nation* described as the "spirit of money-getting which has, since 1868, flowed through all branches of Government like a flood of lava."[19] The first session of the Forty-fourth Congress was an endurance test with the Democratic House and the Republican Senate showing a singular genius for battling to stalemates. A drab presidential campaign, contested by two drab candidates, had been launched on a course that would not be decided on election day, nor for months afterwards, and would end in a compromise that even yet exudes a tainted odor.

Within this context Custer's Last Stand could be seen as just another mockery of the theme proclaimed by the Exposition at Philadelphia, a "Century of Progress." Certainly the bitter political and military controversies that the battle engendered suggest despair and disgust. But there was something more. Custer's Last Stand could also be seen as a moral triumph, a decisive action in a time of indecision, a selfless sacrifice in a time of selfishness. "Let us say what we will about the degradation of the national character, and our Centennial product being corruption and national decadence, the charge of Custer is an answer to it all," the *New York Herald* editorialized. "It shows that manhood and valor, self-denial and absolute consecration to duty, even at the sacrifice of life, all remain with us."[20]

Stripped to its essential element of bravery and isolated as one moment of perfect heroism, Custer's Last Stand was the longed-for proof of an American destiny that transcended current affairs and was more real than reality. It provided a "lesson opportune," as Walt Whitman said, and he accepted it with genuine gratitude:

> As, sitting in dark days,
> Lone, sulky, through the time's thick murk looking
>   in vain for light, for hope,
> From unsuspected parts, a fierce and momentary proof,
> (The sun there at the center, though concealed,
> Electric life forever at the center,)
> Breaks forth, a lightning flash.[21]

One of those "branches from the Whittaker trunk," Captain Willard Glazier's *Heroes of Three Wars* (1878), concluded its sketch of Custer on the same high note: "In the flash of his fame he died as he had lived — for his country. The offering was doubtless a glad one. He desired no better fate than such a death; he could leave no richer inheritance than such an example."[22]

The need for a myth in 1876 helped fashion one. Since that time, the myth has taken on quite different connotations, its subsequent meanings reflecting the prevailing moods of the American people. That this should be so is reasonable. A popular myth must respond to the public's changing interests if it is to remain popular. Custer's Last Stand is no exception, as its relationship to two overriding modern concerns, racism and militarism as factors in the American experience, demonstrates.

In a day of heightened ethnic consciousness, Custer's Last Stand is fast becoming an indispensable anti-heroic myth. The rumblings that presaged the General's tumble from favor in the 1930's included an acerbic essay on "The Custer Myth" by P. E. Byrne, a student of the plains Indian wars who had previously written a popular history of the subject with the telltale dedication "To the Indian Dead." Published in a limited-circulation state historical society quarterly, Bryne's essay was given wider exposure when it was reprinted, with the blessings of the Commissioner of Indian Affairs, as a Congressional document in 1933. Noting that "many absurdities" about Custer had been "set afloat," Byrne proceeded to lay the legends to rest:

> The real Custer at the Little Big Horn must have been a melancholy figure compared with the Custer of legend, the Custer whom the world has been given to know so well throughout these years — the dashing leader before whom all opposition faded; the military spearhead intent upon carrying death and destruction to the hapless Indian hordes. Alas! the dashing leadership was all on the other side in that affair, and the plans for slaughter went awry. Custer and his battalion went in to kill; they remained to die.[23]

Custer was about to become the Glory-hunter.

Almost forty years later, at a time when the First American was regaining a national prominence he had not enjoyed since the days of the Indian New Deal, Alvin M. Josephy, Jr., a student of Indian history and an outspoken champion of Indian rights, wrote an essay also titled "The Custer Myth" for the mass-circulation *Life* magazine. In it, Josephy quoted a Nez Perce on the rationale for selecting Custer as the archetypal bad white man. Because Custer is "the best known hero" of a white cultural myth about the conquest of the West and displacement of the savages, the Nez Perce explained, "to every Indian in the country he is the biggest and most important symbol of all the lies that have been told about us. Destroy the Custer myth, the biggest one of all, and you'll start getting an understanding of everything that happened and an end to the bias against the Indian people."[24]

The onslaught occurs on many fronts. If the movie industry developed an expedient "racial conscience" regarding the Indian in the early 1950's, in the late 1960's it recovered it with a vengeance. The Indian had long been in eclipse, while Mexican banditti substituted as the favorite other-racial villains in a succession of Westerns. But against a background of fish-ins in Oregon, hunt-ins in Oklahoma, marches on Washington, D.C., and sit-ins on abandoned government properties from Alcatraz to Chicago, the Indian re-emerged on the screen with a topical rush. Among the films notable for a certain bloodthirstiness introduced to underline their social concerns — *Cheyenne Autumn, A Man Called Horse, Tell Them Willie Boy is Here, Soldier Blue* — was one which impaled Custer on the cross of cause, *Little Big Man*. Its choice of Custer for vehement denunciation was strategically acute given the prevailing climate of opinion.

Not content with having vanquished Custer in 1876, the Indians appear intent on keeping him pinned to the ground. William Red Fox, an engaging, garrulous old Sioux who once traveled the vaudeville circuit and had not forgotten what he learned, appeared on national television twice in June, 1967, to denounce Custer with a crusading fervor thirty years out of date. "The only thing that made a hero out of Custer," he quipped, "was a picture made for Anheuser-Busch."[25] Far more impassioned were the remarks of a Red Power group that, two months before the pilot film of *Custer* was to debut on television in 1967, protested the glamorization of a man who "endorsed a policy of genocide and massacred village after village of Indians." "General Custer was a madman, the Indian's worst enemy," A. A. Hopkins-Dukes, the group's Kiowa spokesman, asserted.[26] "Custer Died for Your Sins" a much-quoted bumper sticker distributed by the National Congress of American Indians warned white Americans, while another Indian association, United Native Americans, settled for the blunt "Custer Had It Coming."[27] Silverbird, a Navaho rock group, included in its repertoire a song with a message:

> Custer's Last Stand,
> Custer's Last Stand,
> Everyone remembers Custer's Last Stand,
> But who remembers the Indian man?
> Who remembers the Indian man?
> Who remembers the Indian man?[28]

For Indians everywhere, Custer is the core of a complex of white racist beliefs. For guilt-ridden whites, in turn, he is a convenient cultural scapegoat: "Custer died for our sins."[29]

Yet, whatever his faults, Custer was no hardline racial bigot, and in many respects was more enlightened than most of his military contemporaries. To cast him in the form of a zealous racial exterminator is simply to substitute rhetoric for fact. It is completely understandable, however, that Custer should be singled out for this distasteful role. As the civil rights movement in the United States adopted an urgently militant tone in the late 1960's, certain parallels between the situation of the Indian and the Negro, past and present, became more evident. It followed that a mythical-historical figure like George Armstrong Custer should become the red man's Simon Legree and Bull Connor into one.

Instead of demythologizing Custer, the Red Power activists have exploited him, making him the center of their own mythology. In this capacity, as a symbolic rallying point for modern Indian dissent, Custer is not just useful, but essential. The idea is not new. Back in 1925, from the comfort of his own Parisian retreat, Ernest Hemingway had studied the growing vogue of "noble savagery" in the United States with detached bemusement, and he sat down to parody one of its major exponents, Sherwood Anderson, in *The Torrents of Spring: A Romantic Novel in Honor of the Passing of a Great Race*. On the walls of an exclusive club for American Indian veterans, Hemingway wrote, "were framed autographed photographs of Chief Bender, Francis Parkman, D. H. Lawrence, Chief Meyers, Stewart Edward White, Mary Austin, Jim Thorpe, General Custer, Glenn Warner, Mabel Dodge, and a full-length oil painting of Henry Wadsworth Longfellow."[30] Amongst this witty assemblage of heroes and sentimental champions of the red man (whom D. H. Lawrence himself had described as "white savages, with motor-cars, telephones, incomes and ideals!"[31]), one name seems decidedly out of place. Yet Custer had a legitimate claim to membership in such select company, for he had done as much as any of the rest to establish the Indians' position in the twentieth-century American's mind. His was, figuratively speaking, the most celebrated scalp they had ever lifted, and though he is an anti-hero to the red man today, he still serves an undeniably useful function.

Henry Wadsworth Longfellow, given the place of honor in Hemingway's gallery of Indian heroes, raised a second major issue soon after Custer's Last Stand: "Whose was the right and the wrong?" As the foremost poetic champion of the red man since his *Hiawatha* captured the public's imagination in 1855, Longfellow was perhaps obligated to answer that it was the nation's "broken faith" that had "wrought all this ruin and scathe." Another contemporary poet said flatly, "Our greed alone is guilty."[32] But the question of responsibility is not the ultimate one raised by the battle. A Pennsylvania poet, in a meter reminiscent of Longfellow's but with a Quaker simplicity, broached it when he asked in 1909, "Who shall judge, and what the verdict?:"

> Savage deeds of savage natures
> Crouching 'mid the rocks and thickets
> To wreak vengeance on intruders;
> Then came plunder, rapine, murder,
> Homes destroyed and loved ones slaughtered
> Fields laid waste and lands deserted.
> Who will now condone their warfare?
> Racial pride and bold aggression
> Marked the progress of the White-man,
> Claiming all lands as his birthright,
> Using wealth and place and power
> To displace the warlike nomad,
> Drive him to the rocks and sands, where
> Broken health and broken spirit
> Would remove the hated rival.
> Who will now condone such warfare?[33]

War itself is the issue, and its futility the point.

Writing to commemorate the seventy-fifth anniversary of the Little Big Horn, and deeply conscious of the war in which the United States was then involved, Catherine E. Berry echoed the Pennsylvanian's theme:

> Consider now this tragedy of time:
> The white man and the red man both had cause
> In depths of hell and on the heights sublime.
> And both sides lost — as in all wars

136

It must so be — for each a grim defeat.
God in His heaven, looking past the stars,
Must sometimes wonder at the world's conceit
Which places Might so high upon the list,
And seeks to put His blessing on a mailed fist.[34]

In 1965, an amateur poet touched upon the sentiments of Americans perplexed by yet another war when he wrote "The Little Big Horn, War and Progress:"

If progress' cost is freedom lost,
And the threat of war grows worse;
If we're more afraid in each decade,
Then it's progress in reverse. [35]

But Vietnam was to become a continuing fact of national life, and a whole generation of young Americans were raised on the televised coverage of the fighting. "Why didn't he call for air support?," one puzzled boy asks his chum as they emerge from a theater showing "Custer" in a 1971 Whitney Darrow, Jr., cartoon.[36]

Custer's Last Stand is sorrowful proof that all war is wasteful. No blame attaches to one side or any one individual in the strictest sense of the pacifist philosophy, since both sides suffer equally from their participation, and both are equally wrong. Of course, anti-war protest is rarely so equanimous. It requires villains, and Custer has frequently been utilized as a personification of militarism. During the Korean War, a poet writing under the influence of Van de Water allowed a conscience-stricken Custer a defensive soliloquy as he looked about him at the corpses of his troopers:

Alone upon this stony mound of earth,
With fever'd brow and tortur'd mind I stand.
Around me dead men look with sightless eyes;
Were there no bullets shaped and cast for me?
O stare not up at me, ye gallant slain;
The bravest die but once, and ye have died.
Reproach me not, nor chide the lust for fame
That cuts from youth the slender thread of life.[37]

As Vietnam wore on with no end in sight, a distinguished Southwestern novelist lashed out at Custer in biting verse:

General George Armstrong
Custer was a queer
Duck
Who took to killing

137

People at an early
Age.
That's what a career of the army
Can do.
It
Can bend your spirit
Like a pretzel
And make your last stand.
On some hill like Christ the
King.[38]

A 1966 poster put the case against Custer forcefully. Beneath his full-length portrait were the words: "Let's win this war and get the hell out!" Published for the "Little Big Horn Veterans Association," the poster was in the mainstream of anti-war propaganda that issued forth from Berkeley ever since active American involvement in Vietnam became national policy. It is still in print, attesting to the duration of the war and the continuing relevance of the Custer myth to our times, irrespective of the guise under which it appears.

Yet only so much can be done with Custer in this "Fatal Generals" vein before diminishing returns set in, accompanied by a minor backlash. "Custer Died for Your Sins" the message reads. If we can never again accept him on unqualified nineteenth-century terms, we can, perhaps, in this age of the alienated or apathetic individual, see in him a model of commitment. Responsibility for one's fellows has provided the theme for several contemporary Westerns, wherein the reluctant hero sacrifices his own safety for the sake of others. *Custer of the West* portrayed the General as the epitome of rugged individualism. "Whatever I decide to do," he warns an Indian chief, "I will do it because it is right according to my way." The film's musical score was designed to accentuate this idea. Its composer, "acutely aware of the comparison between the need for heroism in the Old West and in today's international crises," concentrated on the "emotionally charged atmosphere of heroism" surrounding the Custer story.[39] Given the context, the comparison seems unfortunate. Yet *Custer of the West* did have a global dimension, and heroic self-sacrifice is always present whenever the Custer story is told. If in his charge to glory Custer sacrificed his command as well, it was in the line of duty and, ostensibly, on society's behalf. He died for his own beliefs, or glory-lust if you will; but he also died for *our* sins. What matters from this perspective is not if what he did was right, but that he risked himself, absolutely and unreservedly, in doing it. It is the act of commitment, apart from consequence, by which we must judge him as a man — and as a model for our times.

The path to the redemption of Custer's personal legend may lie in this direction. But its signposts — unthinking devotion to country and to cause — seem to be pointing backwards to an irrevocable past. With the dropping of the Atom bombs on Japan, the old-fashioned kind of military heroism was rendered obsolete. War's attraction has always been linked

138

to the ideal of a bold individual whose manly virtues are elicited in the heat of combat. Now weaponry has superseded the individual and reduced him to an ultimate impotence. War is depersonalized. There can be no more Custers, and perhaps the world is better off without them. Custer's heroic reputation will not be easily salvaged by reference to his brand of individualistic commitment.

Where Custer goes beyond the pale, beyond all redemption in modern thought, is as the anti-hero of that explosive concept that combines both racism and militarism: genocide. Since Americans engaged in one of their periodic rediscoveries of the Indian while fighting still continued in Vietnam, the logical connection was made. Guerilla warfare in Southeast Asia has brought the soldier back to a "personalized" confrontation with the enemy, and yellow skins now serve to identify the foe just as red skins served a century ago. My Lai, an action in which a platoon under orders to "waste the enemy" destroyed a village of South Vietnamese civilians, slaughtering its occupants without regard to age or sex, stirred the American conscience. From the nation's history certain obscure episodes of the Indian wars were dredged up and made the basis of a usable past.

Arthur Kopit's play *Indians*, a minor critical success when it opened in 1964, chose Buffalo Bill instead of Custer for its symbolic anti-hero. The drama's message was driven home in an interview with an army officer after the Wounded Knee battle of 1890. "Of course innocent people have been killed," he snaps. "In war they always are. And of course our hearts go out to the innocent victims of this. But war is not a game . . . In the long run I believe what happened here at this reservation yesterday will be justified."[40] The next year, a movie, *Soldier Blue*, offered the viewer a simplistically "balanced" version of history. The story opened with the massacre of a cavalry patrol by Indians, and concluded with a far more sanguineous massacre of Indians by soldiers. The inspiration for this climax, according to the director, was the Sand Creek Battle of 1864.[41]

As for George Armstrong Custer, it became clear in *Little Big Man* why he died for our sins: his Last Stand was simply divine retribution for the Washita battle of 1868. Arthur Penn, whose film contained a graphic reconstruction of that wintertime slaughter — a bloodbath in a soft snowfall — confessed that it was his intention to ask Why? of the past. He had been personally staggered by the news of My Lai, and felt deeply that the nation must be reminded of such sordid episodes in its history if it were to avoid their repetition in the future.[42] "I sit with eyes like brown wounds" a part-Seneca poet lamented,

> and remember a yellow-haired laugh
> in a place where
> tumbleweeds blow
> and I think of Dien Bien Phu,
> and Belgian Congo, other Aryan
> last stands, sacrificial totem games,
> and a bitter laugh
> sprawls across my century-wrinkled face.[43]

Among the graffiti scrawled on walls by the American troops in Vietnam was this: "We'll bring peace to this land if we have to kill them all. CUSTER."[44]

Custer's Last Stand is unlikely to attract a latter-day Goya. It offers no horrors that have not been surpassed in the wars of the twentieth-century. But the concept of genocide, like the heroic ideal of Custer's Last Stand, has been compressed into a single work of art. *Custard's Last Stand*, a limited-edition lithograph by Warrington Colescott, a University of Wisconsin fine arts professor, shows a black-faced Custer with orange curls standing alone against the charging Indians beneath the impassive gaze of the four Great White Fathers carved on Mount Rushmore. The implication is clear: Vietnam was a war in which black skins and yellow skins died so that white skins, camped high above, aloof and secure on the summit of their democratic iconography, could continue to enjoy a life of material ease. In a sense, Colescott's lithograph is the visual equivalent of the Charleston *Journal of Commerce*'s suggestion that Doc Adams and Sitting Bull square off in a fight to the finish, thereby settling once and for all the problems of red and black and leaving America a white man's country, freed from the curse of race.

III

Custer's Last Stand has established its credentials as a popular myth by demonstrating the requisite staying power. Without altering the myth, Americans can find in it diverse meanings appropriate to the times. Indeed, because the content never undergoes basic change, the myth remains at once infinitely flexible and absolutely constant. Like that literary genre which has done so much to sustain it, the Western novel, the myth of Custer's Last Stand is a "predictable, serene, and timeless" fantasy.[45]

Adaptability is an essential quality of myth. Present concerns do not obtrude upon the primary image of Custer's Last Stand, but they do inevitably affect its current exchange value for Americans. If this were not so, the myth could not survive. It can endure any amount of critical attack, but it cannot endure prolonged neglect. Neglect, however, is unlikely. Americans need the Custer's Last Stands in their history. They are the stable reference points in a record of breathtaking change.

EPILOGUE

To assess the literature of American heroism and to discover its peculiarities, we must see how in America the compression of time and the extension of space transformed the whole problem.

Daniel J. Boorstin, *The Americans: The National Experience.*

America's Westward trek was marked off neither in miles nor in minutes, for the vastness of the land superseded both. The awesome magnitude of the country dwarfed not only its inhabitants, but the very process of time as caravans creaked into the setting sun. But timelessness was an illusion concealing the fact that time itself was running wild. William Faulkner, in summarizing the history of Yoknapatawpha County, found the words for this:

> There was no time; the next act and scene itself clearing its own stage without waiting for property-men; or rather, not even bothering to clear the stage but commencing the new act and scene right in the midst of the phantoms, the fading wraiths of that old time which had been exhausted, used up, to be no more and never return: as though the mere and simply orderly ordinary succession of days was not big enough, comprised not scope enough, and so weeks and months and years had to be condensed and compounded into one burst, one surge, one soundless roar . . .[1]

So the years rushed by during the course of Westward expansion, until their burst, their surge, their soundless roar were drowned out in the mightier thunder of the Pacific surf. "No place to go, Jody," the grandfather in one of John Steinbeck's California stories sadly remarks. Before, "it was westering and westering . . . Then we came down to the sea, and it was done."[2] All that remains for the man who had grown old with his eyes fixed on the western star is a chair on a porch, and the ocean pounding the cliffs beneath his still-impatient feet.

The West was always perceived as ephemeral, a passing phase in the national development. Hence it was always productive of instant nostalgia. "Few people even know the true definition of the term

141

'West,' " the painter George Catlin observed in the 1830's. "And where is its location? — phantom-like it flies before us as we travel, and on our way is continually gilded, before us, as we approach the setting sun."[3] Francis Parkman, too, showed an eerie awareness of the West's elusiveness. "Looking back, after the expiration of a year, upon Fort Laramie and its inmates," he wrote in 1847, "they seem less like a reality than like some fanciful picture of the olden time; so different was the scene from any which this tamer side of the world can present."[4] How much more vivid the sense of transience for a man who had experienced the West in the 1880's and 1890's. "I knew the derby hat, the smoking chimneys, the cord-binder, and the thirty-day note were upon us in a resistless surge, " Frederic Remington recalled in 1905. "I knew the wild riders and the vacant land were about to vanish forever, and the more I considered the subject the bigger the Forever loomed . . . I saw the living, breathing end of three American centuries of smoke and dust and sweat . . . .[5]

The West, Catlin's "fairy-land," was unreal by virtue of its overwhelming expanse and what Daniel Boorstin has called "the vagueness of the land."[6] Its dimensions were imposed not by geography, but by the American imagination. Like westering, the West itself was movement and change. To Catlin's question — "And where is its location?" — the answer seems to be, in the mind. For the West was an experience, not a region; it was, for Americans, an "adventure of the spirit."[7]

The Eastern reaction to Custer's Last Stand evinced a commitment to that fleeting, distant West which bred so many myths. As the poetess Laura Webb sang in the summer of the disaster,

> Far off they fought, far off they died,
> Afar their fame has spread.
> . . .on the page of future Time
> The eyes to come will see,
> Upon our distant Western wilds,
> A new Thermopylae![8]

Contemporary eyes looked beyond the horror and the death and perceived in Custer's battle a myth of the magnitude of a Thermopylae. Later eyes, removed in time as well as distance, saw only the myth. Henry Steele Commager notes that by the 1890's, "even the most recent past seemed already remote and strange:"

Indian warfare, which for two and a half centuries had been a grim reality, became a game played by children who confused King Philip's War with Custer's Last Stand . . . It had all happened only yesterday, as it were, yet already it was a ripe subject for romantic fiction and for legends . . . [To] thousands of city folk . . . the Wild West was as distant and as exotic as Salem witchcraft.[9]

This sense of removal in time was an emotional one, subject always to the shock of recognition: those events of westering so "distant and exotic" were actually "only yesterday" in history's span.

The past continued to intrude on the present. Mrs. Custer lived through the first third of the twentieth century, a handsome, white-haired woman basking in the warmth and adulation she always inspired, and fiercely devoted to her husband's memory. While she could never bring herself to visit the spot of his martyrdom, she took an active interest in the various anniversary commemorations. In 1926, she pleaded with one of the organizers of the semi-centennial activities to prevent "any memorial of any kind to be placed on that sacred battlefield to so great a coward as Col. Reno!" — and thanked him with "a heart running over with gratitude" for his part in honoring the General.[10] If the world regarded her with tender awe as some quaint relic from an ancient past, Mrs. Custer smiled back at it with an almost equal sense of wonder, marveling over such symbols of modern progress as the phonograph and motor car. Memories ceaselessly swirled through her mind, but she was not out of touch with the present, and she even had a few ideas of her own about the uses to which certain innovations could be put. The cinema, for example, struck her as having distinct possibilities in her defense of the Custer reputation, and until her death in 1933 she toyed with turning her most popular book, "Boots and Saddles;" or, Life in Dakota with General Custer, into a Movie.[11] It never happened, but Errol Flynn accomplished everything she could have hoped for just nine years later.

After Mrs. Custer's death the remaining links with the stirring days of 1876 were precious few. But even the "last great call" for survivors of the Sioux War that was issued in 1936 proved premature. Two old Indians whose boyhood memories stretched back to that bloody June Sunday on the Little Big Horn were on hand to participate in the ceremonies marking the seventy-fifth anniversary of the battle. Life magazine was duly impressed: "Incongruous though it seems in the Atomic Age, Custer's last stand, . . . which marked the last great Indian victory, occurred only 75 years ago last week."[12] Dewey Beard, a Sioux purported to be the sole remaining survivor of the battle, did not die until 1956. Only then was the living link between the present and an impossibly remote past finally snapped.

Custer's Last Stand was the plains Indians' most stunning victory. However, its effect was to hasten the end of the free, wandering life of the plains tribes, and thus the end of the "Wild West" itself. On July 8, 1876, Martin Maginnis, the territorial delegate from Montana, arose in the House of Representatives and expressed the resolution of an aroused populace. "One repulse does not give enemies final victory," he said, "and the safety of the frontiers, the peace of all the other Indian tribes, the blood of our soldiers demand that these Indians shall be pursued until they sue for peace and submit themselves to the authority of the nation."[13] In the autumn of 1876 over nine thousand soldiers, one-third of the United States' entire military strength, were concentrated in the theatre of the Sioux War. By the next spring the Indian resistance was virtually broken. Fifty years after the battle of the Little Big Horn, Mrs. Custer could observe philosophically: "It was a terrible tragedy — so many wonderful lives lost. But perhaps it was necessary in the scheme of things, for the public clamor that rose after the battle resulted in better equipment for the soldiers everywhere, and very soon the Indian warfare came to its end."[14] Very soon, indeed, had the whole nineteenth-century adventure of westering come to its end. The morning star had been eclipsed by the setting sun.

Yet in time's madcap race, a few memories were left behind as permanent mementoes of the Westward trek. Certain individuals became national heroes, and scores of over-night legends sprang up. Occasionally the two fused to produce myth. One prominent historian, annoyed by all of the attention that Custer has received, wondered why so many pages have been "wasted" on the last battle of a man who "did less toward hurrying the occupation of western America than the little-known commanders who won engagements with the Indians."[15] But precisely because it was a deviation from the relentless pace of Western conquest, because it was a temporary impediment in the path of that "resistless restless race" of pioneers, Custer's Last Stand was elevated into a realm apart. Custer, a horseback hero in an increasingly mechanized world. The Little Big Horn, an improbable name evocative of wide open spaces in an era of urbanization. Custer on that ridge above the Little Big Horn, both a distillation and a culmination of one phase of the American experience. Two hundred years after King Philip's War, just over one hundred years after Pontiac's rebellion, on the eve of the nation's Centennial, with America's horizons diminished, its geographical immensity contained, its wilderness tamed, and its youth irrevocably lost, there was Custer, perpetual Boy General, making a Last Stand for all of yesterday.

144

NOTES

Preface

[1]*New York Tribune*, July 8, 1876; quoted in Dee Brown, *The Year of the Century: 1876* (New York, 1966), 177. The reference to Custer's brothers (Tom, a captain in the Seventh, and Boston, a civilian guide) and nephew (Harry A. Reed, along for the fun) is accurate. Custer's brother-in-law, Lieut. James Calhoun, also fell at the Little Big Horn.

[2]"Echoes from the Little Bighorn: Introductory Remarks and Sources on the Sioux Campaign of 1876 and Custer's Last Fight," *Smoke Signal* (Tucson) No. 2 (Fall, 1960), 1.

[3]"The Legend of the Little Bighorn," *Corral Dust* (Washington, D.C.), I (June, 1956), 9. Also see Utley's "But for Custer's Sins," *Western Historical Quarterly*, II (Oct., 1971), 357.

[4]"About Clay Fisher," *Westerners Brand Book* (Chicago), X (Oct., 1953), 59.

[5]See Robin W. Winks' excellent anthology *The Historian as Detective: Essays on Evidence* (New York, 1969), 281.

[6]*The Custer Myth: A Source Book of Custeriana* (Harrisburg, Pa., 1953), vii.

Chapter 1

[1]William Morris, ed., *The American Heritage Dictionary of the English Language* (Boston, 1969), 868-9.

[2]*Virgin Land: The American West as Symbol and Myth* (Cambridge, Mass., 1950), vii. Richard E. Sykes, in "American Studies and the Concept of Culture: A Theory and Method," *American Quarterly*, XV (Summer, 1963, Pt. 2), 253-70, criticizes the use of such imprecise terms as "myth" in cultural studies, but the alternatives that he suggests would substitute a narrow precision for general coherence.

[3]Gregor Sebba, "Symbol and Myth in Modern Rationalistic Societies," *Truth, Myth, and Symbol*, ed. by Thomas J. J. Altizer, William A. Beardslee, J. Harvey Young (Englewood Cliffs, N.J., 1962), 145.

[4]"Theology: Heretic or Prophet?," *Time*, LXXXVIII (Nov. 11, 1966), 64.

[5]See Kent L. Steckmesser, *The Western Hero in History and Legend* (Norman, Okla., 1965), 163-237.

[6]Marshall W. Fishwick, "The Making of a Hero," *Saturday Review*, XLVII (Aug. 1, 1964), 13. See also Fishwick's *American Heroes: Myth and Reality* (Washington, D.C., 1954), 6, and his *The Hero, American Style* (New York, 1969), 1-3.

[7]"Nice Guys and Losers," *Saturday Evening Post,* CCXXXIX (Aug. 27, 1966), 84. Custer is characterized as only one "among our great failures." Orrin E. Klapp, in *Heroes, Villains, and Fools: The Changing American Character* (Englewood Cliffs, N.J., 1962), 47, notes that Custer is often regarded as a martyr, and that to "about one out of four raters" in a poll on social types "the martyr is a fool. . . . General Custer is a hero with the underside of a fool."

[8]Jack Rice, "Custer Fights On, From Bar to Bar," *St. Louis Post-Dispatch,* Dec. 20, 1959. Also see Richard P. Frisbie, *How to Peel a Sour Grape: An Impractical Guide to Successful Failure* (New York, 1965), 3.

[9]"Heroism" (1841), in *The Selected Writings of Ralph Waldo Emerson,* ed. by Brooks Atkinson (New York, 1940), 253.

[10]*Heroes, Villains, and Fools,* 7.

[11]*Trails Plowed Under* (New York, 1927), 191.

[12]J. R. (Bob) Kelly, *The Battle of the Little Big Horn: Requiem for the Men in the Shadows* (Omaha, ca. 1957). This illustrates Dixon Wecter's remark that, while "sainthood or godhead may seem terms too strong from a description of American hero-worship," in the United States "the birthdays of heroes are saints' days, and the scenes of their deeds are shrines." (*The Hero in America: A Chronicle of Hero-Worship* [New York, 1941], 8-9.)

[13]For an annotated bibliography of Custer biography see Appendix A.

[14]Such is the interest in Custer that his court-martial has been the subject of four monographs: Robert A. Murray, "The Custer Court Martial," *Annals of Wyoming,* XXXVI (Oct., 1964), 175-84; Milton B. Halsey, Jr., "The Court-Martial of Brevet Major General George A. Custer," *Trail Guide* (Kansas City), XIII (Sept., 1968); Lawrence A. Frost, *The Court-Martial of General George Armstrong Custer* (Norman, Okla., 1968), which prints verbatim the record of the trial; and John O. Shoemaker, "The Custer Court-Martial," *Military Review,* LI (Oct., 1971), 36-47.

[15]"Military Expedition Against the Sioux Indians," *House Exec. Doc. No. 184,* 44 Cong., 1 sess., 18.

[16]Barry C. Johnson, ed., "With Gibbon Against the Sioux in 1876: The Field Diary of Lt. William L. English," *English Westerners' Brand Book,* IX (Oct., 1966), 5.

[17]Captain Benteen, quoted in P. E. Byrne, *Soldiers of the Plains* (New York, 1926), 174.

[18]Major Reno's testimony in William A. Graham, ed., *The Reno Court of Inquiry: Abstract of the Official Record of Proceedings* (Harrisburg, Pa., 1954), 212. The Court of Inquiry was convened in 1879 at Reno's request to investigate mounting criticism of his conduct at the Little Big Horn. After the battle, Reno was ever on trial before the public, and his version of the last order that he received from Custer was prime evidence in his defense.

[19]Fred Dustin, "Bibliography of the Battle of the Little Big Horn," in William A. Graham, *The Custer Myth: A Source Book of Custeriana* (Harrisburg, Pa., 1953), 382-405. One example of the continuing interest in Custer's Last Stand is the Little Big Horn Associates, a group formed in 1966 devoted to seeking and preserving "the truth about the Battle of the Little Big Horn and all of Custeriana."

[20]Norman Maclean, "Custer's Last Fight a Ritual Drama," *Westerners Brand Book* (Chicago), XV (Oct., 1958), 57. President Kennedy, for example, oriented a German audience to American history by referring to Custer's Last Stand.

[21]"The Revenge of Rain-in-the-Face," *Youth's Companion,* L (Mar. 1, 1877), 68.

[22]*Atlanta Times,* July 9, 1876, 2.

[23]For the mood of this period in American history, see Robert H. Wiebe, *The Search for Order, 1877-1920* (New York, 1967); and Paul F. Boller, Jr., *American*

Thought in Transition: The Impact of Evolutionary Naturalism, 1865-1900 (Chicago, 1969).

[24]"The Hue-and-Cry against the Indians," *Nation*, XXIII (July 20, 1876), 40-1; and "Factory System for the Indian Reservations," *ibid.*, (July 27, 1876), 58-9.

[25]"Expedition to the Black Hills," *Senate Exec. Doc. No. 32*, 43 Cong., 2 sess., 2-3.

[26]Edward Jacker, "Who Is to Blame for the Little Big Horn Disaster?," *American Catholic Quarterly Review*, I (Oct., 1876), 712.

[27]"The Indian War," *Constitution* (Atlanta), July 7, 1876, 2; and *Weekly Commonwealth* (Atlanta), July 18, 1876, 1.

[28]*New York Times*, July 8, 1876, 4.

Chapter 2

[1]"Annual Report of Lieutenant Edward Maguire, Corps of Engineers, for the Fiscal Year Ending June 30, 1876," *Annual Report of the Chief of Engineers to the Secretary of War for the Year 1876*, Pt. III, *House Exec. Doc. No. 1, Pt. 2*, 44 Cong., 2 sess., 702.

[2]"General Custer," *Saturday Review* (London), XLII (July 29, 1876), 135. The author of the *New York Herald* poem, Joseph I. C. Clarke, published his tribute anonymously. It was reprinted under his name in the Boston *Pilot*, a Catholic weekly, for July 29, 1876, and thereafter appeared frequently, usually uncredited and with many of its political references deleted.

[3]*Patriotic Gore: Studies in the Literature of the American Civil War* (New York, 1961), 479.

[4]*The Song of the Indian Wars* (New York, 1925), 134.

[5]"Custer," *New Orleans Republican*, July 23, 1876, 6.

[6]"The Revenge of Rain-in-the-Face," *Youth's Companion*, L (Mar. 1, 1877), 68.

[7]"Custer's Last Charge," *Army and Navy Journal*, July 15, 1876, special sheet.

[8]"Custer's Farewell," *Once Their Home; or, Our Legacy from the Dahkotahs* (Chicago, 1892), 253.

[9]"On the Big Horn," *Atlantic Monthly*, LIX (Apr., 1887), 433.

[10]William Ludlow, "Custer's Last Charge." Unidentified newspaper clipping (1876) in the Elizabeth B. Custer Collection, Custer Battlefield National Monument, "Clippings Enclosed in Correspondence . . ." Hereafter cited as Custer, "Clippings Enclosed."

[11]A. T. Lee, "The Wrath of the Black Hills," *Army and Navy Journal*, Aug. 12, 1876.

[12]"Down the Little Big Horn," *The Poems of Francis Brooks*, ed. by Wallace Rice (Chicago, 1898), 131.

[13]"Little Big Horn," *Poems* (New York, 1895), 236.

[14]Anon., "The Song of Custer and His Men," *Chicago Daily Tribune*, July 22, 1876, 9 (from the *St. Paul Pioneer-Press*).

[15]Whittaker, "Custer's Last Charge," special sheet.

[16]Longfellow, "The Revenge of Rain-in-the-Face," 68.

[17]"Custer's Last Battle," *Thorns and Roses* (Evansville, Ind., 1895), 66.

[18]"The Revenge of Rain-in-the-Face," 68. For a concise, authoritative discussion of the Rain-in-the-Face-killed-Custer fable, see Robert M. Utley,

Custer and the Great Controversy: The Origin and Development of a Legend (Los Angeles, 1962), 126-31.

[19]Thomas Beer, The Mauve Decade: American Life at the End of the Nineteenth Century (New York, 1926), 31.

[20]Thomas Rossman in the New York Daily News, July 31, 1885. From a copy in Benteen's hand, title not indicated (private collection).

[21]"Ballad of the Sabre Cross and 7," In Various Moods: Poems and Verses (New York, 1910), 18. The phrase "Hill of Fear" appeared in a revised version of the poem printed in Wallace and Frances Rice, eds., The Humbler Poets (Second Series): A Collection of Newspaper and Periodical Verse, 1885 to 1910 (Chicago, 1911), 324.

[22]Song of the Indian Wars, 151-3.

[23]J. S. Carvell, "In Memoriam," Campaigns of General Custer in the North-West, and the Final Surrender of Sitting Bull by Judson Elliott Walker (New York, 1966 [1881]), 120.

[24]C. B. Davis, "Custer," Teepee Book, I (June, 1915), 2.

[25]Edmund Clarence Stedman, "Custer," New York Tribune, July 13, 1876, 5.

[26]A. P. Williams, "Custer," New York Mail, ca. June, 1887. Newspaper clipping in Custer, "Clippings Enclosed."

[27]I. E., "Custer's Last Battle," Cincinnati Commercial, July 19, 1876, 5.

[28]Song of the Indian Wars, 105, 141. This represents the Indians' opinion of Custer, not Neihardt's.

[29]See Gerald M. Van Dyke, "Battle of Washita," Singing Wire, II (Nov., 1968); and Maurice Kenny, "Monahsetah . . . A Cheyenne Girl," Akwesasne Notes, VI (Late Autumn, 1972), 48. For positive assessments of the Washita, see Freeman E. Miller, "The Battle of the Washita," Songs from the South-West Country (New York, 1898), 19-26; Jessie G. Eble, "The Battle of the Washita — 1868," The Red Trail (New York, 1931), 42-6; and Daisy Lemon Coldiron, "Custer on the Washita (1868)," Songs of Oklahoma (Dallas, 1935), 32-5.

[30]"Custer," Custer, and Other Poems (Chicago, 1896), 133.

[31]"Custer," 5.

[32]"Custer," 2.

[33]Laura S. Webb, Custer's Immortality. A Poem, with biographical sketches of the chief actors in the late Tragedy of the Wilderness (New York, 1876), 11.

[34]"Custer's Last Charge," 3.

[35]"General Custer," 135.

[36]"Custer and His Three Hundred," Frank Leslie's Illustrated Newspaper, XLII (July 29, 1876), 342.

[37]M. S., "General Custer — In Memoriam," Army and Navy Journal, July 22, 1876.

[38]Whittaker, "Custer's Last Charge," special sheet.

[39]Stedman, "Custer," 5.

[40]"Custer and His Three Hundred," 342.

[41]Edwin Haviland Miller, ed., Walt Whitman: The Correspondence, 1876-1885 (New York, 1964), 53.

[42]"A Death-Sonnet for Custer," New York Tribune, July 10, 1876, 5. Retitled "From Far Dakota's Cañons," Whitman's poem made its first appearance in Leaves of Grass in the book's seventh (1881) edition.

[43]Horace Traubell, With Walt Whitman in Camden, 3 vols. (New York, 1961 [1906-14]), I, 60. Perhaps the "noble motive" was still in Hay's mind four years later when he wrote in "Miles Keogh's Horse," Atlantic Monthly, XLV (Feb., 1880), 214, that

> . . . the sword of Custer,
> In his disastrous fall,
> Flashed out a blaze that charmed the world
> And glorified his pall.

[44]"The Coming Anniversary," New York Herald, July 3, 1876, 4. Ironically, the same page carried an editorial on the Sioux War that expressed some concern about the safety of the troops in the field.

[45]July 8, 1876, in Congressional Record, 44 Cong., 1 sess., 4473.

[46]See Brian W. Dippie, " 'What Will Congress Do about It?:' The Congressional Reaction to the Little Big Horn Disaster," North Dakota History, XXXVII (Summer, 1970), 160-89.

[47]W. E. Pabor, "Little Horn, June 25, 1876," Valley Home Farm (Colo.), July 10, 1876; repr. in Westerners Brand Book (Chicago), XV (Oct., 1958), 64.

[48]Harper's Weekly, XX (July 29, 1876), 617-8.

[49]Custer's Immortality, 7-8, 12-3, 72. Bryant wrote Mrs. Webb on July 26, 1876; facsimile, between pp. 2 and 3.

[50]Wilcox, "Custer," 134. Elizabeth was the General's wife.

[51]See Minnie Dubbs Millbrook, "A Monument to Custer," Montana, the Magazine of Western History, XXIV (Spring, 1974), 18-33.

[52]"Unveiling of Wilson Macdonald's Statue of General George A. Custer at West Point, New York, Saturday, August 30th, 1879" (leaflet in Custer Battlefield National Monument Pamphlet File Cat. Nos. 3778, 3779); leaflet printing of Morford's fourteen-verse song "Hail! and Farewell to Custer" (Cat. No. 3781); and Morford, "Chivalry's Afterglow," in "Address at the Unveiling of a Statue of General Custer at West Point, on August 30, 1879, by Algernon Sydney Sullivan . . .," in Algernon Sydney Sullivan by Anne Middleton Holmes (New York, 1929), 144-7.

[53]Al Duval, Cal Rogers and Marc Fredricks, "Mr. Custer," c. Bamboo Music, Inc. (BMI), ca. 1960.

[54]A. P. Kerr, "Custer's Last Charge: June 25, 1886." Unidentified newspaper clipping (1886) in Custer, "Clippings Enclosed."

[55]Sam T. Clover, "Decoration Day on the Little Big Horn," Army Magazine, June, 1894.

[56]"Where Custer Fell," Songs from the South-West Country, 54.

[57]Wilbur Edgerton Sanders, "On Custer Hill," Contributions to the Historical Society of Montana, VII (1910), 135.

[58]William Stafford, "At the Custer Monument," Oregon Signatures ed. by R. D. Brown, Thomas Kranidas and Faith G. Norris (Monmouth, Ore., 1959), 84.

[59]"Sunrise on Custer Battle Field," Teepee Book, II (June, 1916), 13.

[60]Keogh to his brother Tom, June 1, 1869, in Francis B. Taunton, ed., "The Man Who Rode Comanche," Sidelights of the Sioux War (London, 1967), 77. The best account of Keogh's career is G. A. Hayes-McCoy, Captain Myles Walter Keogh, United States Army, 1840-1876 (Dublin, 1965).

[61]See Barron Brown, Comanche: The Sole Survivor of All the Forces in Custer's Last Stand, the Battle of the Little Big Horn (Kansas City, 1935); Edward S. Luce, Keogh, Comanche and Custer (St. Louis, 1939); and Anthony A. Amaral, Comanche: The Horse That Survived the Custer Massacre (Los Angeles, 1961), for the ascertainable facts about Comanche. Comanche's story is the most popular of the Custer legends possibly because it is basically true. However, it should be pointed out that Comanche was not the only cavalry horse to survive the Last Stand. The Indians captured those in better shape, while the relief column destroyed those in worse shape.

⁶²Edgar I. Stewart, "The Literature of the Custer Fight," *Pacific Northwesterner* (Spokane), I (Winter, 1956-57), 8.

⁶³"Miles Keogh's Horse," 215.

⁶⁴"Old Comanche," *Army and Navy Journal*, Apr. 27, 1878.

⁶⁵"Down the Little Big Horn," 131-2.

⁶⁶"Old Commanche," *Paha Sapa Tawoyake: Wade's Stories* (Mandan, N.D., n.d.), 80. Wade's spelling of Comanche is one common variation; it has also spelled "Comanchee."

⁶⁷See "Kansas 'U' Editor Says 'No' to Hardin Commanche Plan," *Rocky Mountain Husbandman* (Great Falls), Jan. 26, 1939; "Render unto Montana that which Is Montana's," *Montana Standard*, Nov. 1, 1953; and "Comanche's Last Stand," *Newsweek*, XXX (Sept. 15, 1947), 25.

⁶⁸"Cavalry-on-Wheels," repr. in Amaral, *Comanche*, 60-1.

⁶⁹F. Bandy and Johnny Horton, "Comanche (The Brave Horse)," c. Hi-Lo Music, Inc. and Magic Circle Pub. Co. (BMI).

⁷⁰See Michael Goodwin, "Films: *Little Big Man*," *Rolling Stone* No. 77 (Mar. 4, 1971), 58.

⁷¹William J. May, "On the Little Big Horn." A recording of this, sung by Cliff Carl, was released in 1961 under the auspices of the Historical Society of Montana, Helena.

⁷²45 rpm recording by the U. S. Army Band and Chorus; and Verne D. Campbell, "Armor and Cavalry Music," *Armor*, LXXX (Mar.-Apr., 1971), 33-4.

⁷³*San Antonio Express*, July 26, 1876, 3.

⁷⁴Melbourne C. Chandler, *Of GarryOwen in Glory: The History of the Seventh United States Cavalry Regiment* (Annandale, Va., 1960), 412-5.

⁷⁵*Richmond Whig*; repr. in the *Dallas Daily Herald*, July 16, 1876, 3.

⁷⁶See D. W. Brogan, *The American Character* (New York, c. 1954), 181.

⁷⁷Walter Carey, "Custer's Last Ride," *Latrobe* (Pa.) *Advance* (1876?). Undated clipping in the Nettie Bowen Smith *Scrap Book*, 7, Bancroft Library, University of California, Berkeley. Hereafter cited as Smith *Scrap Book*.

⁷⁸Miller, "Custer and His Three Hundred," 342.

⁷⁹Capt. Jack Crawford, "The Death of Custer," *The Poet Scout: A Book of Song and Story* (New York, 1886), 107.

⁸⁰Ludlow, "Custer's Last Charge."

⁸¹Bigney, "Custer," 6.

⁸²Morford, "Chivalry's Afterglow," 146.

⁸³"A Monument to Custer," *New York Herald*, July 12, 1876, 6.

⁸⁴"The Last Charge" (*New York Post*, 1876?). Unidentified clipping, Smith *Scrap Book*, 39.

Chapter 3

¹*The Frontier Re-examined* ed. by John Francis McDermott (Urbana, Ill., 1967), 95.

²See Don Russell, *Custer's List: A Checklist of Pictures Relating to the Battle of the Little Big Horn* (Fort Worth, 1969). No claim to exhaustiveness is made by Russell, whose *Custer's Last* (Fort Worth, 1968) is the best work on the subject of Custer art.

[3]William H. Mace, *A School History of the United States* (Chicago, 1904), v. A count based on Russell's *Custer's List* and my own research turns up fourteen different school texts that included ten different Last Stands in the period 1876-1926. Many of these were standard textbooks used over and over again in various editions.

[4]This is the caption under a painting by Harold Von Schmidt in *Esquire*, XXXIV (Sept., 1950), 53-4.

[5]*San Antonio Express*, July 15, 1876, 2.

[6]*Campaigns of General Custer in the North-West and the Final Surrender of Sitting Bull* (New York, 1966 [1881]), 114.

[7]*Detroit News*; reprinted in the *Denison* (Tex.) *Daily News*, Aug. 13, 1876, 6. Mannion's personal heroics are recounted at great length, and his letter is in effect the very first dime novel about Custer's Last Stand.

[8]Fuch's lithograph and Elder's painting are both reproduced in Russell, *Custer's Last*, 23, 50.

[9]Frederick Whittaker, *A Complete Life of Gen. George A. Custer* (New York, 1876), facing p. 606.

[10]The Steinegger lithograph is discussed and its derivation illustrated in Brian W. Dippie, "Brush, Palette and the Custer Battle: A Second Look," *Montana, the Magazine of Western History*, XXIV (Winter, 1974), 64-5. Cary did a later drawing of the Last Stand that was also turned into a popular print (see *ibid.*, 66), while Waud did a second Last Stand that was fairly widely emulated.

[11]*McClure's Magazine*, XI (Sept., 1898), 447.

[12]For three extensive pictographic accounts of the Little Big Horn, see: Garrick Mallery, "Picture Writing of the American Indians," *Tenth Annual Report of the Bureau of Ethnology, 1888-89* (Washington, D.C., 1893), 563-6, Plates XXXIX-XLVIII (Red Horse); Helen H. Blish, *A Pictographic History of the Oglala Sioux* (Lincoln, Neb., 1967), 35-7, 212-72, Plates 126-85 (Amos Bad Heart Bull); and James H. Howard, *The Warrior Who Killed Custer: The Personal Narrative of Chief Joseph White Bull* (Lincoln, Neb., 1968), 51-62, 69-70, Plates 15-22, 30. White Bull's drawings deal exclusively with his own exploits, while those by Red Horse and Bad Heart Bull provide an overview of the fighting as well.

[13]Atwood Manley, *Some of Frederic Remington's North Country Associations* (Ogdensburg, N.Y., 1961), 17, 23.

[14]Frederic Remington, *Pony Tracks* (Norman, Okla., 1961 [1895]), 14.

[15]Ben Merchant Vorpahl, *My Dear Wister: The Frederic Remington-Owen Wister Letters* (Palo Alto, Calif., 1972), 279. Remington did express his approval of certain subalterns with Reno and Benteen — for example, Lieutenant Luther Hare. See "A Gallant American Officer" (1900), reprinted in Douglas Allen, *Frederic Remington and the Spanish-American War* (New York, 1971), 128-31.

[16]See James D. Horan, *The Life and Art of Charles Schreyvogel: Painter-Historian of the Indian-Fighting Army of the American West* (New York, 1969), 31-40.

[17]*Woman's Home Companion*, XXX (June, 1903), 31.

[18]*Cosmopolitan*, XI (July, 1891), 302.

[19]The oil *Custer's Last Charge* (ca. 1895) is reproduced in the Paine Art Center catalogue *Frederic Remington: A Retrospective Exhibition of Painting and Sculpture* (Oshkosh, Wisc., 1967), Plate 30, and the watercolor *Custer's Last Stand* in Roy Meredith, *The American Wars: A Pictorial History from Quebec to Korea, 1755-1953* (Cleveland, 1955), 203. I am indebted to Edward B. Mayo of The Museum of Fine Arts, Houston, for the opportunity to examine the original watercolor at my leisure.

[20]*Harper's Weekly*, XXXV (Jan. 10, 1891), 23-5.

[21]*American Heritage*, VIII (Feb., 1957), 3. *The Last Stand* has also been used to illustrate the Custer battle on two documentary television programs about the "real West," in the National Geographic Society's *America's Historylands: Touring Our Landmarks of Liberty* (Washington, D.C., 1962), 514-5; and in the popular history ed. by Jay Monaghan, *The Book of the American West* (New York, 1963), 582.

[22]*The Complete Poetical Works of John Greenleaf Whittier* (Library Edition) (Boston, 1904), 470; and *The Way of an Indian* (New York, 1906), facing p. 216.

[23]William A. Allen, *Adventures with Indians and Game; or, Twenty Years in the Rocky Mountains* (Chicago, 1903), facing p. 62. Russell's painting was reproduced a year later as *Custer's Last Stand* in *Outing*, XLV (Dec., 1904), 271, and not again until Dippie, "Brush, Palette and the Custer Battle," 67. The Davis painting (1897), nicely engraved, appeared in Edward S. Ellis, *The History of Our Country . . .* (Cincinnati, 1905), VI, facing p. 1452.

[24]For the correct title of the pen and ink, see H. E. Britzman, "More Custer Pictures," *Westerners Brand Book* (Chicago), IV (July-Aug., 1947), 30.

[25]*Scribner's Magazine*, XXXVII (Feb., 1905), 161.

[26]Wilbur F. Gordy, *A History of the United States for Schools* (New York, 1910 ed.), facing p. 378, used the Russell painting to illustrate "Indian Warfare in the West."

[27]See Dippie, "Brush, Palette and the Custer Battle," 67.

[28]Philip G. Cole, *Montana in Miniature: the Pictorial History of Montana from Early Exploration to Early Statehood* ed. by Van Kirke Nelson and Cato K. Butler (Kalispell, Mont., 1966), 92-105, reproduces Seltzer's seven Custer subjects. Russell's pen drawing can be found in M. I. McCreight, *Firewater and Forked Tongues: A Sioux Chief Interprets U.S. History* (Pasadena, Calif., 1947), facing p. 111.

[29]Dunton's oil was reproduced in *The Mentor* No. 85 (1915), 10; and Elwell's in *Montana: the Magazine of Western History*, VII (Spring, 1957), 41. Both artists did other work on the Custer theme.

[30]See, for example, the Last Stands by Theodore B. Pitman (1923), W. R. Leigh (1939), and Herbert Morton Stoops (1948).

[31]Helen Fitzgerald Sanders, "Edgar Samuel Paxson: Pioneer, Scout and Artist," *Overland Monthly*, Ser. 2, XLVIII (Sept., 1906), 183; and, for a reproduction of the 1906 watercolor, Dippie, "Brush, Palette and the Custer Battle," 61.

[32]M. E. Thalheimer, *The Eclectic History of the United States* (Cincinnati, 1881), 336.

[33]*Harper's New Monthly Magazine*, LXXX (Apr., 1890), 732; George A. Forsyth, *The Story of the Soldier* (New York, 1900), facing p. 327; and *Harper's Weekly*, XLI (Sept. 25, 1897), 949. Bad as it is — and some of its awkwardness might be blamed on an inferior engraving job — Zogbaum's Last Stand has not been entirely without influence. Compare it to the version by A. G. Schmidt in Ella Wheeler Wilcox, *Custer and Other Poems* (Chicago, 1896), facing p. 94.

[34]Cyrus Townsend Brady, "War with the Sioux, Pt. II: The Last of Custer," *Pearson's Magazine*, XII (Sept., 1904), 286.

[35]Cyrus Townsend Brady, *Britton of the Seventh: A Romance of Custer and the Great Northwest* (Chicago, 1914), 366-7.

[36]For Deming's preliminary sketch, see *The Mentor* No. 281 (July, 1926), 56; and, for the finished oil, *New York Times*, June 20, 1926, Sect. 8, 3. It is also reproduced in Russell, *Custer's Last*, 48.

[37]"The Pictorial Record of the Old West, IV: Custer's Last Stand," *Kansas Historical Quarterly*, XIV (Nov., 1946), 390.

[38]"Fact and Fiction in the Documentary Art of the American West," 90-1.

³⁹Pitman's oil was painted expressly for, and first appeared as a plate in, Homer W. Wheeler, *The Frontier Trail: or From Cowboy to Colonel* (Los Angeles, 1923), facing p. 216. For Stephens' Last Stand, see Charles Morris, *A History of the United States of America, Its People, and Its Institutions* (Philadelphia, 1898), 424, or any later edition.

⁴⁰Du Mont's comments appear in his "Theodore Baldwin Pitman — A Tribute," *Westerners Brand Book* (N.Y.), IV, 1 (1957), 12. Du Mont described the painting with particular attention to its details and with equal enthusiasm in "Custer's Last Stand, No. 111," *Westerners Brand Book* (Chicago), IX (Feb., 1953), 90-1. The oil is reproduced in color on the cover of John E. Parsons and John S. du Mont, *Firearms in the Custer Battle* (Harrisburg, Pa., 1953).

⁴¹Eggenhofer's illustrations for Margaret Leighton, *The Story of General Custer* (New York, 1954), included the Last Stand in oil and pen and ink. A different painting appeared in *Adventure*, CXXIX (Sept., 1955), 28-9, while a second pen and ink, with a light color wash over it, illustrated Don Sharkey, Sister Margaret and Philip J. Furlong, *The Making of Our Nation* (New York, 1955), 300. Two other Eggenhofer Last Stands from this period are reproduced in Barron Brown, *Comanche* (New York, 1973 ed.), frontis, xvi-xvii.

⁴²Letter to the author, Aug. 9, 1964. By 1966, there were indications that the wheel of historical interpretation might rotate once again when Cheyenne historian John Stands in Timber revealed that a select "suicide squad" of young warriors did lead a fierce charge up Custer Hill resulting in the total annihilation of the troopers there. ("Last Ghastly Moments at the Little Bighorn," *American Heritage*, XVII [Apr., 1966], 14-21, 72.)

⁴³Color reproductions of *To the Last Man* were distributed with *Westerners Brand Book* (N.Y.), IV, 1 (1957).

⁴⁴The only accessible reproduction is as the frontispiece to Charles Kuhlman, *Legend Into History: The Custer Mystery (An Analytical Study of the Battle of the Little Big Horn)*(Harrisburg, Pa., 1952).

⁴⁵Hoskins' oil was especially commissioned for Graham, *Custer Myth*, and served as both the endpaper and dust jacket illustration. Pp. vii-x discuss the painting's concept and execution and provide a "Key to the Action."

⁴⁶Five Reedstrom drawings, originally distributed individually to members of the Little Big Horn Associates, are sold as a set by The Old Army Press, Ft. Collins, Colo. Reedstrom's oil was reproduced as a postcard by Petley Studios, Phoenix, and is discussed in a leaflet by Jay Charles, *The Custer Exhibit: Private Collection of E. L. Reedstrom* (n.p., ca. 1966).

⁴⁷Wayne Gard, "Joe Grandee: A Painter of the Old West," *American Artist*, XXXI (Summer, 1967), 85; conversation with Grandee, Jan. 25, 1968, Ft. Worth, Tex.; and for reproductions of three of his Custer subjects, Joy Schultz, *The West Still Lives: A Book Based on the Paintings and Sculpture of Joe Ruiz Grandee* (Dallas, 1970), and The R. W. Norton Art Gallery, *The Old West Pictorialized by Joe Ruiz Grandee* (Shreveport, La., 1971), 13.

⁴⁸See *George Armstrong Custer and His 7th Cavalry at the Battle of the Little Big Horn 1876* (Helena, Mont., 1955), 12-5, 23-5.

⁴⁹"Details of the Indian Massacre," *New York Herald*, July 8, 1876, 6.

⁵⁰*New York Herald*, July 15, 1876, 4.

⁵¹*American Heritage*, XXI (June, 1970), 103.

⁵²Letter to the author, Feb. 20, 1963. For a recent selection of Ralston's work on the Custer theme, see Richard Upton, comp., *The Custer Adventure* (Ft. Collins, Colo., 1975).

⁵³*The Hero in America: A Chronicle of Hero-Worship* (New York, 1941), 14.

⁵⁴Von Schmidt anticipated his *Esquire* last Stand in two oils illustrating a short

story and a movie based on the Custer battle. All three paintings are reproduced in Walt Reed, *Harold Von Schmidt Draws and Paints the Old West* (Flagstaff, Ariz. 1971), 131, 134, 135.

[55]*Collier's*, CXXVII (June 30, 1951), 30; and Edgar I. Stewart, *Custer's Luck* (Norman, Okla., 1955), 485, fn. Reusswig's preliminary sketch is reproduced in Frederick J. Dockstader, *The American Indian Observed* (New York, 1971), 30; while a later, less satisfying version is reproduced in Reussig's *A Picture Report of the Custer Fight* (New York, 1967), along with a number of sketches attesting to his continuing interest in the subject.

[56]See *Montana, the Magazine of Western History*, XVI (Spring, 1965), front cover, for a good color reproduction.

[57]The original *Last Rally* was for many years in the possession of the H. J. Heinz Company, Pittsburgh. What might be a later copy, with a number of modifications introduced during its restoration, is in the Memphis Museum, Memphis, Tenn. A smaller version from which a lithograph was made some time between 1881 and 1885 is in the Woolaroc Museum collection, and a color reproduction of it appears in the guidebook *Woolaroc Museum* by Ke Mo Ha [Patrick Patterson] (Bartlesville, Okla., 1965), 52.

[58]"'Custer's Last Rally,'" *Prose Works 1892: Volume I, Specimen Days* ed. by Floyd Stovall (New York, 1963), 275-6, 354. This first appeared in the *New York Tribune*, Aug. 15, 1881, and, along with several other reviews lauding the Americanism of Mulvany's work, was reprinted in *Press Comments on John Mulvany's Great Painting of Custer's Last Rally* (n.p., ca. 1883).

[59] [Young E.] Allison, "Custer's Last Rally," *Courier-Journal* (Louisville, Ky.), ca. Dec. 18, 1881, and *Daily Journal* (Kansas City), Mar. 2, 1881; both quoted in Robert Taft, *Artists and Illustrators of the Old West, 1850-1900* (New York, 1953), 140, 136. Since Mulvany did most of his work on *Custer's Last Rally* in Kansas City, an understandable note of local pride is evident in the *Daily Journal* piece.

[60]*Artists and Illustrators*, 142.

[61]Sanders, "Edgar Samuel Paxson," 83.

[62]Antoinette E. Simons, "Worked Twenty Years on One Picture," *American Magazine*, LXXX (July, 1915), 50.

[63]See Franz R. Stenzel, "E. S. Paxson — Montana Artist," *Montana, the Magazine of Western History*, XIII (Autumn, 1963), 63-5.

[64]"Montana; or The End of Jean-Jacques Rousseau," *An End to Innocence: Essays on Culture and Politics* (Boston, 1955), 138.

[65]Letter from William Edgar Paxson to the author, Mar. 19, 1967. For the painting's sale, see: "Custers' [sic] Last Stand: Painting Battle Settled," *Los Angeles Herald-Examiner*, Dec. 2, 1963, B-5; and "Wyoming Gains 'Custer' Art," *New York Times*, Dec. 3, 1963, 43.

[66]Harold McCracken, quoted in an advertisement for color prints of Paxson's oil, *True West*, XII (Oct., 1964), 55. For the first color reproduction made of the painting see *True West*, XI (Oct., 1963), front cover, and, in the same issue, William Edgar Paxson, "'Custer's Last Stand:' the Painting and the Artist," 14-6, 52-3, for a a brief history that reproduces some of Paxson's preliminary sketches.

[67]Kate Hammond Fogarty, *The Story of Montana* (New York, 1916), 184.

[68]Since an application for the painting's copyright was filed with the Library of Congress on April 26, 1886, it seems reasonable that 1886 was the completion date. Given to the Seventh Cavalry in 1895, stored, rediscovered and restored and then hung in the Officers' Club at Fort Bliss, Tex., in 1938, the Adams oil was destroyed by fire in 1946. But two side panels that had accompanied the original painting, one of Custer as a boy dreaming of martial glory, the other of his body on the battlefield at Little Big Horn, were found in 1967 after disappearing around

154

the turn of the century. See Don Russell, "Those Long-Lost Custer Panels," *Pacific Historian*, XI (Fall, 1967), 28-35.

[69]*Artists and Illustrators*, 129-30. The figure usually quoted is one million copies — an estimate that has more symbolic than literal value. Thomas J. Carroll of Anheuser-Busch, Inc., pointed out to me in a letter dated Feb. 7, 1967, that the million figure has been appearing in newspaper and magazine articles since 1954. The source of this total is Roland Krebs and Percy J. Orthwein, *Making Friends Is Our Business: 100 Years of Anheuser-Busch* (St. Louis, 1953), 39, 329. The figure was quickly picked up by others, for example, "The Baron of Beer," *Time*, LXVI (July 11, 1955), 82. Actually, some 150,000 copies were distributed between 1896 and 1946; since then, "approximately 25 to 30 thousand" more have been sent out by Anheuser-Busch (this, Mr. Carroll writes, is an educated guess). Also, since about 1952, two outside printing firms have handled personal requests for copies, and although no figures are available it is doubtful that enough have been sold to push the total number of prints distributed much past 200,000.

[70]Gerald Carson, "The Saloon," *American Heritage*, XIV (Apr., 1963), 29. Also see Stanton G. Mockler, " 'Custer's Last Stand' Is Still a Popular Painting," in Gurdon Simmons and Ralph Louis Meyer, comps., *This is Your America*, III (New York, 1943), 101-3.

[71]*The Tastemakers* (New York, 1954), 326.

[72]"The Emergence of the Plains Indian as the Symbol of the North American Indian," *Indian Life on the Upper Missouri* (Norman, Okla., 1968), 187-203.

[73]Ralph K. Andrist, *The Long Death: The Last Days of the Plains Indian* (New York, 1964), 3.

[74]"Phonies of the Old West," *American Mercury*, LXVIII (Feb., 1949), 234-5.

[75]"Massacre," *Saturday Evening Post*, CCXIX (Feb. 22, 1947), 142.

[76]*Cavalry Scout* (New York, 1958), 184-5.

[77]Harley Elliott, "Custer Like a Painting in the Greasy Grass," *All Beautyfull & Foolish Souls* (Trumansburg, N.Y., 1974), 22.

[78]*Sitting Bull: Champion of the Sioux* (Norman, Okla., rev. ed. 1957), 178.

[79]"Bigger Than Life," *Time*, LXXXVII (June 17, 1966), 110.

[80]*A Garden of Sand* (New York, 1972), 162, 167.

[81]*For Whom the Bell Tolls* (New York, 1946), 339. Hemingway selected a chapter from Frederic Van de Water's anti-Custer biography *Glory-Hunter* (1934) for inclusion in his anthology *Men at War* (New York, 1942), and among the books in his bedroom-workroom in his home near Havana were two about Custer. (George Plimpton, "An Interview with Ernest Hemingway," *Hemingway and His Critics: An International Anthology* ed. by Carlos Baker [New York, 1961], 21.)

[82]*Travels with Charley in Search of America* (New York, 1962), 143.

[83]"They Built the Saga," *This Is the West* ed. by Robert West Howard (New York, 1957), 182-3.

[84]*An Artist in America* (New York, 1937), 14.

[85]"Benton V. Adams," *Time*, XLVII (Mar. 4, 1946), 49. A color reproduction of Benton's "improved" version appeared in *Coronet*, XXI (Jan., 1947), 68.

[86]*Thomas H. Benton* (New York, 1945), "Foreword."

[87]Paul W. Tredway, "Custer's Last Fight," *St. Louis Globe-Democrat*, July 17, 1949.

[88]Both are reproduced in *Walt Kuhn: An Imaginary History of the West* (Fort Worth, 1964).

[89]"American Realist," *Time*, LVIII (July 16, 1951), 72, 75; and repeated in "Andy's World," *Time*, LXXXII (Dec. 27, 1963), 52.

[90]Three Custer monuments have been erected; the 1879 West Point statue (which Mrs. Custer loathed and succeeded in getting removed), an equestrian

statue in Monroe, Mich. (1910), and a rather "foppish" Custer statue in New Rumley, O. (1932). Others have been proposed. On the statues, see Minnie Dubbs Millbrook, "A Monument to Custer," *Montana, the Magazine of Western History*, XXIV (Spring, 1974), 18-33; and Lawrence A. Frost, *Custer Slept Here* (Monroe, Mich., 1974). The Last Stand itself has been essayed by a few sculptors, notably Dwight Franklin in the 1930's and again twenty years later.

[91]*The Company She Keeps* (New York, 1942), 49.

[92]Krebs and Orthwein, *Making Friends Is Our Business*, 39, also 329.

[93]The Central Federal Savings and Loan Association of Chicago advertised in the *Chicago Tribune*, Sept. 7, 1963; the *New York Times Index* was advertised in the *New York Times Book Review*, Oct. 12, 1969, 62.

[94]*Daily Texan* (Austin), May 10, 1970, 10.

[95]*Harvard Lampoon Parody of Playboy*, 1966, 42. Budweiser maintained its link with Custer's Last Stand in radio ads done in a W. C. Fields voice (1967) and in a television skit featuring Frank Sinatra and Ed McMahon (1968). Another beer, Falstaff, sponsored an advertisement with the theme "Your first one is never your last one," in which an excited sergeant yells, "The Indians are attacking, sir. What shall we do?," and the Custer character replies: "Why, make a stand, Sergeant! What else?" (1970).

[96]*Life*, LVII (Sept. 18, 1964), 18.

[97]*American Magazine*, CXIV (Dec., 1932), back cover.

[98]*Wall Street Journal*, June 10, 1969, 3.

[99] *New York Herald*, July 11, 1876, 3; Atlanta *Constitution*, July 15, 1876, 2; and the *Weekly Ohio State Journal* (Columbus), July 15, 1876, 2.

[100]See "As the Crow Fights," *Newsweek*, LXIV (July 13, 1964), 56; Vine Deloria, Jr., *Custer Died for Your Sins: An Indian Manifesto* (New York, 1969), 149 (several other Custer jokes are recounted); and the Arthur Penn movie *Little Big Man* (1970).

[101]*Red Skelton Hour* (CBS TV, Mar. 11, 1969).

[102]John Ruge, *Saturday Review*, XLVIII (Nov. 13, 1965), 102.

[103]*Cavalier*, XVI (Apr., 1966), 25.

[104]Buck Brown, *Playboy*, XIV (Dec., 1967), 193.

[105]John Ruge, *True*, LI (June, 1970), 90.

[106]Three jokes about Custer's hair are included in *Redeye: A Strip Book* (Akron, O., ca. 1969).

[107]George Lichty, *Grin and Bear It*, Dec. 10, 1967.

[108]L. Herman, *Argosy*, CCCLXIV (Apr., 1967), 114.

[109]David Cobb, "On the Road with Young Canada," *Canadian Magazine*, Oct. 31, 1970, 9.

[110]"Arkansas: Opportunity Regained," *Time*, LXXXVIII (Dec. 2, 1966), 24; and Wick Fowler, "Fowler Fare," *Austin American-Statesman*, Jan. 10, 1970, 4.

[111]"Woman in Mental Institution 97 Years," *New York Times*, Sept. 25, 1973, 16; and Alexander Theroux, "Good Old with Everything," *Esquire*, LXXXIII (Apr., 1975), 148.

[112]Chic Young, *Blondie*, Dec. 22, 1966.

[113]J. R. Williams, *Out Our Way*, Jan. 28, 1967.

[114]Ralph Friar, "White Man Speaks with a Split Tongue, Forked Tongue, Tongue of Snake," *Film Library Quarterly*, III (Winter, 1969-70), 18; *Custard's Last Stand* (dir. by William Watson, 1921); and *Custard's Last Stand (A Physical Culture Comedy)* (dir. by Glen Lambert, 1927).

[115]BIZ, television commercial, Nov., 1968; and Bob Montana, *Archie*, Oct. 20, 1969.

[116]*CBS News* (TV), Oct. 17, 1968.

[117]Hallmark, Coutts Canada, Contemporary Cards B 203-7.

[118]Oz Card, F 138, printed in Canada.

[119]Brant Parker and Johnny Hart, *Wizard of Id*, Dec. 13, 1966.

[120]*Tumbleweeds*, Feb. 4, 1968, Sept. 20, 1969 and Apr. 25, 1971.

[121]*Our Boarding House*, May 20, 1964, Mar. 25 and Mar. 30, 1965, Mar. 15, 1966, May 28, 1967 and July 13, 1968.

[122]Laura S. Webb, *Custer's Immortality. A Poem, with biographical sketches of the chief actors in the late Tragedy of the Wilderness* (New York, 1876), 5.

Chapter 4

[1]*Broken Lance* (New York, 1949) and *Bugles West* (New York, 1954).

[2]*The Pulp Jungle* (Los Angeles, 1967), 185.

[3]"The Art of Fiction," *Realism and Romanticism in Fiction: An Approach to the Novel*, ed. by Eugene Current-Garcia and Walton R. Patrick (Chicago, 1962), 93.

[4]"The Basic Western Plots," *The Writer's 1955 Year Book*, No. 26 (1955), 49. Gruber's account of how he broke into the pulps and made it to the top of the heap by the mid-1930's, *The Pulp Jungle*, demonstrates the same interest in dollars and cents and the same disinterest in what was written to earn them.

[5]"The Wild Western Rides Again," *Saturday Review*, XLVIII (Dec. 11, 1965), 71. Curry's contribution was *Riding for Custer: A "Captain Mesquite" Novel* (New York, 1947), a tale of the Washita battle.

[6]Quoted in Russel Nye, *The Unembarrassed Muse: The Popular Arts in America* (New York, 1970), 280.

[7]"Party of One," *Holiday*, XXXIV (Aug., 1963), 16.

[8]*Jews Without Money* (New York, 1965 [1930]), 29, 136.

[9]Verne Athanas, "Injuns in the Stew," *Roundup*, IV (Feb., 1956), 9.

[10]"The Historical Novel," *Montana Magazine of History*, IV (Fall, 1954), 5.

[11]See Kent L. Steckmesser, "Custer in Fiction: George A. Custer, Hero or Villain?," *American West*, I (Fall, 1964), 47-52, 63-4, and his *The Western Hero in History and Legend* (Norman, Okla., 1965), 211-37, for discussions of Custer's image in fiction.

[12]Marguerite Merington, ed., *The Custer Story: The Life and Intimate Letters of General George A. Custer and His Wife Elizabeth* (New York, 1950), 239.

[13][F. W. Palfrey], "Whittaker's Life of Custer," *Nation*, XXIV (Mar. 22, 1877), 179, 181.

[14]*Nation*, XXIII (Oct. 5, 1876), vi; and *Galaxy*, XXII (Dec. 1876), "Miscellany and Advertiser." Incredibly, Whittaker's *Life* was being announced in the press by July 12. The exact words used in the advertisement were part of Whittaker's tribute "General George A. Custer," *Galaxy*, XXII (Sept., 1876), 363.

[15]*Beadle's Boy's Library of Sport, Story and Adventure* (Octavo Edition) No. 36 (Dec. 10, 1884), 30.

[16]Captain Ralph Bonehill [Edward Stratemeyer], *With Custer in the Black Hills; or, A Young Scout among the Indians* (New York, 1902), iv. See Norman Maclean, "Custer's Last Fight a Ritual Drama," *Westerners Brand Book* (Chicago), XV (Oct., 1958), 57-8; and Steckmesser, *Western Hero*, 218.

[17]Noname [Lu Senarens], *Custer's Little Dead-shot; or, The Boy Scout of the Little Big Horn, Wide Awake Library* No. 826 (May 16, 1888); and Edwin L. Sabin, *On the Plains with Custer* (Philadelphia, 1913).

[18]Fairfax Downey, *The Seventh's Staghound* (New York, 1948), 203.

[19]Dale White [Marian T. Place], *The Boy Who Came Back* (New York, 1966).

[20]Elbridge S. Brooks, *The Master of the Strong Hearts: A Story of Custer's Last Rally* (New York, 1898); Zoa Grace Hawley, *A Boy Rides with Custer* (Boston, 1938); and D. Lange, *The Threat of Sitting Bull: A Story of the Time of Custer* (Boston, 1920).

[21]Bonehill, *With Custer in the Black Hills.*

[22]Custer's Scout [St. George Henry Rathborne], *Custer's Last Shot; or, The Boy Trailer of the Little Horn, Boys of New York* Nos. 51-5 (Aug. 7-Sept. 4, 1876); An Old Scout [Cornelius Shea], *Young Wild West at the Little Big Horn; or, The Last Stand of the Cavalry, Wild West Weekly* No. 108 (Nov. 11, 1904); and Jeff Jeffries, *7th Cavalry* (London, n.d.).

[23]*Buffalo Bill Wild West Annual* (London, 1950), 70.

[24]See Steckmesser, *Western Hero,* 208.

[25]*Britton of the Seventh: A Romance of Custer and the Great Northwest* (Chicago, 1914), ix.

[26]"Billings Man Gives New Version of Custer Battle," Billings (?) *Herald,* June 28, 1951. Clipping in the Billings Public Library folder M-Custer Battle-1941 to date.

[27]Robert Bruce to Capt. Robert G. Carter, Mar., 1930, in John S. duMont, ed., "A Debate of Authors on the Custer Fight," *Westerners Brand Book* (Chicago), XXX (July, 1973), 34.

[28]"The Benteen-Goldin Letters," Feb. 17, 1896, and Apr. 3, 1892, in William A. Graham, *The Custer Myth: A Source Book of Custeriana* (Harrisburg, Pa., 1953), 207, 196.

[29]*Those Fatal Generals* (New York, 1936), 12, 254, 251.

[30]Robert Gessner, *Massacre: A Survey of Today's American Indian* (New York, 1931), 7, 9.

[31]"The Latest Roundup on the Western Range," *New York Times Book Review,* Oct. 3, 1954, 20.

[32]"Custer's New Stand," *New York Times Book Review,* Feb. 13, 1944, 6. It should be noted that the book version was revised and improved over the *Post* serialization.

[33]"Ernest Haycox: An Appreciation," *Roundup,* XII (Apr., 1964), 2.

[34]"The Easy Chair: Phaëthon on Gunsmoke Trail," *Harper's Magazine,* CCIX (Dec., 1954), 16.

[35]*Bugles in the Afternoon* (Boston, 1944), 52, 206.

[36]One yardstick for measuring the "well-knownness" of *Bugles in the Afternoon* is its inclusion in *Saturday Review*'s "Your Literary I.Q." for Jan. 22, 1966. Apparently the reading public is expected to know of the book! It was also included in a 1954 list of "All-Time Books of the West" (Robert West Howard, ed., *This Is the West* [New York, 1957], 230-5), was ranked second among "The Ten Top Western Books" by the Western Writers of America (*Roundup,* IV [Feb., 1956], 2), and came in fourth in an English Westerners' poll of the ten best Western novels (Henry's *No Survivors* was third) (*Westerners Brand Book* [Chicago], XIV [Mar., 1957], 4).

[37]*Bugles in the Afternoon,* 22.

[38]*No Survivors* (New York, 1950), 107.

[39]*Little Big Man* (New York, 1966), xviii.

158

[40]"Paleface in the Cheyenne Camp," *Saturday Review*, XLVII (Oct. 10, 1964), 40.

[41]*Little Big Man*, 396.

[42]"What About the Army Western?," *Roundup*, VIII (June, 1960), 27.

[43]Richard Irving Dodge, *Our Wild Indians: Thirty-three Years' Personal Experience among the Red Men of the Great West* (New York, 1959 [1882]), 518.

[44]"The Secret of the Sioux" in *Redman Echoes: Comprising the Writings of Chief Buffalo Child Long Lance and Biographical Sketches by His Friends* comp. by Roberta Forsberg (Los Angeles, 1933), 39; the story originally appeared in *Hearst's International . . . Cosmopolitan*, LXXXII (June, 1927), 40-3, 208-11.

[45]William Christie Macleod, *The American Indian Frontier* (London, 1928), 497-9; and Hans Olson, "Custer Killed Himself!," *Denver Post Empire Magazine*, Dec. 28, 1958, 4-5.

[46]*The Dauntless and the Dreamers* (New York, 1963), 182.

[47]*Winter Count* (Denver, 1968), 110. The Custer suicide theory earlier found a place in fiction, in James Warner Bellah, "Massacre," *Saturday Evening Post*, CCXIX (Feb. 22, 1947), 146, but since this told the story of Major Owen Thursday's Last Stand, and was only loosely modelled on history, the implication was obscure.

[48]*The Way of an Indian* (New York, 1906), 220-1.

[49]"General Denies Suicide Story Told Here," *Denver Post*, June 23 (?), 1918, 12. Clipping in George A. Custer folder, B-C 96g, Western History Research Center, University of Wyoming, Laramie (hereafter cited as WHRC). The Officer was Edward S. Godfrey.

[50]Fred Dustin, *The Custer Tragedy: Events Leading Up To and Following the Little Big Horn Campaign of 1876* (Ann Arbor, Mich., [1939] 1965), 150; and Stewart H. Holbrook, "Phonies of the Old West," *American Mercury*, LXVIII (Feb., 1949), 234.

[51]T. J. (Tim) Mahoney, "Was It Really Gen. Custer's Last Stand?," big *Wyoming*, Sect. I, *Casper Star-Tribune*, Mar. 20, 1966, 23, 26-7. The story is replete with impeccable credentials: it was told to Mahoney by Mrs. Alta Rowe Barnes, who in turn heard it from Judge George Layman. Supposedly, the Judge, who was involved in the semi-centennial arrangements, had a man walk into his office in 1926 who, he concluded, was Custer himself. An earlier version had Layman hearing the story from "a brother attorney," R. E. McNally, and the time was supposedly 1936 — three years after Mrs. Custer's death! ("General Custer Alive Today?," *Winners of the West*, XV [Feb., 1938], 3; reprinted from the *Sheridan News*, Dec. 8, 1937.) For more examples of such tales, see Jay Jackson, "Last Stand of the Last Stand," *Argosy*, CCCXLIII (Dec., 1956), 9; and Edgar I. Stewart, "Which Indian Killed Custer?," *Montana, the Magazine of Western History*, VIII (Summer, 1958), 31-2. The opposite tack is taken by Fred Mitchell, "Custer's Death: A New Theory," *ibid.*, XI (Summer, 1961), 71, who heard from an Assiniboine aunt living in Sitting Bull's camp in 1876 that Custer was killed in the Indian village two or three days *before* the battle!

[52]See Don Russell, *The Lives and Legends of Buffalo Bill* (Norman, Okla., 1960), "The Dime Novels (a List)," 494-503.

[53]*Beadle's Dime Library*, No. 682 (Nov. 18, 1891), 2 (reprint).

[54]See Russell, *Lives and Legends*, 407-8; and Steckmesser, *Western Hero*, 214-6.

[55]*The Autobiography of Frank Tarbeaux* as told to Donald Henderson Clarke (New York, 1930), 74-5.

[56]Gilbert Parker, *Tarboe: The Story of a Life* (Toronto, 1927), 1-5, 61-2, 188-9.

[57]Untitled clipping about Joseph Sinsel, *Billings Times,* Apr., 1925, in the Billings Public Library folder M-Custer Battle to 1940.

[58]*Autobiography,* 75.

[59]*Life and Adventures of Frank Grouard* ed. by Edgar I. Stewart (Norman, Okla., 1958 [1894]), 123-4.

[60]Wallace David Coburn, "The Battle of the Little Big Horn," *Montana, the Magazine of Western History* VI (Summer, 1956), 36.

[61]Mrs. A. B. Conway, letter in *Life,* XXV (July 12, 1948), 8. Mrs. Conway was fortunate enough to possess an affidavit signed by Nixon verifying this tale.

[62]"Famous Scout Dies Boots On; Lift Kills Him," *Billings Gazette,* Apr. 18, 1923; and "'Lone Star' Claims He Was First on Battlefield Upon Which Custer Command Fell," *Enterprise* (n.p.), Feb. 23, 1923. Clipping in Custer's Battle file 2, C 96, WHRC. In his incredible book *The Great Sioux Nation* (Chicago, 1907), pirated in most part from popular histories of the Indian wars, Hans had the good sense not to press his claim to having discovered the bodies of Custer's men, though his other pretensions were included, lovingly elaborated. Lone Star's adventures are also recounted by his daughter Montana Helena Weyer in *Trailing the Teepees* (New York, 1968).

[63]Paul K. Heerwagen, *Indian Scout — Western Painter: Captain Charles L. Von Berg* (Little Rock, 1969), 78; and Philip Steele, "Captain Charles Louis Von Berg," *True Frontier,* II (Mar., 1970), 26-9.

[64]*Copies of Calamity Jane's Diary and Letters* (N.p.[Billings, Mont.], 1951). The letter and the daughter (by Wild Bill Hickok) are equally spurious. See J. Leonard Jennewein, *Calamity Jane of the Western Trails* (Mitchell, S.D., 1953), 28-33, for a delightful discussion of the subject. The gruesome description of mutilations in all likelihood derives from Thomas B. Marquis, *Two Days After the Custer Battle: The Scene there as Viewed by William H. White, a soldier with Gibbon in 1876* (Hardin, Mont., 1935), 5-6.

[65]*Only the Earth and the Mountains: A Tale of the Cheyenne Nation* (New York, 1964). Heinzman notes in his preface that Ben Kane is modeled upon Frank Grouard, among others.

[66]"Custer Warrior Dead," *Billings Gazette,* Mar. 9, 1929.

[67]"Mon Tana Lou" Grill, "Old-Timers of the Days When Men Were Men Recall Early Incidents at Meeting in Miles City," *Midland Empire Farmer,* updated clipping in the Billings Public Library folder M-Custer Battle-"no date" or undated clippings.

[68]"Harvey Faucett, Custer's Scout, Dies after Fall," *New York Herald Tribune,* undated clipping (ca. Sept. 26, 1936[?]) in the Billings Public Library folder M-Custer Battle-Anniversaries.

[69]*Cache la Poudre: The Romance of a Tenderfoot in the Days of Custer* (New York, 1905), 177-8.

[70]For example, John Clayton of *No Survivors* and Tony Newman and Doug Phillips of television's *Time Tunnel* suffer such treatment at the General's hands. The underlying assumption that Custer's obstinacy would deafen him to advice receives some support from history. Among others, scouts "Lonesome Charley" Reynolds, the part Arikara Bloody Knife, the Crow Half Yellow Face and the half-breed Mitch Bouyer were all extremely pessimistic about the Seventh's chances at the Little Big Horn, and expressed their doubts. Custer ignored them, and even taunted Bouyer with the suggestion that, in consideration of his Sioux blood, he would perhaps prefer not to fight. His courage questioned, Bouyer resolved to go into battle beside the General and, ironically, was the only one of the four to fall with him (though Reynolds and Bloody Knife died in the valley with Reno). If they

were not actually threatened with arrest, then, Custer's scouts were subjected to the lash of his scorn.

[71]"Famous Indian Scout Is Dead," *Billings Gazette*, undated clipping (1920's) in the Billings Public Library folder M-Custer Battle to 1940.

[72]*Summer of the Sioux* (New York, 1967), 157.

[73]"Custer's Slaughter," *Charleston Journal of Commerce*, July 13, 1876, 1.

[74]Ridgeley's tale first appeared in the Sept. 8, 1876, Minneapolis *Pioneer-Press and Tribune*, and the refutation in the Sept. 25 edition. See E. L. Reedstrom, "The 17 Day Hero," *Guns*, XVII (Feb., 1971), 30-1, 51-2. But the original lies were remembered long after their refutation was forgotten.

[75]Max Miller, *It Must Be the Climate* (New York, 1941), 95.

[76]"Killing of Custer Seen by Saugus Man," unidentified clipping in George A. Custer folder, B-C 96g, WHRC.

[77]Graham, *Custer Myth*, 355.

[78]Berger, *Little Big Man*, 396.

[79]F. A. Kinsey, "Some interesting Sidelights on the Custer Massacre," *Hunter-Trader-Trapper*, Jan., 1920, 48-50.

[80]Eldon K. Everett, "Gower Gulch!: When the Old West Came to Hollywood," *Classic Film Collector* No. 43 (Summer, 1974), 12.

[81]*Little Smoke: A Tale of the Sioux* (New York, 1891), 288.

[82]"Report of Major M. H.[sic] Reno," July 15, 1876, in *Annual Report of the Secretary of War for the Year 1876*, 44 Cong., 2 sess., 477-8.

[83]"Custer Betrayed by a Crow Scout," Cheyenne (Wyo.) *Sun*; reprinted in Denison (Tex.) *Daily News*, Aug. 13, 1876, 6.

[84]John Benteen, *Taps at Little Big Horn* (New York, 1973).

[85]*Custer Myth*, 80.

[86]Steckmesser, *Western Hero*, 204.

[87]N.B., Essex, England, in *The West*, V (June, 1966), 43.

[88]*Custer Myth*, 267-78, 354-5. The story of John Martin and the last message is told on pp. 287-300.

[89]"Custer's Orderly a Murderer," Anaconda (Mont.) *Standard*, Dec. 14, 1904.

[90]"Another Final Custer Scout Bites the Dust," *Billings Gazette*, Mar. 13, 1926; and "Death of Survivor of Custer Massacre," unidentified clipping in the Billings Public Library folder M-Custer Battle to 1940.

[91]J. C. Ryan, ed., *Custer Fell First* (San Antonio, 1966), 47-8. Earlier, Lockwood had merely claimed to be a "civilian packer attached to the pack train of the Seventh" at the Little Big Horn. ("Old Packer on Hand to Attend Big Show," *Independent Record* [Helena, Mont.], June 18, 1926.)

[92]Anthony A. Amaral, *Comanche: The Horse That Survived the Custer Massacre* (Los Angeles, 1961), 33-4, fn.

[93]Helena (Mont.) *Daily Herald*, July 15, 1876; reprinted in Graham, *Custer Myth*, 10-1.

[94]"Vanishing Indian Types: The Tribes of the Northwest Plains," *Scribner's Magazine*, XXXIX (June, 1906), 662. Early newspaper articles and histories gave the Curly story full play, but later historians — with the exception of Charles Kuhlman — have tended to discount it.

[95]*Custer's Luck*, 490.

[96]Dustin, *Custer Tragedy*, 150.

[97]Holbrook, "Phonies of the Old West," 235.

[98]"Custer Indian Scout Dies at 96," *New York Times*, Feb. 4, 1923, Sect. II, 1.

[100]"Another Man Who Saw Custer Die Bobs Up to Awe Natives," *Billings Gazette*, June 9, 1930. It was a common tactic to disarm skeptics by declaring other poseurs frauds. William Fellew, who was busy carrying dispatches from Terry to

161

Custer and Custer to Gibbon, and talking with Bloody Knife, Billy Cross and Curly about the defeat, self-righteously denounced "an ex-soldier at the world's fair in Chicago, who posed as a soldier in the Seventh Cavalry, who escaped from the fatal field. He was an imposter, for none but Curley left the ground alive. He may have dreamed it and believed in dreams." ("One More Witness of What Happened in the Custer Field," *Anaconda* [Mont.] *Standard*, July 25, 1899.)

[101]Stewart, *Custer's Luck*, 491-2; and Charles Kuhlman, *The Frank Finkel Story* ed. by Michael J. Koury (Omaha, 1968).

[102]Pandy and Mason are, respectively, old and young heroes of *Custer's Last Shot*. Young Wild West's exploits are recorded in *Young Wild West at the Little Big Horn*, and Tom Carleton's in an unknown writer's story *Sitting Bull on the War-Path; or, Custer in the Black Hills*, serialized in *The Fireside Companion* Nos. 461-76 (Aug. 28-Dec. 11, 1876).

[103]Berger, *Little Big Man*, 440.

[104]Heerwagen, *Indian Scout — Western Painter*, 7, 65.

Chapter 5

[1]Norman Maclean, "Custer's Last Fight a Ritual Drama," *Westerners Brand Book* (Chicago), XV (Oct., 1958), 57-8.

[2]Don Russell, *The Lives and Legends of Buffalo Bill* (Norman, Okla., 1960), 214-35.

[3]"Wood's Museum," *New York Herald*, Aug. 15, 1876, 10.

[4]*Story of the Wild West and Camp-Fire Chats* (Boston, 1888), 689. The Battle of War Bonnet Creek was captured for posterity in a 1913 film, *The Indian Wars*, made by the Col. W. F. Cody (Buffalo Bill) Historical Pictures Company. Posterity, however, has been ill-served. Only a fragment of the film could be located in 1961 according to Don Russell, "Buffalo Bill — In Action," *Westerners Brand Book* (Chicago), XIX (July, 1962), 33-5, 40, and it did not include the Yellow Hand episode.

[5]Don Russell, *The Wild West; or, A History of the Wild West Shows* (Fort Worth, 1970), mentions Last Stand re-enactments in other early Wild West shows, and discusses Cody's Wild West at length.

[6]*Buffalo Bill's Wild West and Congress of Rough Riders of the World — Historical Sketches, and Programme* (Chicago, 1893).

[7]This is based on a British reporter's account of the show (1887) reprinted in Buffalo Bill, *Story of the Wild West*, 753-4.

[8]Henry Blackman Sell and Victor Weybright, *Buffalo Bill and the Wild West* (New York, 1955), 156.

[9]*Buffalo Bill's Wild West and Congress of Rough Riders of the World. Madison Square Garden, 3 Weeks and 4 Days, Commencing Wednesday, March 30* ([New York], 1898), 18, 23.

[10]"The Crow Celebration," *Weekly Times* (Billings), July 11, 1891, 5. For contemporary reactions to the tenth anniversary, see the letter from C. H. Barstow, June 24, 1886, in Lawrence Bond Romaine, "Custer's Last Stand — 10th Anniversary," *Hobbies*, L (Oct., 1945), 110, 114; and Pvt. James O. Purvis' column "Fort Custer News" in the *Billings Daily Gazette*, as reprinted in Richard Upton, ed., *Fort Custer on the Big Horn, 1877-1898* (Glendale, Calif., 1973), 100-12.

[11]H. H. Thompson to Grace Raymond Hebard, May 16, 1916, in Custer's Battle Memorials folder, C 96-m, WHRC, which contains a number of newspaper clippings pertaining to the fortieth anniversary ceremonies.

[12]"Fortieth Anniversary Memorial," *Teepee Book*, II (June, 1916), 4; and "Paleface and Redskin Join in Commemorating Fortieth Anniversary Custer Battle," *Billings Gazette*, June 26, 1916, 1, 8.

[13]"The Custer Battle," *Billings Gazette*, Nov. 10, 1920.

[14]"Custer's Last Stand Is Mystery Battle of West; Big Observance to Honor Hero Occurs Saturday," unidentified clipping, ca. June 18, 1921, in the Billings Public Library folder M-Custer Battle-Anniversaries.

[15]*The Custer Semi-Centennial Ceremonies, 1876 — June 25-6 — 1926* (Casper, Wyo., 1926), 33; and see the following folders in the WHRC; Custer's Battle, C 96; Custer's Battle file 2, C 96 (includes several notebook pages, hand-written and typed, by Grace Hebard labelled "Custer Battle Field, Crow Agency, Montana, June 24, 25, 26, 1926"); and, particularly, Custer's Battle Memorials, C 96-m.

[16]"To Name Coolidge 'Leading Eagle,' " *New York Times*, July 19, 1927, 6; "Coolidge to be 'Leading Eagle,' " *ibid.*, July 31, 1927, 2xx; "Coolidge Becomes Chief of the Sioux," *ibid.*, Aug. 5, 1927, 1,3; and "Coolidge Becomes 'Leading Eagle' of the Sioux Nation," *Lead* (S.D.) *Daily Call*, Aug. 4, 1927, 1.

[17]"Schedule Custer Battle Program Thursday June 25," *Billings Gazette*, Apr. 21, 1936; "Custer Celebration Plans" and "Hardin, Crow Agency Set to Greet Visitors," *ibid.*, June 23, 1936; and "Custer Celebration Draws Big Crowd," *Midland Review* (Billings), July 3, 1936, 1. The *Review* carried detailed itineraries of the commemorative activities in its June 19 issue.

[18]"Historian Terms Celebration of Battle 'Last Great Call,'" *Billings Gazette*, June 23, 1936.

[19]See "Colorful Ceremony Marks 75th Anniversary of Custer's Last Stand," *Denver Post*, June 29, 1951; "It Was Only 75 Years Ago: Custer Anniversary Is Observed," *Life*, XXXI (July 9, 1951), 41-4; and Josephine O'Keane, "The Band Played Garryowen," *Villager*, Nov., 1951, 21-1, 43-5.

[20]Olin D. Wheeler, "The Custer Battlefield," in *Wonderland: 1901* (St. Paul, 1901), 40.

[21]"On the Bloody Field Where Custer Fell," *Anaconda* (Mont.) *Standard*, May 26, 1901.

[22]"To Reproduce Sham Battle," *Billings Daily Gazette*, Sept. 23, 1909, 3. Also see [John A. Cockerill], *Custer Battlefield on the Burlington Route* (n.p., n.d.), for the railroad's use of the attraction in its advertising.

[23]Nora B. Kinsley, "Custer Memorial Highway," *American Review of Reviews*, LXIV (Aug., 1921), 184-6; and Paul L. Hedren, "On the Trail of Elusive Custeriana," *Little Big Horn Associates Research Review*, VIII (Summer, 1974), 9-13.

[24]"46th Anniversary of the Day When Gallant Custer Died," unidentified clipping (Sheridan, 1922), in Custer's Battle Memorials folder, C 96-m, WHRC.

[25]Division of Publicity, Dept. of Agriculture, Labor and Industry, *Carrying on for Fifty Years with the Courage of Custer, 1876-1926* (Helena, Mont., 1926). Also see the "Custer Fight Anniversary Program" distributed by the Hardin Chamber of Commerce, *Information descriptive of the resources and location of Big Horn County, Montana, in the Crow Indian country, made habitable and famous by General George A. Custer and his immortal band of brave soldiers* (Hardin, Mont., 1926).

[26]Liz Wilson, " Recreation — The BIG Way (Big Horn Area)," *Billings Gazette*, Sept. 13, 1964, 13.

[27]"Montana Territorial Centennial," *Playgrounds of the Rockies*, VII (June-July, 1964), 37.

[28]"As the Crow Fights," *Newsweek*, LXIV (July 13, 1964), 56; "America's Greatest Moment of Living History" / Custer's Last Stand / June 19-20 & 26-27 /

Crow Agency, Montana (Hardin, Mont., 1965); and "Custer's Last Last Stand," *Newsweek*, LXXXIII (Mar. 11, 1974), 15. The re-enactment also received national coverage in *Saturday Evening Post, Ford Times, Holiday* and *Sunset*; its checkered career can be traced in a clipping file in the Billings Public Library, M-Custer Battle Re-Enactment.

[29]"Crazy Horse Pageant: World's Largest Indian Pageant," *Playgrounds of the Rockies*, VII (June-July, 1965), 51; and the brochure *Crazy Horse Pageant* (Hot Springs, S.D., ca. 1966).

[30]Austin C. Wehrwein, "In Dakota of Old: Clash between Sitting Bull and Custer Re-enacted in Huge Amphitheatre," *New York Times*, Aug. 13, 1961, xx19.

[31]*Buffalo Bill's Wild West* (1898), 23.

[32]Robert Welles Ritchie, "Resurrection Spoils Drama," unidentified clipping (reprinted from the *Cleveland Plain Dealer*) in Custer's Battle Memorials folder, C 96-m, WHRC. Frackelton told the story at greater length and with numerous changes in detail to Herman C. Seely in *Sagebrush Dentist* (Chicago, 1941), 196-218. Now he claimed to have personally captured the flag.

[33]"On the Little Big Horn; or, Custer's Last Stand," *Moving Picture World*, V (Nov. 27, 1909), 773.

[34]F. N. Shorey, "Making a Selig Film," *Film Index*, IV (Jan. 30, 1909); reprinted in Kalton C. Lahue, ed., *Motion Picture Pioneer: The Selig Polyscope Company* (South Brunswick, N.J., 1973), 48, 50.

[35]"Great Custer Massacre Graphically Repeated," *Billings Daily Gazette*, Sept. 26, 1909, 2.

[36]"To Reproduce Sham Battle," 3.

[37]"Great Custer Massacre Graphically Repeated," 2.

[38]James E. McQuade, "Making 'Selig' Pictures," *Film Index*, IV (Nov. 20, 1909); reprinted in Lahue, ed., *Motion Picture Pioneer*, 58.

[39]S. G. Dewell, "Custer's Last Fight," *National Guard Magazine*, IV (Dec., 1909), 515-6.

[40]"A Marvelous Reproduction of Custer's Last Fight" in *Around the World With a Camera* (New York, 1910); copies of the advertising poster are on display at Wall Drug, Wall, S.D.

[41]"Custer Fight," *Daily Capital-Journal* (Pierre, S. D.), Oct. 4, 1909, 1.

[42]"A Marvelous Reproduction of Custer's Last Fight."

[43]A photo of the poster appears in George N. Fenin and William K. Everson, *The Western from Silents to Cinerama* (New York, 1962), 267; it probably dates from the movie's re-issue as a five-reeler in 1925. A copy of the program, *"Custer's Last Fight"/ in three reels / "101"* — Bison Film — *"101"* (Brooklyn, 1912), is in Pamphlet File Cat. No. 3234, Custer Battlefield National Monument.

[44]Alice Ward Bailey, "Custer's Last Fight: Founded upon the True Story of the Battle of the Little Big Horn," *Photoplay Magazine*, III (Sept., 1912), 30.

[45]Mrs. D. W. Griffith (Linda Arvidson), *When the Movies Were Young* (New York, 1925), 218, linked *The Massacre* to Custer's Last Stand, and others have followed suit.

[46]*New York Times*, May 2, 1921, 12. Jack Spears, *Hollywood: The Golden Era* (London, 1971), 293, claims that the film was shot on location at Fort Huachuca, Arizona.

[47]Frank Elliott, "The Scarlet West," *Motion Picture News*, XXXII (July 25, 1925), 460.

[48]*The Flaming Frontier*, a two-page advertisement in *Motion Picture News*, XXXIII (May 15, 1926).

[49]"'Flaming Frontier,' Depicting Custer Battle, Here This Week," *Billings Theatre and Town*, June 26-July 2, 1926, 5, quoting Col. George L. Bryam; and

George T. Pardy, "The Flaming Frontier," *Motion Picture News*, XXXIII (Apr. 17, 1926), 1934.

[50]"National Drive on 'Flaming Frontier,' " *Motion Picture News*, XXXIII (May 1, 1926), 2105; and "Cleveland Witnesses a Model Campaign," *ibid.*, XXXIV (Aug. 7, 1926), 494.

[51]Mordaunt Hall, "The Custer Massacre," *New York Times*, Apr. 5, 1926, 24; " 'Flaming Frontier,' Opening," *Motion Picture News*, XXXIII (Apr. 17, 1926), 1787; "'Flaming Frontier' Makes Bow," *ibid.*, 1807; and "National Drive on 'Flaming Frontier,'" 2105.

[52]Clipping in Custer's Battle file 2, C 96, WHRC.

[53]" 'Red Horse,' Sioux Indian Who Says He Struck Custer Last, Visits Here — General Killed Himself as Redmen Closed in Declares Warriors Passing through Sheridan," *Sheridan Post*, June 23, 1926.

[54]Fenin and Everson, *The Western*, 156.

[55]"Forty Chieftains and Scores of Tribes Reported Mobilized at 'Little Big Horn,' " *Sheridan Post*, June 23, 1926.

[56]"Big Horn Battle Subject for Much Controversy," *Rapid City* (S.D.) *Daily Journal*, Jan. 20, 1957, 8.

[57]Kalton C. Lahue, *Sinners of the West: The Sagebrush Heroes of the Silent Screen* (New York, 1970), 127-8.

[58]"With General Custer at the Little Big Horn," *National Board of Review Magazine*, I (Dec., 1926), 17-8.

[59]Fenin and Everson, *The Western*, 231; and Ken Weiss and Ed Goodgold, *To Be Continued . . .* (New York, 1972), 82.

[60]Andrew Bergman, *We're in the Money: Depression America and Its Films* (New York, 1971), 88-91, is good on this point.

[61]Walter C. Clapham, *Western Movies: The Story of the West on Screen* (London, 1974), 21.

[62]*Following the Guidon* (Norman, Okla., 1966 [1890]), 160-2. Custer was just as enthusiastic about Wild Bill in his *My Life on the Plains; or, Personal Experiences with Indians* (New York, 1874), 33-4.

[63]Lewis R. Freeman, "Calamity Jane and Yankee Jim," *Sunset Magazine*, XLIX (July, 1922), 52.

[64]See Paul T. Nolan's excellent "An Experiment in Myth-Making," which introduces J. W. (Capt. Jack) Crawford, *Three Plays* (The Hague, Netherlands, 1966), 13-86.

[65]*The Poet Scout: A Book of Song and Story* (New York, 1886), 106, 50. Also see Paul T. Nolan, "Jack Crawford's Account of Wild Bill," *Real West*, XIV (Sept., 1971), 27-30.

[66]A 1958 list of the "Best 10 Western Movies" included *The Plainsman* (*Westerners Brand Book* [Chicago], XV [Mar.,1958], 8).

[67]See Tony Thomas, Rudy Behlmer and Clifford McCarty, *The Films of Errol Flynn* (New York, 1969), 97-100.

[68]Robert M. Utley describes the Last Stand scene at length in "The Legend of the Little Bighorn," *Corral Dust*, I (June, 1956), 9, and two stills from the film illustrate his *Custer and the Great Controversy: The Origin and Development of a Legend* (Los Angeles, 1962), 115-6, while one illustrates Bruce A. Rosenberg, *Custer and the Epic of Defeat* (University Park, Pa., 1974), 61. *Time*, LXXXVIII (July 22, 1966), 95, assumed its readers would know the movie when it began a book review with a colorful account of Custer's Last Stand, concluding: "That was the way Errol Flynn did it in *They Died With Their Boots On* in 1941." *Life*, LXX (Apr. 2, 1971), 62A, parodied the dramatic scene in an essay on "Films that Will Offend Nobody."

[69]"Errol Flynn Custer," *Newsweek*, XVIII (Dec. 1, 1941), 70, *New York Times*, Nov. 21, 1941, 23, and Rosenberg, *Custer and the Epic of Defeat*, 62, make this point.

[70]Douglas W. Churchill, "A Cowboy's Feud with Hollywood," *New York Times*, Oct. 19, 1941, X5.

[71]Quoted in Jean Mitry, *John Ford* (Paris, 1954), 132.

[72]"Massacre," *Saturday Evening Post*, CCXIX (Feb. 22, 1947), 146. Frank Nugent, who wrote the screenplay for *Fort Apache*, remarked on the extensive liberties that were taken with the original Bellah story; see Philippe Haudiquet, *John Ford* (Paris, 1966), 125.

[73]See the reviews in *Time* LI (May 10, 1948), 102, 104; *Newsweek*, XXXI (May 17, 1948), 95; and the *New York Times*, June 25, 1948, 16.

[74]*Your Campaign Plan . . . Little Big Horn* (San Francisco, 1951).

[75]"Story of Custer's Massacre Told by El Paso, Texas, Visitor, *Winners of the West*, XVI (May, 1939), 7.

[76]"Authentic Indian Version of Custer Battle Revealed," *Yellowstone News* (Billings), July 19, 1951, 8-9.

[77]"Covered Wagons Roll along Old Bozeman Trail," *Great Falls Tribune*, undated clipping (ca. Sept., 1950), in the Billings Public Library folder M-Custer Battle-1941 to Date. Also see the *Tribune* for June 24, 1951.

[78]*Time*, LIX (Feb. 11, 1952), 97.

[79]This simile appeared in an interview with Sitting Bull in the *New York Herald*, Nov. 16, 1877, reprinted in William A. Graham, *The Custer Myth: A Source Book of Custeriana* (Harrisburg, Pa., 1953), 73. *Life*, XI (Dec. 8, 1941), 78, applied it to the Last Stand scene in *They Died With Their Boots On*.

[80]*National Board of Review Magazine*, XVI (Nov., 1941), 19.

[81]Fenin and Everson, *The Western*, 265-6.

[82]Bosley Crowther in the *New York Times*, Nov. 16, 1954, 24.

[83]*Time*, LXV (May 30, 1955), 86.

[84]*Ibid.*

[85]Saleh Sadiq, Jamaica, N.Y., in *True*, XL (Dec., 1959).

[86]Edward S. Luce, letter in the *Westerners Brand Book* (Chicago), XV (Nov., 1958), 72.

[87]See Buena Vista Film Distribution Co., *Walt Disney's TONKA* (New York, 1958), 2-3, 5; and "Tonka," *Screen Stories*, LXVIII (Feb., 1959), 63.

[88]"Injun Sal," *Newsweek*, LIII (Jan. 5, 1959), 69. For very different reactions to the Last Stand scene, see Howard Thompson's review in the *New York Times*, Mar. 26, 1959, 27; and *Monthly Film Bulletin*, XXVI (May, 1959), 62, which deplored the "vicious savagery" of the "massacre scenes."

[89]Charles N. Heckelmann, "Along Publisher's Row: The Movie and TV Front," *Roundup*, XII (Mar., 1964), 13. However, an Italian Western directed by Alfredo De Martino, *Le Carica del 7° cavalleggeri (The Charge of the Seventh Cavalry)* was released in 1964.

[90]The American premieres were held in Dallas and Houston in June, 1968. See William A. Payne, "Custer Rides West to His Last Stand," *Dallas Morning News*, Jan. 26, 1968, 14A.

[91]Fenin and Everson, *The Western*, 11-2.

[92]Marvin Levy, *"CUSTER OF THE WEST:"* Production Notes (New York, n.d. [ca. 1968]), 6.

[93]Helen Clark, "Little Big Man," *Western Horseman*, XXXVI (Feb., 1971), 22-3, 104, 106; and John K. Hutchens, "One Thing and Another," *Saturday Review*, LII (Oct. 4, 1969), 42-3.

[94]For examples of the buildup, see: "People," *Time*, XCIV (Aug. 1, 1969), 36;

"Newsmakers," *Newsweek*, LXXIV (Oct. 27, 1969), 67; Sally Kempton, "Little Big Man Clings to Life," *Esquire*, LXXIV (July, 1970), 78-81, 40, 42, 48; "The Old Age of Dustin Hoffman," *Life*, LXIX (Nov. 20, 1970), 75-9; and Gerald Astor, "The Good Guys Wear Paint," *Look*, XXXIV (Dec. 1, 1970), 56-61.

[95]"Little Big Man as Seen by Arthur Penn," *Great American Dream Machine* (NET, Jan. 13, 1971).

[96]Jean de Baroncelli, "Custard-pie Custer," *Guardian* (Manchester, Eng.), Feb. 9, 1974, 16; from *Le Monde*, Jan. 25, 1974, 21.

[97]Conversation, Sept. 10, 1965, at Billings. Mrs. Ralston was referring to the abortive *The Day Custer Fell* production.

[98]Brander Matthews, "The Kinetoscope of Time," *Scribner's Magazine*, XVIII (Dec., 1895), 733-44.

[99]"The Last Word: News from Unwithit Press," *New York Times Book Review*, Sept. 5, 1971, 23.

[100]"Axe Custer, Indians Tell TV Sponsor," *Edmonton* (Alberta) *Journal*, Sept. 12, 1967.

[101]"Custer at Bay Again," *Newsweek*, LXX (Aug. 7, 1967), 51.

[102]"A TV Critique . . .," *Westerners Brand Book* (Chicago), XVII (Aug., 1960), 41.

[103]Joe Hyams, "The Western He Wanted to Do," *Lively Arts and Book Review*, New York Herald Tribune, Mar. 26, 1961, 23.

[104]*Time* (Canada Edition), LXXXIV (Nov. 6, 1964), 2.

[105]"A Blunderer, but Not a Coward," *San Francisco Chronicle-Examiner*, Mar. 12, 1967.

[106]Andrew A. Rooney, "If It Had Been a Term Paper, I'd Have Failed," *TV Guide*, XXIII (June 28, 1975), 34.

[107]"Wait Till Next Year?," *Newsweek*, LXIV (Dec. 28, 1964), 40.

Chapter 6

[1]*Glory-Hunter: A Life of General Custer* (Indianapolis, 1934), 122.

[2]*A Complete Life of Gen. George A. Custer* (New York, 1876), 599-600.

[3]Robert M. Utley, *Custer and the Great Controversy: The Origin and Development of a Legend* (Los Angeles, 1962), 155-8.

[4]Foreword to Joseph A. Altsheler, *The Last of the Chiefs: A Story of the Great Sioux War* (New York, n.d.), iii-iv. This is a later reprint with West's Foreword added.

[5]*Custer's Last Stand* (New York, 1951), 180.

[6]*Glory-Hunter*, 129, 355.

[7]Elbridge S. Brooks, *The American Soldier: Being the Story of the Fighting Man of America* (Boston, 1899 ed.), 287.

[8]"Custer's Last Charge," *Army and Navy Journal*, July 15, 1876, special sheet.

[9]A. A. Whitman, "Custar's Last Ride," *Not a Man, and Yet a Man* (Springfield, O., 1877), 227.

[10]Lawrence Turnbull McAtee, "Custer's Last Stand," *A Poetry Concert* ed. by Henry Harrison (New York, 1935), 119.

[11]"The Last Cavalier," *Primer for America* (New York, 1943), 42-3.

[12]William A. Graham, *The Custer Myth: A Source Book of Custeriana* (Harrisburg, Pa., 1953), xiii. A photograph of Franklin's model serves as the frontispiece to this volume.

[13]*Bob Hampton of Placer* (Chicago, 1906), 367, 373-4.

[14]*No Survivors* (New York, 1950), 305-6.

[15]*Little Big Man* (New York, 1964), 412-3.

[16]*Time*, XXXVIII (Dec. 22, 1941), 47. Vincent Mercaldo, "Cessilly [*sic*] Adams and His Custer Painting," *Westerners Brand Book* (N.Y.), IV, 1 (1957), 17, mentions that Warner Brothers distributed photographs of the Adams painting to promote *They Died With Their Boots On*.

[17]For the relationshp between the movie and the Paxson painting, see William Edgar Paxson's advertisement in *True West*, XII (Oct., 1964), 55.

[18]Will Carleton, "The Heart and the Sword," *Monroe* (Mich.) *Record Commercial*, June 23, 1910.

[19]*Nation*, XXI (Dec. 30, 1875), 414.

[20]"The Monument for Custer," *New York Herald*, July 13, 1876, 4.

[21]"A death-Sonnet for Custer," *New York Tribune*, July 10, 1876, 5.

[22]*Heroes of Three Wars: Comprising a Series of Biographical Sketches . . .* (Philadelphia, 1882 ed.), 446.

[23]"The Custer Myth," *North Dakota Historical Quarterly*, VI (Apr., 1932), 187-200; and ".When War Came to the Indian: A Chapter of Neglected Truth in American History, with a Letter from the Commissioner of Indian Affairs," *Senate Doc. No. 68*, 73 Cong., 1 sess., 6-7. Byrne's history was *Soldiers of the Plains* (New York, 1926).

[24]"The Custer Myth," *Life*, LXXI (July 2, 1971), 52, 55.

[25]*The Tonight Show* (NBC TV, June 26, 1967). The comment is repeated in *The Memoirs of Chief Red Fox* (New York, 1971), 207-8.

[26]Charles Hillinger, "US Indian Group Protests Projected Custer Series," *Austin American-Statesman*, July 22, 1967, 25.

[27]See Vine Deloria, Jr., *Custer Died for Your Sins: An Indian Manifesto* (New York, 1969), 148.

[28]Reuben Ortiz, "Custer's Last Stand," *Silverbird: Broken Treaties* (Capitol Records, Hollywood, ca. 1970). Also: "Silverbird: The Birth of a Navaho Rock Group," *Fanfare* (NET, May 2, 1971).

[29]The Print Mint, Berkeley, 1970, issued a poster by Norman Orr titled *Custer Died for Our Sins*, and buttons with this slogan have been manufactured in New York and Houston. The first booklength treatment of the Red Power movement, Stan Steiner, *The New Indians* (New York, 1968), 292, whole-heartedly embraced this imputation of racial guilt: "Whichever way the visitor [to the Indians] seeks to declare his honesty, no matter how nakedly he attempts to strip himself of the past, he comes with the burden of that past on his back, like a curse he cannot easily exorcise." Even Custer's blood sacrifice was insufficient atonement.

[30]Reprinted in *The Hemingway Reader* ed. by Charles Poore (New York, 1953), 69.

[31]*Studies in Classic American Literature* (New York, 1964 [1923]), 33.

[32]Louis Belrose, Jr., "To 'Sitting Bull,' on receiving the news of his victory over U.S. troops," *Thorns and Flowers* (Philadelphia, 1879), 121.

[33]A. M. Gher, "The Conflict," *The Old Trail and the New: A Tale of the Kittatinnies* (N.p.[Pa.?], 1909), 10-1.

[34]"Look Past the Stars," *Denver Post Empire Magazine*, June 24, 1951, 33. The commemorative activities at the Battlefield in 1951 featured a number of speakers, and "the theme which predominated in all talks was PEACE." (Mrs. E. R. Burleigh, "Little Big Horn, 1876-1951," *Montana Treasure*, Mar., 1952, 3.)

[35]Arthur Z. Oliver, "The Little Big Horn, War and Progress," *Bits and Pieces* (Newcastle, Wyo.), I (May, 1965), 17.

[36]*New Yorker*, XLVII (June 26, 1971), 37.

[37]Quentin Waight, "The Golden Eagle," *Prelude to Glory* (Seattle, 1951), 29.

[38]William Eastlake, "red muslims and uncle tomahawks," *A Child's Garden of Verses for the Revolution* (New York, 1970), 56.

[39]*The Original Motion Picture Soundtrack CUSTER OF THE WEST* (ABC Records, New York, ca. 1968), album jacket notes.

[40]*Indians: A Play* (New York, 1969), 84.

[41]See "Fallen Angel on Location," *Time*, XCV (Feb. 2, 1970), 71.

[42]"*Little Big Man* as Seen by Arthur Penn," *Great American Dream Machine* (NET, Jan. 13, 1971).

[43]Fred Red Cloud, "A Tale of Last Stands," *Prairie Schooner*, XLIV (Spring, 1970), 22.

[44]Ken Same and Irving Breslauer, comps., "The View from Kilroy's Head: A Compendium of Vietnam Graffiti," *Playboy*, XVIII (Aug., 1971), 203.

[45]Wallace Stegner, "History, Myth, and the Western Writer," *American West*, IV (May, 1967), 62. While John G. Cawelti points out that Westerns do in fact reflect the social concerns of their times, he adds that, "generally, the Western's treatment of these issues is ritualistic rather than original . . . . Consequently, the Western rarely makes a truly profound or transcendent statement about the conflicts it expresses." (*The Six-Gun Mystique* [Bowling Green, O., ca. 1971], 74, 86.)

Epilogue

[1]*Requiem for a Nun* (New York, 1951), 222.

[2]*The Red Pony* (New York, 1963 [1937]), 91.

[3]*Letters and Notes on the Manners, Customs, and Condition of the North American Indians*, 2 vols. (New York, 1841), I, 62.

[4]*The Oregon Trail* (New York, 1964 [1849]), 82.

[5]*Collier's Weekly*, XXIV (Mar. 18, 1905), 16; quoted in Robert Taft, *Artists and Illustrators of the Old West, 1850-1900* (New York, 1953), 248.

[6]*The Americans: The National Experience* (Kew York, 1965), Pt. Five: "The Vagueness of the Land."

[7]See A. B. Guthrie, Jr., " 'THe West Is Our Great Adventure of the Spirit,' " *Life*, XLVI (Apr. 13, 1959), 93.

[8]*Custer's Immortality. A Poem, with biographical sketches of the chief actors in the late Tragedy of the Wilderness* (New York, 1876), 10, 14.

[9]*The American Mind: An Interpretation of American Thought and Character Since the 1880's* (New Haven, Conn., 1950), 44.

[10]Elizabeth Custer to J. A. Shoemaker, Mar. 19 and May 16, 1926. Copies in the Billings Public Library folder M-Biography-Custer, Elizabeth B.

[11]"Widow of Gen. Custer Recalls Stirring Days of Old West," unidentified clipping (1926) reprinting a story by Marie de Nervand in the *Boston Transcript*, in the Custer file, The Jennewein Western Library, (July 9, 1951), 41.

[12]*Congressional Record*, 44 Cong., 1 sess., 4478.

[13]"No Bitterness in Mrs. Custer Over Tragedy," *Billings Gazette*, June 25, 1926. Also see John B. Kennedy, "A Soldier's Widow," *Collier's*, LXXIX (Jan. 29, 1927), 10, 41; and Ishbel Ross, "Mrs. Custer Turns Pages of the Past," *New York Herald-Tribune*, June 25, 1929.

[14]Ray Allen Billington, "The New Western Social Order and the Synthesis of Western Scholarship," *The American West: An Appraisal. Papers from the Denver Conference on the History of Western America* ed. by Robert G. Ferris (Santa Fe, 1963), 12.

BIBLIOGRAPHICAL ESSAY

The materials upon which a study such as this is based do not accommodate themselves readily to bibliographical listing. The citations in the text indicate the range of my research. My primary sources are often secondary works, for I am as much interested in the impact of and reactions to popular Custeriana as in the Custeriana itself. For example, what people have said about the Anheuser-Busch lithograph is, for my purposes, almost as important as the lithograph. My concern, then, is with popular culture, not history; with attitudes toward an event, not the event.

Admittedly, my study is an impressionistic one. Attitudes have been divined from extensive but not exhaustive research. Indeed, I would contend that the pervasiveness of the Custer's Last Stand myth makes exhaustiveness a practical impossibility. One writer has noted that a week rarely goes by without Custer's name appearing in some context in any given American newspaper. The comic strips delight in it. Military analysts would be at a loss without it. Ann Landers tells "Withered Orange Blossoms" that she needs Clyde "like Custer needed more Indians." Jim Murray and his fellow sportswriters have made Custer's Last Stand an integral part of their vocabularies. On television, Johnny Carson has a whole repertoire of particularly leaden one-line Custer jokes that he regularly draws upon in his opening monologue, tossing them off with abandon. In fact, one index to the familiarity of Custer's name is not so much the frequency as the inevitability of its appearance. In my study, I have selected among the Custer references that I have encountered; those that have been missed are only further proof of the Last Stand's popularity.

As might be apparent from the text, I have methodically scanned the file of a single periodical, *Time*. Examining one American magazine over an extended run reveals something of the quantity and kind of its Custer reference, thereby serving to demonstrate the continuing vitality — and growth — of the Last Stand myth. *Time* is ideally suited to this purpose because, over the years, the Luce publications have retained a consistent, openly hostile attitude towards Custer which makes their Custer material one of a piece, with the bias understood.

I HISTORICAL BACKGROUND

The bibliography of Custer's Last Stand is immense, and it seems more

171

practical here to mention a few of the works on Custer literature than to prepare an extensive list of that literature. Fred Dustin's "Bibliography of the Battle of the Little Big Horn," first compiled in 1938 and updated twice thereafter, was published in three parts in William A. Graham, *The Custer Myth: A Source Book of Custeriana* (Harrisburg, Pa.: The Stackpole Company, 1953), 382-405. The quality of Dustin's "Bibliography" is uneven. His is primarily a compilation of materials in his personal collection (including private correspondence), not a scholarly bibliography. While 641 numbered items are listed, the actual total is well below this figure since Dustin often cross-referenced items under different numbers. But Dustin's is the necessary pioneering work. It provides a solid core of materials for a study of the Little Big Horn battle. Too, because Dustin was an extreme Custerphobe, his annotations can serve the wary reader as an enlightening guide to the intensity of emotion that has colored so much of the writing on Custer. Even better for assessing the almost unbelievable personal animosity between Custerphiles and Custerphobes of the past is John S. duMont, ed., "A Debate of Authors on the Custer Fight," *Westerners Brand Book* (Chicago), XXX (July, Aug., 1973), 33-5, 37-48. T. N. Luther, a Shawnee Mission, Kansas, bookdealer, has been carrying on a worthwhile project in his catalogues since 1964: a listing of Custer items (mostly books) published before 1953, but not included in Dustin's "Bibliography." Luther's annotations are incisive, and it is to be hoped that when he completes his supplement he will have it published as a whole. The task then facing some ambitious bibliographer will be to bring the compilation up to date. Since 1953, an amazing amount of relevant material has appeared, and while most of it is secondary, some of it is of high quality. For a selective appraisal of Custeriana, see Luther's *Custer High Spots* (Ft. Collins, Colo.: The Old Army Press, 1972).

There are three useful essays on Custer literature which throw light on the personal-historical controversies that have engaged the attention of the students of the battle: Edgar I. Stewart, "The Literature of the Custer Fight," *Pacific Northwesterner* (Spokane), I (Winter, 1956-57), 1-8; T. N. Luther, "Flags or Pigeons: Source Problems in the Literature of Custer's Last Stand," *Trail Guide* (Kansas City), VI (Mar., 1961); and Robert M. Utley, *Custer and the Great Controversy: The Origin and Development of a Legend* (Los Angeles: Westernlore Press, 1962), 147-66.

For the reader who wishes to learn something about the Last Stand without confronting its voluminous bibliography, a few standard works can be recommended. William A. Graham's *The Custer Myth* and *The Reno Court of Inquiry: Abstract of the Official Record of Proceedings* (Harrisburg, Pa.: The Stackpole Company, 1954) both contain primary materials that must underlie any study of the Little Big Horn. Two older syntheses, still worthwhile, are Graham's *The Story of the Little Big Horn: Custer's Last Fight* (Harrisburg, Pa.: Military Service Publishing Co., 1952 [1926]) and Dustin's *The Custer Tragedy: Events Leading Up To And Following the Little Big Horn Campaign of 1876* (Ann Arbor: Edwards Brothers, 1965 [1939]). Graham always maintained an admirable objectivity towards the various officers of the Seventh Cavalry, though he was less impartial in assessing the relative merits of Indian and white evidence. Custerphobia very much flavored Dustin's *The Custer Tragedy*, just as it does E. A. Brininstool's *Troopers With Custer: Historic Incidents of the Battle of the Little Big Horn* (Harrisburg, Pa.: The Stackpole Company, 1952), but both include important first-hand information. Edgar I. Stewart's *Custer's Luck* (Norman: University of Oklahoma Press, 1955) is the best of the syntheses, objective, accurate and broad in scope. For the reader interested in dipping into the conjecture and controversy that surrounds the Last Stand, Charles Kuhlman's *Legend Into History: The Custer Mystery (An Analytical Study of the Battle of the Little Big Horn)* (Harrisburg, Pa.: The Stackpole Company, rev. ed., 1952) is an excellent starting point. Though *Legend Into History* may not reflect the heat of the debate, it certainly testifies to the kind — and, in this case, quality — of mental exertion that has been expended on solving the riddles of Custer's Last Stand.

II. GENERAL CULTURAL STUDIES

Lord Raglan, *The Hero: A Study in Tradition, Myth, and Drama* (London: Watts & Co., 1949), is a dogmatic, stimulating analysis of the traditional hero. Raglan delineates twenty-two points that generally constitute the hero's biography — and, while he does not feel that historical figures can ever fit this pattern (the most points he grants one, Alexander the Great, is seven), those familiar with the Custer story will find that the General meets at least fourteen of Raglan's conditions, more than Pelops, Apollo, Joseph, Siegfried and Robin Hood! Dixon Wecter, *The Hero in America: A Chronicle of Hero-Worship* (New York: Charles Scribner's Sons, 1941) and Marshall W. Fishwick, *American Heroes: Myth and Reality* (Washington, D.C.: Public Affairs Press, 1954) both examine the facts and fictions about a number of America's heroes, and formulate several generalizations about the hero-making process in the United States. Also see Fishwick's *The Hero, American Style* (New York: David McKay Company, 1969), and Gerald W. Johnson's less useful *American Heroes and Hero-Worship* (New York: Harper & Brothers, 1943). Leo Gurko, *Heroes, Highbrows and the Popular Mind* (Indianapolis: Charter Books, rev. ed., 1962) is an interpretative study of the kinds of heroes Americans choose, and what these choices reflect about the American mind. Orrin E. Klapp, for his part, thinks that the "social types" Americans respond to may be keys to the national character. His *Heroes, Villains and Fools: The Changing American Character* (Englewood Cliffs, N.J.: Prentice-Hall, 1962) is useful because it is based on opinion polls and includes a few hard facts on what a sampling of Americans think of Custer and his Last Stand. Klapp's *Symbolic Leaders: Public Dramas and Public Men* (Chicago: Aldine Publishing Company, 1964) is more impressionistic and less helpful, though it does contain generalizations about the transformation of a man (and an event) into a symbol. Theodore P. Greene, *America's Heroes: The Changing Models of Success in American Magazines* (New York: Oxford University Press, 1970), includes many useful observations on American heroes and the concept of success as revealed in popular periodicals during four periods in American history. Many of the broader works on American culture have also considered the importance of heroes in the nation's life, for example, Daniel J. Boorstin, *The Americans: The National Experience* (New York: Random House, 1965), Pt. Seven: "Search for Symbols."

Henry Nash Smith's *Virgin Land: The American West as Symbol and Myth* (Cambridge: Harvard University Press, 1950) not only shows how myth has been a potent force throughout America's history, but also how, very early, the American Dream became associated with the geographical fact of free land to the West. Arthur K. Moore's *The Frontier Mind: A Cultural Analysis of the Kentucky Frontiersman* (Lexington : The University of Kentucky Press, 1957) is not as limited as its subtitle might indicate, and, while less unified and persuasively argued than *Virgin Land*, does contain some provocative insights into the relationship between the frontier-forest environment and the American character. "The Western Myth and a Last Frontier," the opening chapter of Robert G. Athearn's *Westward the Briton* (New York: Charles Scribner's Sons, 1953), provides a concise and lucid commentary on the myth of the Wild West. John G. Cawelti, "Cowboys, Indians, Outlaws," *American West*, I (Spring, 1964), 28-35, 77-9, briefly chronicles how the West came to be mythicized — from Leatherstocking to TV Westerns — and includes a useful bibliography. A. B. Guthrie, Jr., " 'The West Is Our Great Adventure of the Spirit,' " *Life*, XLVI (Apr. 13, 1959), 78-80, 93-4, 97-8, is an eloquent statement on the continuing significance of the West for modern Americans. Of course, no study of Western Myth can neglect Frederick Jackson Turner's seminal essay, "The Significance of the Frontier in American History," *Annual Report of the American HIstorical Association for the Year 1893* (Washington, D.C.: Government Printing Office, 1894), 199-227.

Besides *Virgin Land*, I have found Frank R. Kramer, *Voices in the Valley: Mythmaking and Folk Belief in the Shaping of the Middle West* (Madison: The University of Wisconsin Press, 1964), and Gregor Sebba, "Symbol and Myth in Modern Rationalistic Societies," *Truth, Myth, and Symbol* ed. by Thomas J. J. Altizer, William A. Beardslee and J. Harvey Young (Englewood Cliffs, N.J.: Prentice-Hall, 1962), 141-68, of assistance in clarifying my own understanding of myth and its role in American life.

III. THE CUSTER MYTH

A. Custer

William A. Graham's *The Custer Myth* is a collection of diverse source materials on the Little Big Horn battle. Graham's "myth" is implicit in these materials, existing in the very contradictions, seemingly impossible of reconciliation, contained in them. What Graham meant by "myth," Robert M. Utley and Kent L. Steckmesser call "legend." Utley's "The Legend of the Little Bighorn," *Corral Dust* (Washington, D.C.), I (June, 1956), 9-12, and *Custer and the Great Controversy* are excellent analyses of some of the fallacies, truths and half-truths that have emerged from the continuing historical debate over the Last Stand. Steckmesser's *The Western Hero in History and Legend* (Norman: University of Oklahoma Press, 1965), 163-237, examines the two Custers, historical and legendary. Steckmesser directs his efforts to separating fact from fiction, and to a study of the General's reputation in juvenile and adult novels. "Custer's Last Fight A Ritual Drama," *Westerners Brand Book* (Chicago), XV (Oct., 1958), 57-8, is the summary of a talk given by Norman Maclean, and presents many perceptive insights into the Custer myth. So also does Chp. VII, ". . .'A trumpet note for heroes,'" in Dee Brown, *The Year of the Century: 1876* (New York: Charles Scribner's Sons, 1966), 167-97, and the first section of Don Russell, *Custer's Last* (Fort Worth: Amon Carter Museum of Western Art, 1968), "The Legend," 3-11. Bruce A. Rosenberg, *Custer and the Epic of Defeat*, (University Park, Pa.: The Pennsylvania State University Press, 1974), is an overdue examination of the creation of the Last Stand myth that is especially good in elucidating the common elements in this American version of the universally-cherished legend of total annihilation.

B. Poetry

Virtually no attention has been paid to Custer poetry. An earlier version of Chapter Two of this book appeared as "Bards of the Little Big Horn," *Western American Literature*, I (Fall, 1966), 175-95; a compendium with the same title is scheduled to be published by The Old Army Press, Ft. Collins, Colorado, in 1976. Rosenberg, *Custer and the Epic of Defeat*, includes a discussion of "Instant Heroic Epics." Robert C. Steensma has written on Walt Whitman's "From Far Dakota's Cañons" in "Whitman and General Custer," *Walt Whitman Review*, X (June, 1964), 41-2. "The Poet Scout," Captain Jack Crawford, has been ably treated by Paul T. Nolan in a number of articles and, particularly, in "An Experiment in Myth-Making" which introduces *Three Plays* by J. W. (Capt. Jack) Crawford (The Hague, The Netherlands: Mouton & Co., 1966), 13-86. James T. King, "The Sword and the Pen: The Poetry of the Military Frontier," *Nebraska History*, XLVII (Sept., 1966), 229-45, also emphasizes Crawford's work. Robert H. Walker, *The Poet and the Gilded Age: Social Themes in Late 19th Century American Verse* (Philadelphia: University of Pennsylvania Press, 1963) mentions the Custer battle in passing, and offers some background to the verse of the time. Aaron Kramer, *The Prophetic Tradition in American Poetry, 1835-1900* (Rutherford, Pa.:

Fairleigh Dickinson University Press, 1968), 241-67, has much to say on poetry about the Little Big Horn but is disappointingly superficial. Lucy Lockwood Hazard, *The Frontier in American Literature* (New York: Thomas Y. Crowell Company, 1927), 126-37, and Albert Keiser, *The Indian in American Literature* (New York: Oxford University Press, 1933), 264-78, include critical dissections of John C. Neihardt's *The Song of the Indian Wars* in which a complaint common to both is that "the figure of General Custer never assumes heroic proportions" in the poem. The related subject of the Last Stand in song has also been largely ignored. One exception is Austin and Alta Fife, "Ballads of the Little Big Horn," *American West*, IV (Feb., 1967), 46-9, 86-9, which prints the words and music of six Custer ballads.

C. Painting

The Anheuser-Busch lithograph and the Cassilly Adams painting it was based upon have inspired a sizable bibliography extremely uneven in quality. Serious research came to the fore in 1946, perhaps stimulated by the destruction of the Adams' oil in a fire.

Two important essays on Custer art appeared that year: Robert Taft, "The Pictorial Record of the Old West, IV: Custer's Last Stand," *Kansas Historical Quarterly*, XIV (Nov., 1946), 361-90; and Don Russell, "Sixty Years in Bar Rooms; or 'Custer's Last Fight,'" *Westerners Brand Book* (Chicago), III (Nov., 1946), 61-3, 65-8. The two are discussed in Peter Caswell, "The Bar Room Custer," *Military Affairs*, XI (Spring, 1947), 50-1. Taft's article, slightly condensed, serves as Chapter IX of his *Artists and Illustrators of the Old West, 1850-1900* (New York: Charles Scribner's Sons, 1953). Russell, as editor of the Chicago *Westerners Brand Book*, has brought much information on Custer paintings into print over the years, and his *Custer's Last*, published in conjunction with a 1968 exhibition of pictorial Custeriana at the Amon Carter Museum of Western Art, Fort Worth, Texas, is an entertaining and informative introduction to the subject, while his *Custer's List: A Checklist of Pictures Relating to the Battle of the Little Big Horn* (Fort Worth: Amon Carter Museum of Western Art, 1970) is indispensable for the student of pictorial Custeriana. Lists of movie re-enactments and cartoons about Custer's Last Stand are also included. Harold McCracken, *Portrait of the Old West* (New York: McGraw-Hill Book Company, 1952), has a chapter on Custer artists, while Harrison Lane, "Brush, Palette and the Little Big Horn," *Montana: the Magazine of Western History*, XXIII (Summer, 1973), 66-80, is an interpretive discussion. For a rebuttal, see Brian Dippie, "Brush, Palette and the Custer Battle: A Second Look," *ibid.*, XXIV (Winter, 1974), 55-67.Vincent Mercaldo, "Cessilly [*sic*] Adams and His Custer Painting," *Westerners Brand Book* (N.Y.), IV, 1 (1957), 17, 23, and William Edgar Paxson, " 'Custer's Last Stand:' The Painting and the Artist," *True West*, XI (Oct., 1963), 14-6, 52-3, are concerned with the Last Stands of, respectively, Cassilly Adams and E. S. Paxson, but discuss others as well. Several Last Stand paintings are reproduced in "Speaking of Pictures . . . Artists Had a Field Day with Custer's Famous Stand," *Life*, XXIV (June 21, 1948), 12-4; Lawrence A. Frost, *The Custer Album: A Pictorial Biography of General George A. Custer* (Seattle: Superior Publishing Company, 1964), 8-16; "Little Big Horn: A Massacre Captured Forever by the Artists of the West," *Westerner*, I (Nov.-Dec., 1969), 33-7; and Editors of Time-Life Books, *The Soldiers* (New York: Time-Life Books, 1973), 222-31. An expanded version of my discussion of Custer humor, " 'Have you heard the one about Custer's Last Words?' " is scheduled to appear in Paul Hutton, ed., *Little Big Horn Associates Annual*, 1976.

D. Fiction

The word "Western" usually connotes "cowboy story" and that whole body of high-appeal, low-quality formula fiction set in te late nineteenth-century West. Certainly, most articles on the Western have meant what Wallace Stegner termed the "large 'W' Westerns." In the past, informal, sometimes reminiscent essays comprised the bulk of available literature on the genre. For example: W. H. Hutchinson, "Virgins, Villains, and Varmints, " *Huntington Library Quarterly*, XVI (Aug., 1953), 381-92; Bernard De Voto, "The Easy Chair: Phaëthon on Gunsmoke Trail," *Harper's Magazine*, CCIX (Dec., 1954), 10-11, 14, 16; and Clifton Fadiman, "Party of One," *Holiday*, XXXIV (Aug., 1963), 10, 12-7. Writers of formula Westerns have occasionally paused to analyze their craft: Frank Gruber, "The Basic Western Plots," *The Writer's 1955 Year Book*, No. 26 (1955), 49-53, 160; and Tom Curry, "The Wild Western Rides Again," *Saturday Review*, XLVIII (Dec. 11, 1965), 70-1, 78. So dominant is the cowboy story in this genre that Will Chamberlain was led to ask, "What About the Army Western?," *Roundup*, VIII (June, 1960), 27-8, 30. The file of *Roundup*, the monthly journal of the Western Writers of America, is a major source of anyone interested in the popular Western since it offers the opinions of the practitioners of the art.

Today, a more scholarly, analytical approach to the Western is common. For example, five essays on the subject were published in the *Journal of Popular Culture*, IV (Fall, 1970), 453-526. Russel Nye, *The Unembarrassed Muse: The Popular Arts in America* (New York: The Dial Press, 1970), Chp. XII: "Sixshooter Country," 280-304, is a good introduction to the formula Western, while John G. Cawelti, *The Six-gun Mystique* (Bowling Green, O.: Bowling Green University Popular Press, ca. 1971), is an essential, if occasionally ponderous, study. Cawelti places the Western within the context of formula fiction generally, assesses previous theories on the subject of its mass appeal and includes a valuable bibliography of critical literature.

A spokesman for one branch of the small "w" western is A. B. Guthrie, Jr., "The Historical Novel," *Montana: the Magazine of Western History*,

IV (Fall, 1954), 1-8. Also see John Milton, "Interview: Michael Straight," *South Dakota Review*, VI (Winter, 1968-69), 3-13. Wallace Stegner discusses the future of the western with mixed emotions in "History, Myth and the Western Writer," *American West*, IV (May, 1967), 61-2, 76-9. Two booklength treatments of Western literature are James K. Folsom, *The American Western Novel* (New Haven, Conn.: College & University Press, 1966), and Robert Edson Lee, *From West to East: Studies in the Literature of the American West* (Urbana: University of Illinois Press, 1966). The scholarly quarterlies *South Dakota Review* and *Western American Literature* are exploring a relatively untouched field in critical depth.

Custer fiction has received general coverage in Kent L. Steckmesser, "Custer in Fiction: George A. Custer, Hero or Villain?," *American West*, I (Fall, 1964), 47-52, 63-4, which appeared in a slightly different form in *The Western Hero in History and Legend*. Norman Maclean, "Custer's Last Fight a Ritual Drama," also makes some pertinent comments on the Custer fiction. Specific Custer novels have rarely received extended comment. Thomas Berger's *Little Big Man* is the exception. See L. L. Lee, "American, Western, Picaresque: Thomas Berger's *Little Big Man*," *South Dakota Review*, IV (Summer, 1966), 35-42; William T. Pilkington, "Aspects of the Western Comic Novel," *Western American Literature*, I (Fall, 1966), 209-17; Delbert E. Wylder, "Thomas Berger's *Little Big Man* as Literature," *ibid.*, III (Winter, 1969), 273-84; Jay Gurian, "Style in the Literary Desert: *Little Big Man*," *ibid.*, 285-96; Brian W. Dippie, "Jack Crabb and the Sole Survivors of Custer's Last Stand," *ibid.*, IV (Fall, 1969), 189-202; and Leo E. Oliva, "Thomas Berger's *Little Big Man* as History," *ibid.*, VIII (Spring and Summer, 1973), 33-54. Ernest Haycox's *Bugles in the Afternoon* is often favorably mentioned in discussions of the popular Western, and Haycox himself has been accorded a high position by his fellow writers: Luke Short [Frederick D. Glidden], "Ernest Haycox: An Appreciation," *Roundup*, XII (Apr., 1964), 1-3. See also Richard Etulain, "Ernest Haycox: The Historical Western, 1937-43," *South Dakota Review*, V (Spring, 1967), 35-54. Henry W. Allen's work, published under the pennames Will Henry and Clay Fisher, is intelligently appraised in a long review by Arnold E. Needham, *Western American Literature*, I (Winter, 1967), 297-302, while Anne Falke, "Clay Fisher or Will Henry?: An Author's Choice of Pen Names," *Journal of Popular Culture*, VII (Winter, 1973), 692-700, concentrates on *Red Blizzard* (Fisher) and *No Survivors* (Henry).

The dime novel is a specialized field wherein the non-expert ventures with trepidation. I have been fortunate in finding capable guides. Albert Johannsen, *The House of Beadle and Adams and His Dime and Nickel Novels: The Story of a Vanished Literature*, 2 vols. (Norman: University of Oklahoma Press, 1950), provided precise bibliographical information on the Custer dime novels published by Beadle and Adams. Steckmesser's work has been helpful, as has Don Russell, *The Lives and Legends of Buffalo Bill* (Norman: University of Oklahoma Press, 1960). I am very much indebted to Mr. Russell for additional information on the Custer dime novels in general, and the Buffalo Bill-Custer stories in particular. Thomas A. Frazier, "Custer, the Man and the Legend," *Real West*, XI (Aug., 1968), 18-9, 54-6, 70, 76, provides plot outlines of a few early Custer stories. The bibliography "Custer in Popular Fiction," *ibid.*, 6, was compiled by Edward T. LeBlanc, publisher of the monthly *Dime Novel Round-up* , and a most generous and knowledgeable correspondent. William A. Settle, Jr., "Literature as History: The Dime Novel as an Historian's Tool," in *Literature and History* ed. by I. E. Cadenhead, Jr. (Tulsa, Okla.: The University of Tulsa, Monograph Series No. 9, 1970, 9-20), is an interesting essay for the student of Western myth.

E. Re-enactments

There is no comprehensive study of the Custer's Last Stand re-enactments, though Don Rickey, Jr., deals with several of them in *History of Custer Battlefield* (Billings,, Mont.: Custer Battlefield Historical and Museum Association, 1967), 74-84. Don Russell's *The Lives and Legends of Buffalo Bill* and Henry Blackman Sell and Victor Weybright's *Buffalo Bill and the Wild West* (New York: Oxford University Press, 1955) pay some attention to the Wild West Show's re-enactment, while Don Russell, *The Wild West: A History of the Wild West Shows* (Fort Worth: Amon Carter Museum of Western Art, 1970), and "The Golden Age of Wild West Shows," *Westerners Brand Book* (Chicago), XXVI (Feb., 1970), 89-91, 96, include information on other early Wild West Shows, some of which also featured re-enactments of Custer's Last Stand. The clipping files of the Western History Research Center at the University of Wyoming, Laramie, contain much on the various anniversary observances, particularly the fortieth and fiftieth.

Considerable interest has been aroused by the Crow Indian re-creation of the battle staged annually since 1964 just outside Hardin, Montana: "As the Crow Fights," *Newsweek*, LXIV (July 13, 1964), 56; Anne Chamberlin, "Bad Day Ahead for the Army's Greatest Loser," *Saturday Evening Post*, CCXXXIX (Aug. 27, 1966), 70-3 (illustrated with color photographs); Dorothy M. Johnson, "Custer Rides Again," *Montana: the Magazine of Western History*, XVII (Spring, 1967), 53-63 (also mentions some of the earlier re-enactments and anniversary celebrations), and her "Where Custer Fell," *Ford Times*, LXI (June, 1968), 7-11; and Richard Atcheson, "Montana Is the Message," *Holiday*, XLV (May, 1969), 56-9, 78-9.

Probably no subject lends itself more grudgingly to conventional historical research techniques than cinematic history. It has not been possible for me to see any of the really early Custer films apart from Ince's *Custer's Last Fight* and Griffith's *The Massacre*, though I have seen all of those that have appeared since *The Plainsman* courtesy of that much-deprecated institution, the late-night TV show, and thus I am especially grateful for George N. Fenin and William K. Everson's excellent work,

The Western from Silents to Cinerama (New York: Orion Press, 1962). Also see William K. Everson, *A Pictorial History of the Western Film* (New York: The Citadel Press, 1969). Allen Eyles' compendium *The Western: An Illustrated Guide* (London: A. Zwemmer Limited, 1967) is useful, and includes a list of the cinematic Custers.

The Western movie or television series is, like its literary counterpart, usually approached as a cowboy story. But such essays as Robert Warshow, "Movie Chronicle: The Westerner," *The Immediate Experience: Movies, Comics, Theatre & Other Aspects of Popular Culture* (Garden City: Doubleday & Company, 1962), 135-54; Janet Graves, "They Never Miss," *American Gun*, I (Spring, 1961), 65-80; Peter Homans, "The Western: The Legend and the Cardboard Hero," *Look*, XXVI (Mar. 13, 1962), 82-4, 86-7, 89; Larry McMurtry, "Cowboys and Cadillacs: Realism in the Movies," *Riata: Student Literary Magazine of the University of Texas*, Fall, 1966, 4-9; John A. Barsness, "A Question of Standard," *Film Quarterly*, XXI (Fall, 1967), 32-7; and John G. Cawelti, "The Gunfighter and Society," *American West*, V (Mar., 1968), 30-5, 76-8, all include interesting generalizations about the Western. Jack Spears, "The Indian on the Screen," *Films in Review*, X (Jan., 1959), 18-35; and Robert Larkins, "Hollywood and the Indian," *Focus on Film* No. 2 (Mar.-Apr., 1970), 44- 53, are useful guides to a once-neglected subject, now heavily studied. For a discussion focusing on the Custer movies that cites a good number of the recent studies of the Indian on the screen, see Brian Dippie, "Popcorn and Indians: Custer on the Screen," *Cultures*, II, 1 (1974), 139-68.

The best known Custer movie, *They Died With Their Boots On* (1941), has received much comment over the years. "Custer's Last Stand: 'They Died With Their Boots On' Glorifies a Rash General," *Life*, XI (Dec. 8, 1941), 75-8, is particularly worthwhile since it reproduces a number of stills from the movie and parallels these romanticized scenes with actual photographs of General Custer. Also see Tony Thomas, Rudy Behlmer and Clifford McCarty, *The Films of Errol Flynn* (New York: The Citadel Press, 1969), 106-11. *Little Big Man* also occasioned much critical interest and comment. The best review is Philip French's intelligent, highly informative discussion in *Sight and Sound*, XL (Spring, 1971), 102-3.

The television series *Custer*, under almost continual attack by various Indain rights groups from the moment of its conception, got a great deal of press coverage *before* it began its run. See, for example, Charles Hillinger, "US Indian Group Protests Projected Custer Series," *Austin American-Statesman*, July 22, 1967, 25; Harriet Peters, "Real Indians Take Pot Shots at New Series on Col. Custer," *Cleveland Press*, Aug. 15, 1967; "Custer TV Show Protested," *The Edmonton* (Alberta) *Journal*, July 22, 1967, 43; and "Custer at Bay Again," *Newsweek*, LXX (Aug. 7, 1967), 51. With its first appearance on the screen, however, interest quickly waned. *Custer* did inspire an amusing article by P. M. Clepper, "He's Our George," *TV Guide*, XV (Sept. 23, 1967), 32-4.

Appendix A:

A CHRONOLOGICAL BIBLIOGRAPHY
OF CUSTER BIOGRAPHY

1874.   George A. Custer. *My Life on the Plains; or, Personal Experiences with Indians.* New York: Sheldon & Company.

A readable account of Custer's experiences on the Southern Plains. To get a better balanced picture of the events described, however, one should consult another contemporary work, W. B. Hazen's "Some Corrections of *Life on the Plains*," which serves as an appendix to an edition of Custer's book ed. by Edgar I. Stewart (Norman: University of Oklahoma Press, 1962). An edition ed. by Milo Milton Quaife has been reprinted twice: New York: The Citadel Press (A Citadel Pioneer Book), 1962; and Lincoln: University of Nebraska Press (Bison Series), 1966.

1876.   Frederick Whittaker. *A Complete Life of Gen. George A. Custer.* New York: Sheldon & Company.

Based in large part on *My Life on the Plains*, this is a complete whitewash of the General. Popular in its time, it caused considerable controversy, for in shifting the blame for the Little Big Horn off Custer's shoulders it indicted Major Reno and Captain Benteen as the two individuals most directly responsible for the disaster. Whittaker's book was widely read, and it set the heroic tone for future works on Custer.

1882.   Frederick Whittaker. *The Dashing Dragoon; or, The Story of Gen. George A. Custer from West Point to the Big Horn. Beadle's Boy's Library of Sport, Story and Adventure* (Quarto Edition) No. 20 (Apr. 26, 1882).

A condensation of the 1876 biography with all of the heroism left intact. Reprint: *Beadle's Boy's Library of Sport, Story and Adventure* (Octavo Edition) No. 36 (Dec. 20, 1884).

1885.   Elizabeth B. Custer. *"Boots and Saddles;" or, Life in Dakota with General Custer.* New York: Harper & Brothers.

The first volume in Mrs. Custer's trilogy. All three are well-written paeans to the General's memory. Of the books, *"Boots and Saddles"* has been particularly influential, and Mrs. Custer's dedication is worth quoting: "Dedicated to my husband, the echo of whose voice has been my inspiration." Rebrint: Norman: University of Oklahoma Press (The Western Frontier Library), 1961.

1887.   Elizabeth B. Custer. *Tenting on the Plains; or, General Custer in Kansas and Texas*. New York: Charles L. Webster & Company.
Reprint: Norman: University of Oklahoma Press (The Western Frontier Library), 1971.

1890.   Elizabeth B. Custer. *Following the Guidon*. New York: Harper & Brothers.
Reprint: Norman: University of Oklahoma Press (The Western Frontier Library), 1966.

1901.   Mary E. Burt, ed.; as told by Elizabeth B. Custer. *The Boy General: Story of the Life of Major-General George A. Custer*. New York: Charles Scribner's Sons.
A juvenile biography culled from Mrs. Custer's three books.

1917.   Frederick S. Dellenbaugh. *George Armstrong Custer*. New York: The Macmillan Company.
Another juvenile biography in the hero-worshipping vein.

1928.   Frazier Hunt. *Custer: The Last of the Cavaliers*. New York: Cosmopolitan Book Corporation.
This was apparently intended as a "reply" to criticisms of Custer that were raised during the semi-centennial observance (1926). Inaccurate and flimsy, as its title indicates it is an adulator's account. It was also serialized as "The Romantic Soldier," *Red Book Magazine*, LI (Aug., Sept., Oct., 1928).

1929   Milton Ronsheim. *The Life of General Custer*. Cadiz, O.: Cadiz Republican.
Another biography in the Whittaker tradition. Ronsheim's book had limited circulation and thus has been of slight importance, though it has an unusually good bibliography.

1934.   Frederic F. Van de Water. *Glory-Hunter: A Life of General Custer*. Indianapolis: The Bobbs-Merrill Company.
This is not only the classic anti-Custer biography, but also a brilliantly-written analysis of Custer's character. The General is shown as a man of courage, but also as a perpetual adolescent who was ruled by a single passion throughout his life: a craving for glory. Van de Water's book (which appeared the year after Mrs. Custer's death) still exerts a strong influence. Reprinted: New York: Argosy-Antiquarian, 1963.

1944.   Shannon Garst. *Custer: Fighter of the Plains*. New York: Julian Messner.

Like most of the juvenile biographies, Mrs. Garst's book remains faithful to the tradition of a heroic Custer.

1946.   Fred Dustin. "George Armstrong Custer," *Michigan History Magazine*, XXX (Apr.-June, 1946), 226-54.
The blackest, severest account of Custer's life ever written. Dustin was a bitter Custerphobe, and his hatred sometimes dominated his historical judgment.

1950.   Marguerite Merington, ed. *The Custer Story: The Life and Intimate Letters of General George A. Custer and His Wife Elizabeth.*
Marguerite Merington was for years Mrs. Custer's private secretary. Her collection of The Custer letters in the form of a "story" makes the book a readable joint-biography of the General and his wife. At the same time, because of Miss Merington's discreet selection and editing of the letters, we get a one-sided, totally glamorous picture of the Custers.

1951.   Quentin Reynolds. *Custer's Last Stand.* New York: Random House.
Reynolds in this juvenile biography has so thoroughly exploited the heroic tradition of the Boy General that his is more an account of a legend than a study of a life.

1954.   Margaret Leighton. *The Story of General Custer.* New York: Grosset & Dunlap.
A straightforward juvenile biography of the heroic Custer. The illustrations by Nicholas Eggenhofer are noteworthy.

1959.   Nelle Deex. *Glory Trek: The Story of General George Custer's Last Stand.* New York: The William-Frederick Press.
Written by a grandmother whose hobby happens to be Custeriana, *Glory Trek*, is little more than a pastiche of excerpts from Mrs. Custer's books — and these badly pieced together. It is a complete whitewash, of course.

1959.   Jay Monaghan. *Custer: The Life of General George Armstrong Custer.* Boston: Little, Brown and Company.
The best modern life of the General. Monaghan's book is well-written, and while the author inclines markedly in Custer's favor, he is not an indiscriminate hero-worshipper. The book gives the best coverage of Custer's Civil War career available. It is weak chiefly in its discussion of Custer's years on the Northern plains. Reprint: Lincoln: University of Nebraska Press (Bison Series), 1971.

1960.   Lauran Paine. *The General Custer Story: The True Story of the Battle of the Little Big Horn.* London: W. Foulsham & Co.
This is primarily a discussion of the Little Big Horn campaign and only secondarily a biography.

1963.   Augusta Stevenson. *George Custer: Boy of Action.* Indianapolis: The Bobbs-Merrill Company.

Despite its title and its inclusion in a series on the childhood of famous Americans, this book covers Custer's entire life. Intended for very young readers, it is surprisingly objective in treatment.

1964.   Lawrence A. Frost. *The Custer Album: A Pictorial Biography of General George A. Custer.* Seattle: Superior Publishing Company.

The pictures in this album are excellent, but the text is disappointing. Dr. Frost, curator of the Custer Room in the Monroe, Michigan, County Museum, is the best known Custerphile of our time, but he exhibits slight skill as a writer, and his book is not the well-argued defense of Custer that the reader has a right to expect.

1967.   D. A. Kinsley. *Favor the Bold.* Vol. 1: *Custer: The Civil War Years.* New York: Holt, Rinehart and Winston.

1968.   D. A. Kinsley. *Favor the Bold.* Vol. 2: *Custer: The Indian Fighter.* New York: Holt, Rinehart and Winston.

This two-volume biography depicts Custer as an "epic hero, a legend even in his own time," who "still lives enshrined by all the mystery and glamour that immortalize a man transcended into myth." Neither its scholarship nor its style are equal to Jay Monaghan's, whose *Custer* remains the standard work.

1968.   William Heuman. *Custer: Man and Legend.* New York: Dodd, Mead & Company.

Intended primarily for teenagers, this is a relatively sophisticated biography with only a mild pro-Custer bias.

Appendix B:

BIBLIOGRAPHY OF CUSTER POEMS

CBNM: Custer Battlefield National Monument, Crow Agency, Montana.

"Clippings Enclosed:" "Clippings Enclosed in Correspondence: Catalogued and Cross-referenced," E. B. Custer Collection, CBNM.

Smith *Scrap Book*: Mrs. Nettie Bowen Smith *Scrap Book*, Bancroft Library, University of California, Berkeley.

Anderson, Clarence. "The Battle of the Little Big Horn," *Little Big Horn Associates Newsletter*, II (Jan., 1968), 8.

Anon. "Custer. To The Heroes of the Custer Tie. *Dedicated to the gallant Gen. Custer*," *Chicago Daily Tribune*, July 10, 1876, 2. A Civil War poem, datelined "Six miles from Alexandria, Va., May 30, 1865."

——. "The Song of Custer and His Men," *St. Paul Pioneer-Press*, July 14, 1876; reprinted in the *Chicago Daily Tribune*, July 22, 1876, 9.

——. "Custer," *Charleston Journal of Commerce*, July 19, 1876, 3.

——. "Romance and Reality," *Harper's Weekly*, XX (July 29, 1876), 618.

——. "Old Comanche," *United States Army and Navy Journal*, Apr. 27, 1878.

——. "The Legend of Old Tennessee," *Little Big Horn Associates Newsletter*, I (Jan., 1971), 3-4.

AtLee, T. S. "In Memory of General Custer," *Washington Star* (?), July, 1876; reprinted in S. Goodale Price, *Saga of the Hills* (Hollywood: Cosmo Press, 1940), 51-2.

B., H. G. "General Custer," unidentified clipping (*The Vedette* [?]) dated "Philadelphia, August 13, 1876," in the Smith *Scrap Book*, 10.

Bacheller, Irving. "Ballad of the Sabre Cross and 7," *In Various Moods: Poems and Verses* (New York: Harper & Brothers, 1910), 14-9. Reprinted, revised, in Wallace and Frances Rice, eds., *The Humbler Poets (Second Series): A Collection of Newspaper and Periodical Verse, 1885 to 1910* (Chicago: A. C. McClurg, 1911), 323-5.

Barber, Raymond T. "Massacre at Little Big Horn," *Bits and Pieces*, I (Aug., 1965), 22.

Beede, A. McG. *Sitting Bull-Custer* (Bismarck, N.D.: Bismarck Tribune, 1913). A drama in four scenes and in verse.

Bellville, John Oliver. "Custer's Last Battle," *Thorns and Roses* (Evansville, Ind.: Keller Printing, 1895), 65-7.

Belrose, Louis, Jr. "To 'Sitting Bull,' on receiving the news of his victory over U.S. troops," *Thorns and Flowers* (Philadelphia: privately printed [S. A. George & Co.], 1879), 121. Dated "Eaux-Bonnes, Basses Pyrénées, Sept. 9, 1876."

Bénet, Rosemary, and Stephen Vincent Bénet. "Crazy Horse," *A Book of Americans* (New York: Farrar and Rinehart, 1933), 79.

Berry, Catherine E. "Look Past the Stars," *Denver Post Empire Magazine*, June 24, 1951, 33.

Bigney, M. F. "Custer," *New Orleans Republican*, July 23, 1876, 6.

Black Elk. [Sioux kill songs], *Black Elk Speaks: Being the Life Story of a Holy Man of the Ogalala Sioux* by John G. Neihardt (New York: William Morrow, 1932), 134.

Brautigan, Richard. "General Custer Versus the Titanic," *The Pill Versus the Springhill Mine Disaster* (New York: Dell, 1973 [1968]), 3.

Brooks, Francis. "Down the Little Big Horn," *The Poems of Francis Brooks* ed. by Wallace Rice (Chicago: R. R. Donnelley, 1898), 123-32.

Buck, Audrey Souder. "Custer's Grave," Postcard 8715, Robbins-Tillquist Co., Spokane, Wash., n.d.

"Buckskin." *The Passing of the Buffalo* (Vancouver, B.C.: The Selkirk Press, 1916). Sitting Bull's Sioux in Canada; a verse play.

Carey, Walter. "Custer's Last Ride," *Latrobe* (Pa.) *Advance* (1876), in the Smith *Scrap Book*, 7.

Carleton, Will. "The Heart and the Sword," *Monroe* (Mich.) *Record Commercial* June 23, 1910. Clipping in the CBNM Pamphlet File #4322, E. B. Custer Scrap Book.

Carvell, J. S. "In Memoriam," *Campaigns of General Custer in the North-West, and the Final Surrender of Sitting Bull* by Judson Elliott Walker (New York: Argonaut Press, 1966 [1881]), 120-1. The peom was dated July 8, 1876.

Chapman, Arthur. "Sunrise on Custer Battle Field," *Teepee Book*, II (June, 1916), 13.

[Clarke, Joseph I. C.], "Custer's Last Charge," *New York Herald*, July 15, 1876, 3. This poem was frequently reprinted, usually with passages deleted, sometimes with additions.

Clover, Sam T. "Decoration Day on the Little Big Horn," *Army Magazine*, June, 1894.

——— . "Where Custer Fell," *On Special Assignment: Being the Further Adventures of Paul Travers* (New York: Argonaut Press, 1965 [1903]), 67-8.

Coffin, Robert P. Tristram. "The Last Cavalier," *Primer for America* (New York: Macmillan, 1943), 42-3.

Coldiron, Daisy Lemon. "Custer on the Washita (1868)," *Songs of Oklahoma* (Dallas: The Kaleidograph Press, 1935), 32-5. Also: "The Death of Brave Bear," pp. 117-8.

Cowdrey, Mary Boynton. "The Second Departure of Custer," *The North American Book of Verse*, Vol. IV (New York: Henry Harrison, 1939), 396-7.

Crawford, Captain Jack [John Wallace Crawford]. "The Death of Custer,"

The Poet Scout: A Book of Song and Story (New York: Funk & Wagnalls, 1886), 106-8. Also: "Wild Bill's Grave," pp. 49-50; "The Dying Scout," p. 94; "Comrade, Why this Look of Sadness?," pp. 108-10; "'God Bless Ye, Gener'l Custer,' " pp. 112-3; and "Custer," pp. 133-4.

Davis, C. B. "Custer," *Teepee Book*, I (June, 1915), 2. Poem copyrighted 1912.

E., I. "Custer's Last Battle," *Cincinnati Commercial*, July 19, 1876, 5.

Eastlake, William. "red muslims and uncle tomahawks," *A Child's Garden of Verses for the Revolution* (New York: Grove Press [Black Cat Book], 1970), 46, 53, 56-9.

Eble, Jessie G. "The Battle of the Washita — 1868," *The Red Trail* (New York: Henry Harrison, 1931), 42-6.

Eccard, Eva (Shillingburg), "Ballad of the 7th," *Little Big Horn Associates Research Review*, VII (Fall, 1973).

Ee-Soshke-Oah-Bush [Herbert Coffeen]. "The Las' Stan'," *Teepee Book*, II (June, 1916), 59.

Elliott, Harley. "Custer Like a Painting in the Greasy Grass," *All Beautyfull & Foolish Souls* (Trumansburg, N.Y.: The Crossing Press, 1974), 22-3. Also: "Crazy Horse Returns to South Dakota," pp. 10-1.

Fatchen, Max. "High Noon on Oxford Street," *Denver Post*, Oct. 2, 1966. A humorous poem on the BBC's decision to cancel all Westerns on its television network; reprinted from the *Adelaide* (Australia) *Advertiser*.

Gardner, Orpha M. "With Custer," *Frontier*, XIII (May, 1933), 310.

Gesell, William, "The Battle of Little Big Horn, June 25, 1876," *Monroe County Weekly* (Mich.), Feb. 20, 1936.

Gher, A. M. "The Conflict," *Old Trail and the New: A Tale of the Kittatinnies* (Carlisle, Pa., 1909), 8-12.

Green, Charles P. ("Soldier"). "Custer Framed," *Ballads of the Black Hills* (Boston: The Christopher Publishing House, 1931), 123-5. Also: "General Custer," p. 131; "Crazy Horse," p. 136; and "Sitting Bull," pp. 138-9.

Guerrier, George P. "Custer and His Men," *Bivouac*, II (Feb., 1884).

Haggard, Robert E. "'Cavalry-on-Wheels,'" *New York Herald Tribune*, Sept. 12, 1949; reprinted in Anthony A. Amaral, *Comanche: The Horse That Survived the Custer Massacre* (Los Angeles: Westernlore Press, 1961), 60-l.

Harriman, Alice. "To a Wild Rose from the Custer Battlefield," *Pacific History Stories: Montana Edition* (San Francisco: The Whitaker & Ray Company, 1903), 100.

[Hay, John]. "Miles Keogh's Horse," *Atlantic Monthly*, XLV (Feb., 1880), 214-6.

Hazell, Audrey J. "Commanche," *Custer's Last Battle* by Charles King (Grand Rapids, Mich.: Custer Ephemera Publications, 1975), 11.

Hersey, Harold. "Chilled-Steel Custer," *Singing Rawhide: A Book of Western Ballads* (New York: George H. Doran, 1926), 37-41. Also: "The Lay of the Last Frontier," pp. 185-9.

Holley, Frances Chamberlain. "Custer's Farewell," *Once Their Home; or, Our Legacy from the Dahkotahs* (Chicago: Donohue & Henneberry, 1892), 253.

Hunt, Leavitt. "The Last Charge," unidentified clipping (*New York Post,* 1876) in the Smith *Scrap Book,* 39.

Hutchinson, Percy Adams. "Little Big-Horn," *The Lyric Year: One Hundred Poems* ed. by Ferdinand Earle (New York: Mitchell Kennerley, 1912), 131.

Jenkins, Paul. "Custer's Last Stand," *Massachusetts Review,* XIV (Spring, 1973), 306-7.

Kenny, Maurice. "Monahsetah . . . A Cheyenne Girl," *Akwesasne Notes,* IV (Late Autumn, 1972), 48.

—— . "Black Kettle," *Bits and Pieces,* IX (Mar.-Apr., 1973), inside back cover. Both of Kenny's poems deal with the Washita.

Kerr, A. P. "Custer's Last Charge: June 25, 1876," unidentified clipping (Indianapolis, 1886) in "Clippings Enclosed."

LeCaine, John (Woonkapi-sni). "Custer's Day," *The Sioux Indians in Canada* by Gontran LaViolette (Regina, Sask.: The Marian Press, 1944), 77-9.

Lee, A. T. "The Wrath of the Black Hills," *United States Army and Navy Journal,* Aug. 12, 1876.

Lenhart, William. "Our Hero." One sheet, printed, n.p. [N.Y.?], n.d. Copy in CBNM Pamphlet File #2711.

Linton, Kent. "The Last Battle of the Century — Fought June 25th, 1876," *Decatur* (Ill.) *Republican,* July 20, 1876.

Lockwood, Betty. "The Night on Reno Hill," *Little Big Horn Associates Newsletter,* III (Summer, 1969), 8-9.

Longfellow, Henry Wadsworth. "The Revenge of Rain-in-the-Face," *The Youth's Companion,* L (Mar. 1, 1877), 68.

Lovelace, Katherine Kerns. "The Battle (June 1876)," *The Eagle's Cry* (Philadelphia: Dorrance & Company, 1967), 38.

Low, Charles H. "Custer and His Brave Men," *Winners of the West,* Feb. 28, 1931.

Lucas, Harry A. "The Saga of General George Custer," *Ballads of Arizona* (New York: Exposition Press, 1952).

Ludlow, William. "Custer's Last Charge," unidentified clipping in "Clippings Enclosed" and in the Smith *Scrap Book,* 50.

McAtee, Lawrence Turnbull. "Custer's Last Stand," *A Poetry Concert* ed. by Henry Harrison (New York: Henry Harrison, 1935), 117-20.

McClure, William J. "Extermination," *The Pilot* (Boston), Aug. 26, 1876, 6.

McGaffey, Ernest. "Little Big Horn," *Poems* (New York: Dodd, Mead, 1895), 235-7.

McGregor, James H. "A Chief's Last Thoughts," *Voices from Tepee Land* (Philadelphia: Dorrance & Company, 1944), 17-9.

Madden, John. "The Custer Flower," *American Indian,* II (Jan., 1928), 9.

Mayfield, Ben. "Trooper's Dilemma," *Little Big Horn Associates Research Review,* V (Fall, 1971), 54.

———. "'Talk T' Me,'" *Little Big Horn Associates Reserach Review*, VI (Spring, 1972), 12.

Miller, Freeman E. "Where Custer Fell," *Songs from the South-West Country* (New York: The Knickerbocker Press, 1898), 54-5. Also: "The Battle of the Washita," pp. 19-26; and "Slaughtering the Ponies," pp. 32-5.

Miller, Joaquin [Cincinnatus Hiner Miller]. "Custer and His Three Hundred," *Frank Leslie's Illustrated Newspaper*, XLII (July 29, 1876), 342.

———. "Custer," *In Classic Shades and Other Poems* (Chicago: Belford-Clarke, 1890), 52. Also: "The Battle Flag at Shenandoah," 34-6.

Morford, Henry. "Chivalry's Afterglow," *Algernon Sydney Sullivan* by Anne Middleton Holmes (New York: The New York Southern Society, 1929), 146-7. Morford's poem concluded Sullivan's "Address at the unveiling of a statue of General Custer at West Point, on August 30, 1879 . . ."

Neihardt, John G. *The Song of the Indian Wars* (New York: Macmillan, 1925).

Norris, P. W. "The Cal-u-met of the Coteau," *The Calumet of the Coteau, and Other Poetical Legends of the Border* (Philadelphia: J. B. Lippincott, 1883), 17-39. Also: "Gallant Charley Reynolds," pp. 60-2; and "Reynolds' Dirge," 138.

Oliver, Arthur M. "The Little Big Horn, War and Progress," *Bits and Pieces*, I (May, 1965), 17.

Orton, May. *Custer's Last Battle: A Poem* (Detroit: Friesema Brothers, 1891).

Osterlund, Steven. "George Armstrong Custer," *Massachusetts Review*, XII (Spring, 1971), 240.

Pabor, W. E. "Little Horn, June 25, 1876, " *Valley Home Farm* (Colo.), July 10, 1876; reprinted in the *Westerners Brand Book* (Chicago), XV (Oct., 1958), 64.

Pond Samuel William. "Speech of a Dakota Chief: Custer's Charge," *Legends of the Dakotas, and Other Selections from the Poetical Works of Reverend Samuel William Pond* (Minneapolis: K. C. Holter, 1911), 30-1. Also: "The Triumph," pp. 31-2.

Ralston, James K. *The Custer Mystery* (Crow Agency, Mont.: Custer Battlefield Historical and Museum Association, 1960).

Red Cloud, Fred. "A Tale of Last Stands," *Prairie Schooner*, XLIV (Spring, 1970), 21-2.

Remak, Mrs. Gustavus. "In Memoriam: Lieutenant Benajmin H. Hodgson. *Respectfully inscribed to his Relatives, Friends and Comrades*," *United States Army and Navy Journal*, July 29, 1876.

Rossman, Thomas. ["Brave Benteen"], *New York Daily News*, July 31, 1885.

[Rowland, Don]. "Custer," *Poet of the Big Horns* (N.p., 1927), 48-51.

S., M. "General Custer — In Memoriam," *United States Army and Navy Journal*, July 22, 1876.

Sanders, Wilbur Edgerton. "On Custer Hill," *Contributions to the Historical Society of Montana*, VII (1910), 135-7.

Shields, Angeline. "Custer Battlefield," *Bits and Pieces*, II (Sept., 1966), 16.

Shillingburg, Eva. [Visit to the Custer gravesite at West Point], *Little Big Horn Associates Newsletter*, VI (Aug., 1972).

Simmerlee, Maud M. "War with the Sioux (1876)," *United States History in Rhyme* (New York: Hermann Lechner, 1911), 212.

Sissman, L. E. "Mouth Organ Tunes: The American Lost and Found, V: Good Indians," *New Yorker*, XLVII (Feb. 27, 1971), 43.

Skyhawk, White Fox. "Battle of the Little Big Horn (June 25th, 1876)," *Pony Express Courier*, IX (Apr., 1943), 4.

Sprague, Kurth. "Garryowen, 25 June 1876," *The Promise Kept* (Austin, Tex.: the Encino Press, 1975), 72-5.

Stafford, William E. "At the Custer Monument," *Oregon Signatures* ed. by R. D. Brown, Thomas Kranidas and Faith G. Norris (Monmouth: Oregon State College, 1959), 84-5.

Stanley, Benoin Jacques. "Battle of Little Bighorn," *The Men of Ormolu* (Dallas: The Kaleidograph Press, 1935), 70-2.

Staunton, Ruth Gillespie. "On Visiting Custer Battlefield," *Montana Magazine of History*, IV (Summer, 1954), 16.

Stedman, Edmund C. "Custer," *New York Tribune*, July 13, 1876, 5.

Stokes, William. "The Ghosts that Ride with Custer," *United States Army and Navy Journal*, Aug. 10, 1895.

Taylor, W. O. "On the Rosebud," unidentified clipping (ca. 1890) in "Clippings Enclosed." See Edward S. Luce, ed., "Our Last Camp on the Rosebud," *Montana Magazine of History*, II (July, 1952), 5-9, for background to this poem.

Tibbs, Ben. "To Custer, Crazy Horse, et al," *Little Big Horn Associates Research Review*, V (Winter, 1971), 77.

VanDyke, Gerald M. "Battle of the Washita," *Singing Wire*, II (Nov., 1968).

Wade, William V. "Old Commanche," *Paha Sapa Tawoyake: Wade's Stories* (Mandan, N. D.: Cresecent Printing, n.d.), 80.

Waight, Quentin. "The Golden Eagle," *Prelude to Glory* (Seattle: Superior Publishing, 1951), 11-34.

Ward, William Henry, "Memory of the Custer Massacre," *All Sides of Life: A Volume of Prose and Poetry* (Des Moines: Iowa Printing, 1886), 112-3.

Warner, Charles. "Custer and His Battlefield," *Old Coins of the Sweet Grass Hills and Some Shreds of Wiregold* (Kalispell, Mont.: Thomas Printing, 1965), 62-3.

Webb, Laura S. *Custer's Immortality. A Poem, with biographical sketches of the chief actors in the late Tragedy of the Wilderness* (New York: New York Evening Post Steam Presses, 1876).

White, John. "Custer and Sons," *Wassaja*, I (Feb.-Mar., 1973).

White Buffalo Man, Frank. "Sioux," *Indians at Work*, III (July 1, 1936).

Whitman, A. A. "Custar's Last Ride," *Not a Man, and Yet a Man*

(Springfield, O.: Republic Printing, 1877), 225-7. First appeared in the *Zanesville (O.) Courier*.

Whitman, Walt. "A Death-Sonnet for Custer, " *New York Tribune*, July 10, 1876, 5.

——. "From Far Dakota's Cañons,"*Leaves of Grass: Comprehensive Reader's Edition* ed. by Harold W. Blodgett and Sculley Bradley (New York: New York University Press, 1965), 483-4.

Whitson, John H. "Our Fallen Heroes: Tribute to the Memory of General Geo. A. Custer and His Gallant Men," *Cincinnati Daily Times*, July 13, 1876, 3.

Whittaker, Frederick. "Custer's Last Charge," *United States Army and Navy Journal*, July 15, 1876, special sheet.

Whittier, John Greenleaf. "On the Big Horn," *Atlantic Monthly*, LIX (Apr., 1887), 433-4.

Wilcox, Ella Wheeler. "Custer," *Custer, and Other Poems* (Chicago: W. B. Conkey, 1896), 94-134.

Williams, A. P. "Custer," unidentified clipping (*New York Mail*) datelined "Rutherford, N.J., May 30, 1887," in "Clippings Enclosed."

Witherup, Mary E. "Custer Battle Memorial Celebration: June 25, 1926," *Down the Trail with the Buffalo Herds: Western Miscellanea* by Mary E. Witherup and Others (Philadelphia: Dorrance and Company, 1972), 38-9.

Woodyard, Darrel. "Custer," *Dakota Indian Lore* (San Antonio: The Naylor Company, 1968), 153-7.

Appendix C:

BIBLIOGRAPHY OF CUSTER FICTION

1. Dime Novels

This biliography is confined to first appearances in either serial or novel form. For a full bibliography, listing variant titles and editions, see Edward T. LeBlanc and Brian W. Dippie, "Bibliography of Custer Dime Novels," *Dime Novel Round-up*, XXXVIII (July 15, 1969), 66-70.

Anon. *Sitting Bull on the War Path; or, Custer in the Black Hills. The Fireside Companion*, XVIII, 461-76 (Aug. 28-Dec. 11, 1876).

Author of Buffalo Bill [Prentiss Ingraham]. *Buffalo Bill's Unknown Ally; or, The Brand of the Red Arrow. Buffalo Bill Stories* No. 15 (Aug. 24, 1901). Custer interest is slight.

——. *Buffalo Bill's Galant Stand; or, The Indian's Last Victory. Buffalo Bill Stories* No. 95 (Mar. 7, 1903).

——. *Buffalo Bill's Creek Quarrel; or, Long Hair's Long Shot. Buffalo Bill Stories* No. 248 (Feb. 10, 1906). Custer interest is slight.

author of "Kit Carson's Last Raid" [H. Llewellynn?]. *Custer's Last Charge; or, The Ravine of Death. Champion Novels* No. 39 (Dec. 20, 1876).

Braddon, Paul. *The Boy Prairie Courier; or, Custer's Youngest Aide. Boys of New York* Nos. 902-9 (Nov. 26, 1892-Jan. 14, 1893).

Burr, Dangerfield [Prentiss Ingraham]. *Buffalo Bill's Secret Service Trail; or, Major Mephisto, the Soldier's Foe. A Romance of Red-Skins, Renegades and Army Rencounters. The Banner Weekly*, V, 220-32 (Jan. 29-Apr. 23, 1887). Custer interest is slight.

——. *Custer's Shadow; or, The Red Tomahawk. The Banner Weekly*, V, 247-59 (Aug. 6-Oct. 29, 1887). Custer interest is slight.

Cody, William F. ("Buffalo Bill") [Could be by Prentiss Ingraham]. *The Crimson Trail; or, On Custer's Last War Path. A romance Founded upon the Present Border Warfare as Witnessed by Hon. William F. Coey, "Buffalo Bill." New York Weekly*, XXXI, 45-50 (Sept. 25-Oct. 30, 1876).

Custer's Scout [St. George Henry Rathbone]. *Custer's Last Shot; or, The Boy Trailer of the Little Horn. Boys of New York* Nos. 51-5 (Aug. 7-Sept. 4, 1876).

Forrest, Frank. *The Gallant Trooper; or, Fighting for Uncle Sam. A Story of* the Indian Uprising of 1876. *Happy Days* Nos. 24-31 (Mar. 30-May 18, 1895).

Garne, Gaston. "Custer to the Rescue." Short story in *Boys of New York* No. 694 (Dec. 1, 1888).

Harbaugh, T. C. *Plucky Phil of the Mountain Trail; or, Rosa, the Red Jezebel. A Tale of Siouxdom. Beadle's Half-Dime Library* No. 231 (Dec. 27, 1881). After the Custer battle.

——. *Roving Rifle, Custer's Little Scout; or, From the Plains to West Point. Beadle's Boy's Library of Sport, Story and Adventure* (Quarto Edition) No. 96 (Oct. 10, 1883). Washita battle of 1868.

Ingraham, Prentiss. *Buffalo Bill's Grip; or, Oath-Bound to Custer. Beadle's Weekly*, I, 9-17 (Jan. 13-Mar. 10, 1883).

Lawrence, Maj. Ashley [Alfred Rochefort Calhoun]. *The Custer Avenger. A story of the Present Sioux War. Saturday Night*, XIV, 3-15 (Sept. 30-Dec. 23, 1876).

Lieut. Col. ——. *Jack Mosby, the Guerilla Chief.* New York: T. R. Dawley. Custer in the Civil War.

Manly, Marline. *Custer and His Men; or, The Bold Riders of Virginia. The War Library* No. 65 (Dec. 8, 1883). Custer in the Civil War.

Maynard, Robert. *Facing the Death Circle; or, the Boy Scout of the Little Big Horn. Happy Days* Nos. 755-8 (Apr. 3-Apr. 24, 1909).

Morton, Ralph. *The Girl he Left Behind; or, the Hero of the 7th. Happy Days* Nos. 58-66 (Nov. 23, 1895-Jan. 18, 1896).

Noname [Lu Senarens]. *Custer's Little Dead-shot; or, The Boy Scout of the Little Big Horn. Wide Awake Library* No. 826 (May 16, 1888).

Old Scout, An [Cornelius Shea]. *Young Wild West at the Little Big Horn; or, The Last Stand of the Cavalry. Wild West Weekly* No. 108 (Nov. 11, 1904).

Rochefort, Maj. Alfred [Alfred Rochefort Calhoun]. *Sitting Bull's Revolt; or, Through Fire and Flood. Saturday Night*, XIII, 50-XIV, 9 (Aug. 26-Nov. 11, 1876).

White, Grace Miller. *Custer's Last Fight, A Thrilling Story Based upon Hal Reid's Famous Play of the Same Name. Play Book Series* No. 68 (1905).

2. Comic Books

"Custer's Massacre," *Westerners Comics* (St. Louis: Patches Publications) No. 19 (Mar., 1949). "Wild Bill Pecos" at the Little Big Horn.

"Custer's Last Stand," *Cadet Gray* (New York: Dell) No. 1 (Apr., 1958). West Point Cadet Gray imagines himself at the Little Big Horn.

Walt Disney's TONKA (New York: Dell, 1958).

"Custer's Report," *Cheyenne Kid* (Derby, Conn.: Charlton Comic Group) No. 39 (Apr., 1963). Cheyenne Kid; prelude to the Little Big Horn.

"The Most Daring Disguise," *The Lone Ranger* (Poughkeepsie, N. Y.: K. K. Publications, 2nd ed.) No. 3 (Dec. 1965 [c. 1958]). Prelude.

"Massacre at Medicine Bend," *Rawhide Kid* (New York: Atlas Magazines) No. 60 (Oct., 1967). The Rawhide Kid; prelude to the Little Big Horn.

The LEGEND OF CUSTER (New York: Dell) No. 1 (Jan., 1968). Two fictional stories based on the television show *Custer*.

"Custer," *Tiger Annual* (London: IPC Magazines Ltd., 1970), 78-85. Based on the television show *Custer*.

General "Tete Jaune": Une Aventure du Lieutenant Blueberry by Jean-Michel Charlier and Jean Giraud (Paris: Dargaud Editeur, 1971). Fiction turning on the Washita battle.

"Colonel Caldwell's Last Stand!," *The Twilight Zone* (Poughkeepsie, N.Y.: Western Publishing) No. 54 (Jan., 1974). Science fiction story with a Custer-type.

3. Juvenile Fiction

Allan, Iris. *White Sioux: Major Walsh of the Mounted Police* (Sidney, B.C.: Gray's Publishing, 1969). Sitting Bull in Canada after Custer's Last Stand.

Altsheler, Joseph A. *The Last of the Chiefs: A Story of the Great Sioux War* (New York: D. Appleton, 1909).

——— . *The Horsemen of the Plains: A Story of the Great Cheyenne War* (New York: Macmillan, 1910). The Washita battle.

Annixter, Jane, and Paul Annixter [Mr. and Mrs. Howard Allison Sturtzel]. *Buffalo Chief* (New York: Holiday House, 1958).

Anon. "The First Train Through: A Story of Gallant Custer and Sitting Bull the Sioux Chief," *Stories of Scouts and Redskins* ed. by Wingrove Willson (London: Aldine, n.d.), 5-16.

Appel, David. *Comanche* (New York: World, 1951).

[Baring, Peter?]. "You Have Found What You Were Seeking," *Great Cowboy Adventures* ed. by Peter Baring (London: Weidenfeld and Nicolson, 1958), 217-55. Perhaps the craziest story ever written about Custer's Last Stand.

Beecher, Elizabeth. *Walt Disney's TONKA* (New York: Golden Press, 1959).

Benchley, Nathaniel. *Only Earth and Sky Last Forever* (New York: Harper & Row, 1972).

Bonehill, Captain Ralph [Edward Stratemeyer]. *With Custer in the Black Hills; or, A Young Scout among the Indians* (Rahway, N.J.: The Mershon Company, 1902).

Brooks, Elbridge S. *The Master of the Strong Hearts: A Story of Custer's Last Rally* (New York: E. P. Dutton, 1898).

Clover, Samuel Travers. *On Special Assignment; Being the Further Adventures of Paul Travers; Showing How He Succeeded as a Newspaper Reporter* (New York: Argonaut Press, 1965 [1903]). Includes a visit to the Custer Battlefield.

Custer, Elizabeth. "The Kid," *St. Nicholas* XXVII (Sept., 1900), 964-79. A story about the cavalry; of interest because of its author.

Downey, Fairfax. *The Seventh's Staghound* (New York: Dodd, Mead, 1948).

Goble, Paul, and Dorothy Goble. *Red Hawk's Account of Custer's Last Battle: The Battle of the Little Bighorn, 25 June 1876* (London: Macmillan, 1969).

Groom, Arthur. "Custer's Last Stand," *Buffalo Bill's Wild West Annual* (London: The Popular Press, 1950), 69-78.

Hart, William S. *Injun and Whitey to the Rescue.* (New York: Grosset & Dunlap, 1922).

—— . *Hoofbeats* (New York: The Dial Press, 1933). Prelude to the Little Big Horn.

Hawley, Zoa Grace. *A Boy Rides with Custer* (Boston: Little, Brown, 1938).

Inman, Henry. *The Ranche on the Oxhide: A Story of Boys' and Girls' Life on the Frontier* (New York: Grosset & Dunlap, 1898). The Washita battle, Custer on the Southern plains.

Jeffries, Jeff [Jeffrey Boatfield]. *7th Cavalry* (London: The Children's Press, n.d.).

Lange, D. *The Threat of Sitting Bull: A Story of the Time of Custer* (Boston: Lothrop, Lee & Shepard, 1920).

MacKaye, Loring. *The Great Scoop* (New York: Thomas Nelson, 1956).

Morecamp, Arthur [Thomas Pilgrim]. *Live Boys in the Black Hills; or, The Young Texan Gold Hunters* (Boston: Lee and Shepard, 1880). An early hard-cover juvenile set in the Black Hills in 1877. Many references to Custer's Last Stand.

Mueller, John Theodore. *Heroes of the Black Hills: A Tale of the Conquest of the Black Hills in 1876* (Columbus, O.: The Book Concern, ca. 1935).

Neal, Bigelow. *The Last of the Thundering Herd* (New York: The Junior Literary Guild and Sears Publishing, 1932).

Regli, Adolph. *Fiddling Cowboy in Search of Gold: A Ross Gordon Story* (New York: The Junior Literary Guild and Franklin Watts, 1951). Prelude to the Sioux campaign of 1876.

Sabin, Edwin L. *On the Plains with Custer* (Philadelphia: J. B. Lippincott, 1913).

Smith, Terry. *Reprieve from Little Big Horn: A Novel of General Custer's Cavalry* (New York: the Exposition Press, 1957).

Sneve, Virginia Driving Hawk. *High Elk's Treasure* (New York: Holiday House, 1972).

Stoddard, William O. *Little Smoke: A Tale of the Sioux* (New York: D. Appleton, 1891).

Tilgham, Zoe A. *Maiom: The Cheyenne Girl* (Oklahoma City: Harlow Publishing, 1956). Custer on the Southern plains.

Van de Weter, Frederic F. *Thunder Shield* (Indianapolis: Bobbs-Merrill, 1933).

White, Dale [Marian T. Place]. *Boy Who Came Back* (New York: Criterion Books, 1966).

4. Adult Fiction

Annixter, Paul [Howard A. Sturtzel]. "Red Begle of the Seventh," *Overland Monthly*, Ser. 2, LXXIV (Oct., 1919), 327-9. Same as Will Levington Comfort's "Red Brennan of the Seventh," with only the names changed.

Benteen, John. *Dakota Territory* (New York: Leisure Books, 1972). Prelude to the Little Big Horn.

——. *Taps at Little Big Horn* (New York: Leisure Books, 1973).

Berger, Thomas. *Little Big Man* (New York: The Dial Press, 1964).

Brady, Cyrus Townsend. "Custer of the Cavalry: A Romance of the Little Big Horn," *All-Story Cavalier Weekly*, XXXVI-XXXVII (Sept. 26-Oct. 24, 1914).

——. *Britton of the Seventh: A Romance of Custer and the Great Northwest* (Chicago: A. C. McClurg, 1914).

Catlin, Don. *The Bow and the Lance* (Derby, Conn.: Monarch Books, 1962). Prelude to the Little Big Horn.

Chief Eagle, D. *Winter Count* (Denver: Golden Bell Press, 1968).

Cody, Al [Archie L. Joscelyn]. *Renegade Scout* (New York: Avalon Books, 1954).

Comfort, Will Levington. "Red Brennan of the Seventh," *Trooper Tales: A Series of Sketches of the Real American Private Soldier* (New York: Street & Smith, 1899), 95-104.

Cooper, Courtney Ryley. *The Last Frontier* (Boston : Little, Brown, 1923). Custer on the Southern plains.

Curry, Tom. *Guns of the Sioux* (New York: Arcadia House, 1945). With Custer in the Black Hills.

——. *Riding for Custer: A "Captain Mesquite" Novel* (New York: Arcadia House, 1947). The Washita battle.

——. *Riding for Custer: A Rio Kid Western* (New York: Curtis Books, ca. 1973). A slightly revised version of the 1947 novel with a newly-named hero.

Drago, Harry Sinclair. "Guns of the Little Big Horn," *Big-Book Western Magazine*, II (Nov., 1935), 6-67.

——. *Montana Road* (New York: William Morrow, 1935).

Evarts, Hal G. "The Shaggy Legion," *Saturday Evening Post*, CCII (Nov. 30, 1929-Jan. 4, 1930).

——. *The Shaggy Legion* (Boston: Little, Brown, 1930). References to Custer on the Southern plains.

Ferber, Richard. *The Hostiles* (New York: Dell Publishing, 1958). Prelude to the Little Big Horn.

Fisher, Clay [Henry W. Allen]. "Yellow Hair," *Zane Grey's Western*, VII (July, 1953), 3-60.

——. *Yellow Hair* (Boston: Houghton Mifflin, 1953). The Washita battle.

——. *Yellowstone Kelly* (Boston: Houghton Mifflin, 1957). Another slant on the Sioux campaign of 1876.

Foreman, L. L. "Riddle for a Red Man," *Adventure*, CV (July, 1941), 77-85.

——. *The Renegade* (New York: E. P. Dutton, 1942).

——. *Decision at Little Big Horn* (New York: Belmont Books, 1971). *The Renegade* under a new title.

Fox, Norman A. "Only the Dead Ride Proudly," *Blue Book*, LXXXVII (June, 1948), 52-8.

——. "Only the Dead Ride Proudly," *The Valiant Ones* (New York: Dodd, Mead, 1957), 175-92.

Frazee, Steve. "Payroll of the Dead," *Bar 6 Roundup of Best Western Stories* ed. by Scott Meredith (New York: E. P. Dutton, 1957), 88-131.

Fuller, Robert G. "13th Cavalry's Mad March into Hell — Major Devlin, Commanding," *Stag*, XII (Sept., 1961,) 16-7, 68-81. Pure fiction about the Sioux War of 1876.

——. "Powder River Showdown of Cannon-Crazy Major Malenfant," *Stag*, XIII (Aug., 1961), 32-3, 48-50, 52, 54, 56. Comic book stuff about an expedition sent out to avenge Custer.

Garfield, Brian. "The Glory Riders," *With Guidons Flying: Tales of the U.S. Cavalry in the Old West by Members of the Western Writers of America* ed. by Charles N. Heckelmann (Garden City, N. Y.: Doubleday, 1970), 55-72. References to Custer, 1869.

Goshe, Frederick, and Frank Goshe. *The Dauntless and the Dreamers* (New York: Thomas Yoseloff, 1963).

Gruber, Frank. *Broken Lance* (New York: Rinehart, 1949).

——. *Bugles West* (New York: Rinehart, 1954).

Gulick, Bill. "Tear Up the Orders!," *With Guidons Flying* ed. by Heckelmann, 97-111. Prelude to the Little Big Horn.

Haines, William Wister. *The Winter War* (Boston: Little, Brown, 1961). The campaigning following Custer's defeat.

Halleran, E. E. *Warbonnet Creek* (New York: Ballantine Books, 1961). Campaigning against the Sioux in the summer of 1876.

Haycox, Ernest. "Bugles in the Afternoon," *Saturday Evening Post*, CCXVI (Aug. 21-Oct. 9, 1943).

——. *Bugles in the Afternoon* (Boston: Little, Brown, 1944).

Heckelmann, Charles N. *Trumpets in the Dawn* (Garden City: Doubleday, 1958).

Heinzman, George. *Only the Earth and the Mountains: A Novel of the Cheyenne Nation* (New York: Macmillan, 1964).

Henry, Will [Henry W. Allen]. *No Survivors* (New York: Random House, 1950).

——. *The Last Warpath* (New York: Random House, 1966). The Washita battle.

——. *The Bear Paw Horses* (Philadelphia: J. B. Lippincott, 1973). Aftermath of the Little Big Horn — Sioux and Nez Perce.

Hill, Lee Trex. *The Golden Years* (New York: Vantage Press, 1951). The Custers are characters in this novel set in Montana and the Dakotas in the 1870's and 1880's.

Idell, Albert E. *Centennial Summer* (New York: Henry Holt, 1943). A story set in Philadelphia in 1876; frequent references to the Custer battle.

King, Charles. *"Laramie;" or, The Queen of Bedlam, A Story of the Sioux War of 1876* (Philadelphia: J. B. Lippincott, 1889). The subtitle is deceptive, for this conventional romance has nothing to do with the Sioux war. At the same time, King, an officer with General Crook in 1876, does capture the gossipy life in a Western fort of Custer's era.

Matthews, Brander. "The Kinetoscope of Time," *Scribner's Magazine*, XVIII (Dec., 1895), 733-44.

Meigs, Cornelia Lynde. *Railroad West* (Boston: Little, Brown, 1937). Custer plays a minor role in this novel about the building of the Northern Pacific Railroad.

Moorehead, Warren K. *Wanneta, the Sioux* (New York: Dodd, Mead, 1890). Custer and Rain-in-the-Face are prominent in this Indian love story set in the years before Custer's Last Stand.

——. *Tonda: A Story of the Sioux* (Cincinnati: Robert Clarke, 1904).

Mowery, William Byron. "The Constable of Lone Sioux," *Tales of the Mounted Police* (New York: Airmont Publishing, 1962 [1953]), 108-44. Sitting Bull's Sioux in Canada after the Little Big Horn.

Myrick, Herbert. *Cache la Poudre: The Romance of a Tenderfoot in the Days of Custer* (New York: Orange Judd, 1905).

Neihardt, John G. *When the Tree Flowered: An Authentic Tale of the Old Sioux World* (New York: Macmillan, 1951). Published in England as *Eagle Voice: An Authentic Tale of the Sioux Indians* (London: Andrew Melrose, 1953).

Overholser, Wayne D. *Summer of the Sioux* (New York: Dell Publishing, 1967). Campaigning with Crook in 1876.

Parkhill, Forbes. *Troopers West* (New York: Farrar & Rinehart, 1945). The Ute uprising in Colorado of 1879; Custer's Last Stand is introduced to build up suspense: Will this be a re-enactment, etc?

Parrish, Randall. *Bob Hampton of Placer* (Chicago: A. C. McClurg, 1906).

——. *Molly McDonald: A Tale of the Old Frontier* (Chicago: A. C. McClurg, 1912). The Washita battle.

Patten, Lewis B. *The Red Sabbath* (Garden City: Doubleday, 1968).

Remington, Frederic. *John Ermine of the Yellowstone* (New York: Macmillan, 1902). Scouting against the Sioux during the summer of 1876.

——. "The Way of an Indian," *Cosmopolitan Magazine*, XL (Nov., 1905-Mar., 1906).

——. *The Way of an Indian* (New York: Fox Duffield, 1906).

Rodney, George Bridges. "Bad Medicine," *Adventure*, Nov. 1921. Custer, the Sioux and Deadwood, D. T., in the summer of 1876.

Sale, Richard. *The White Buffalo* (New York: Simon and Schuster, 1975). A mystical confrontation between Crazy Horse and Wild Bill Hickok.

Shrake, Edwin. *Blessed McGill* (Garden City, N.Y.: Doubleday, 1968). Includes Custer on the Southern plains.

Smith, Martin. *The Indians Won* (New York: Belmont Books, 1970). Opens with Custer's Last Stand and develops the "What if the Indians had won the war?" hypothesis.

Steelman, Robert. *Winter of the Sioux* (New York: Ballantine Books, 1959).

—— . *Cheyenne Vengeance* (Garden City, N.Y.: Doubleday, 1974). An educated Cheyenne in the 1880's sets out to revenge his people for the Washita massacre.

Sundstrom, Harold W. "Prelude at the Big Horns," *The American West in Prose, Poetry, and Pictures* (Tokyo: The Hokuseido Press, 1956), 49-59. Prelude to the Custer battle.

Ulyatt, Kenneth. *Custer's Gold* (London: Collins, 1971).

Weibe, Rudy. *The Temptations of Big Bear* (Toronto: McClelland and Stewart, 1973). Includes Sitting Bull in Canada.

—— . "Bluecoats on the Sacred Hill of the Wild Peas," *Where is the Voice Coming From?* (Toronto: McClelland and Stewart, 1974), 103-11.

White, Stewart Edward. *The Westerners* (New York: McClure, Phillips, 1901). Includes chapters on Rain-in-the-Face, ending with his killing Custer.

5. Stories Modelled upon Custer's Last Stand

Bellah, James Warner. "Massacre," *Saturday Evening Post*, CCXIX (Feb. 22, 1947), 18-9, 140, 142, 144, 146.

—— . "Massacre," *Reveille* (Greenwich, Conn.: Fawcett Publications, 1962), 69-83. Major Owen Thursday's Last Stand.

Birney, Hoffman. *The Dice of God* (New York: Henry Holt, 1956). Colonel Frederic C. Tuthill's Last Stand.

Brown, Dee. *Cavalry Scout* (New York: Perma Books, 1957). Colonel Charles Crawford Comstock's Last Stand.

Harrison, C. William. *Ride the Wild Wind* (New York: Avon Books, 1962). Colonel Maxwell Cady's Last Stand.

6. Adult Semi-Fiction

Since most juvenile treatments of Custer, Comanche and the battle of theLittle Big Horn are fictionalized to the extent that conversations — and often incidents — are fabricated, I have confined this list to adult semi-fiction.

Burdick, Usher L. *Tragedy in the Great Sioux Camp* (Baltimore: The Proof Press, 1936). A novelette based on the exploits of Sgt. James Butler, who fell at the Little Big Horn.

Dallas, David. *Comanche Lives Again* (Manhattan, Ka.: The Centennial Publishing Co., 1954).

Garland, Hamlin. "The Silent Eaters," *The Book of the American Indian* (New York: Harper & Brothers, 1923), 157-274. A fictionalized biography of Sitting Bull.

Kaufman, Fred S. *Custer Passed Our Way* (Aberdeen, S.D.: North Plains Press, 1971).

Peterson, H. L. *Dusty Trails and Iron Rails: 60 Years on the Dakota Prairie* (Sioux Falls, S.D.: O'Connor Printers, 1972). Includes the Indian story of Custer's Last Stand.

Ryan, Man Mountain Ed (The Old Prospector); as told to Brad Slack. *Me and the Black Hills* (Rapid City, S.D.: Holmgren's, 1950). Includes a Last Stand survivor tale. The title page wisely cautions "This story is fictional in part."

Shiflet, Kenneth E. *The Convenient Coward* (Harrisburg, Pa.: The Stackpole Company, 1961). A fictionalized biography of Maj. Marcus A. Reno.

INDEX

X

Y

Z